Gathering Moments in Time

ADVENTURES OF A TIMELESS TRAVELER

Ramani Rangan
with Jenny Rangan

To order additional copies of this book, contact:
Xlibris
1-888-795-4274
www.Xlibris.com
Orders@Xlibris.com
730481

Shree Ganesha as the Messenger, Ramani Rangan

Author's Note

I started writing before I could put down a proper sentence, when grammar was an abstraction for me. I left school before my fifteenth birthday. As I was very quiet and unable to understand any of the classes except religion and art, the teachers gave up on me. They didn't know, and I didn't know, that I was suffering from Post Traumatic Stress Disorder from living in war-torn London from 1942 to 1945, when bombs were dropping and food was scarce. My reading improved with the help of British comic books like *Beano and Dandy* and *Dan Dare*, plus the American *Donald Duck* and *Mickey Mouse*. This progressed to the superheroes *Superman*, *Marvelman*, and *Batman*. As I got older, I began to love books of all kinds, especially science fiction, religion, history, and books about real people and places.

My two uncles came from India to stay with us when I was twelve, and their influence propelled me into a big leap forward. I started to feel that I was not alone. Finally, my mother, my father, and I were not the only Indians in my vicinity. They went to college, and I would regularly visit them there. I was received as an equal, and we would gather with their fellow students and discuss all subjects for hours. My confidence grew, and as a result, I began to write ferociously. My writings then were mostly poems and thoughts on philosophical subjects.

Over the years, I have written volumes of pages by hand, evolving to a typewriter, and currently a laptop. Going over past writings, it is obvious that until recently, I didn't understand the basics of the written word and was writing as if copying the spoken word onto paper. There is still great room for improvement.

In my sixty-ninth year, I joined a memoir writing group. I am still in it. It is a small group comprised of four to ten people. We are between sixty and ninety-five years of age and meet every first and third Thursday of the month. It is out of the dynamics of this group, with their extraordinary talent, skill, and humor, in the laid-back environment of our gatherings, that this series of reflective postcards of my past came into being.

I hope my voice can be detected through the bridge of the written word and remind us that those who came before sat in circles and while fire's light flickered across their faces, shared their experiences and stories through the spoken word. These stories were passed down from generation to generation, as hopefully mine will be too. It is my wish that you, the reader, will know that within the chapters of your life, there are stories of value, and that you will be encouraged to seek them out and share them with us and with future generations as well.

Privacy Note

In telling the story of one's life, the full complexity and volume of experience can't possibly be included. With respect for privacy, certain pivotal stories have been omitted, and the names of all living important individuals (except my current wife's) have been changed, or they are referred to without being named. Some names of deceased individuals have also been changed. The names of some locations or institutions have been omitted, obscured, or changed. All claims and statements herein reflect the perspective and experience of the author or events as told to him by family members and other individuals.

Prologue

The Beloved, Ramani Rangan

₁ Search of Sabu

My mother was born Dorothy Matilda Maud Parke into a Christian home in Bombay, India, in 1919. At twelve years old, she passionately wanted to attend afternoon Indian classical dance and song classes for girls, and her father reluctantly agreed. One day, a talent scout from Raj Film Studios, now known as Bollywood, wanted some girl dancers for extra work. She was chosen and got many casting roles for small parts that developed into bigger ones.

At the time, Raj Studios was producing more films than Hollywood, so she had plenty of work. By the time she reached the age of fourteen, she was a star. The family had been struggling, and her income was a welcome addition. At seventeen, she made a film that was chosen to show alongside the Indian premiere in Bombay of *Jungle Boy*, a British production that was a big hit, starring the teenager Sabu. My mother had, like most young girls, fallen in love with Sabu. He was the first international Indian film star. She dreamt of being in a film as his love interest.

During the reception, she was introduced to the producer of *Jungle Boy*, and he remarked that he liked her performance. She convincingly posed her idea to him. He said she needed to come to England for a screen test and to meet the director. That was going to be impossible, even on the money she was earning. At the same time, there was a large theatrical revue called *Tropical Express*, touring India. Afterwards, they would carry on to Europe. This presented the opportunity she needed to get herself to England.

She approached her father, but he was strongly opposed. The director of *Tropical Express* came specially to speak to him. He assured him that she would be well chaperoned, her income would greatly improve the family situation and, of course, this was the opportunity of a lifetime. Finally, her father agreed, as long as her sister, Irene, accompanied her.

In 1937, both under contract, they sailed for Europe and toured there for about two and a half years. As the show was so successful, a second company was formed, and her sister went with them to England. On the third of September 1939, while Dorothy was performing with

Tropical Express in Germany, war broke out. All foreigners were given thirty-six hours to leave the country. With only the clothes on her back, a small purse, and a little money, she traveled on several trains packed with soldiers headed for their station. These young boys in uniform bought her meals, treated her with a great deal of respect, and protected her till she reached Holland. Her money ran out, but she pleaded her case to the Dutch consulate, who finally gave her enough for a ferry ticket to England. There, she was interrogated because she was carrying love letters written to her by Helmut, a handsome German pilot, and also by Bill, a British lad who had seen her show and had become a fan. They asked her if she was secretly passing information between Bill and Helmut. Was she a spy? After two days, when they were finally satisfied she was "too scattered, young, and not intelligent enough," she was released and granted refugee status.

Despite the chaos of the time, she managed to trace the *Tropical Express* company in England, join them, and reunite with her sister, my Auntie Irene. Thus the stage was set for her to meet my father, Sonnee, and for our story to unfold.

How My Parents Met

My mother told me the first time she set eyes on him—just seeing a dark face, another Indian, in this mad world at war—was shocking. Shocking, she said, in that it was so out of place that she turned away as though it were a dangerous mirage. At his first glimpse of her, my father felt a sharp pain like a bolt of lightning. She reminded him of his mother and his sisters thousands of miles away. His impulse was to speak to her immediately, but she exuded a sense of being unapproachable, so he hesitated and kept his distance.

It was England, 1940. World War II was nearly a year old, and both my parents, still strangers to each other, were now performers in *Tropical Express*. On tour, the whole company—performers, technicians, stage people, orchestra, and management—lived and worked together all the time, especially as it was wartime. There were nightly bombing raids. Industrial cities were targeted. London was aflame. Hundreds of civilians were killed and maimed. Many of the cities and towns where they performed were quiet, with no sign of the war. People would glue themselves to the radio for the first morning news from the BBC Home Service to hear where the bombs had fallen, anxious to know if it were in a place where their loved ones lived. Each loss echoed throughout the community and was felt by all.

Tropical Express performed for the boys and girls in the army, the navy, and the air force, hospitals, civil defense, and all the others who needed cheering up. They traveled by train, lorry, and bus, thousands of miles around England. They played in theaters, airplane hangars, barrack halls, and out in the open, but only during the day because of the no-lights ordinance at night. This was so the enemy bombers couldn't see them as a target. They were told that even a lit cigarette could be seen by a plane flying over, and just a few people lighting up could signal to the enemy that there was a town, train station, or something to report back to command.

My mother and her sister, Auntie Irene, performed both together and in their own featured acts. My father not only sang solos but also filled in on large scenes with the full assembly. He was perfect in his role as an exotic prince in a scene with a tiger and an elephant. Dorothy had one act where she danced with a python. One night, as she was dancing, the python got startled and began to constrict and squeeze her. She thought she was going to faint, and worse still, she knew it was strong enough to kill her. At the last moment, just before her cue to leave the stage, it loosened its grip. At the same time, it broke her bra strap. As she continued to dance and get her balance back, her bra fell off, but she didn't know it because of the pressure of her partner around her body. She said that the audience went wild and stood up and she couldn't understand why. As she took the snake off her body and into her arms, she first realized that she was showing her bare chest to the audience. She bowed and quickly ran off the stage, with the audience clamoring for more. She said she was told that it was a big hit and was asked to keep it in. "I was so mad that they asked me and so embarrassed at the same time. But later, we all laughed about it, along with all the other funny, strange, and embarrassing things that happened on stage."

News came in of another theater group who were lodged together in one house to sleep. During the night, there was a direct hit by an incendiary fire bomb that killed everyone. As a result, all touring theaters were told that they had to split up the staff and performers to avoid too many being killed or injured at one time. This tragedy was devastating to the whole company, as many were friends and colleagues.

A few days later there was an air raid, and bombs were dropped on a train depot near to where *Tropical Express* was performing. That night the show was over, and some of the cast with my mother and Auntie Irene had taken up an offer by the owner of a local hotel to go over and have a nightcap and play some music on a record player. All was quiet, so when they were tired, they returned to their lodgings, called "digs" at the time. Sonnee had gone off with some others for a drink. My mother said he always followed the chorus girls, and that is also why she didn't want to speak to him. "I was not brought up to be one of those kinds of girls." During the night, there was a hum of planes, and everyone awake thought it was "our boys." It was not. Bombs began to fall on the town. When the enemy bombers hadn't used all their bombs, they would just drop them before crossing back over the British Channel on their way back home, and this was what happened that night.

In the morning, when the cast, musicians, and staff assembled, eight members were missing. The director announced that during the night, a bomb exploded on one of the digs, and all were lost. My mother was so shocked that she couldn't move. Everyone looked to see who was missing. People were screaming and hugging each other for impossible comfort, and many just collapsed in the street. My mother cried out for her grandmother, who she was closest to as a child, then for her father and her mother. As she looked around, she found herself searching for a break in the faces, a different face, a face that was dark like hers, but it was not to be found. She had a sinking feeling. She didn't know why. She could still feel all the other feelings of terror and loss, but this was different. Sonnee wasn't there. It was important that she see his face. It was as though his face could make all this madness less horrific. But where was he? She dared not think . . .

By this time, Irene had come over, and they lay down on the pavement and held each other like conjoined twins returning to the womb, not wanting to come out into this insane world. After a few minutes, she felt a presence. Still in her sister's embrace, she looked up and saw Sonnee looking down at her. As their eyes met directly for the first time, he fell back, overwhelmed. His first thought when he found out what happened was of Dorothy and Irene. He had already lost so many friends, and he missed his family, especially his mother. The two Parke Sisters, though they had never spoken, had become his home away from home.

"The show must go on." If the boys on the front line had to go on no matter what, they must too. The director, with tears, said it was going to be hard, but it was important for no one in the audience to know. They rehearsed right up to the lifting of the curtain, with eight beloved members missing, but not missing from their hearts. Acrobats, comedians, dancers, the knife thrower, the animal acts—they all did "what they do." After the show, they had to pack up and travel to the next engagement, a theater somewhere up north. Everyone was very quiet but for a few necessary words each time communication was needed. They arrived and unloaded, the stage people started the setup, and the performers went to their digs to change, wash up, rest a little, dress for rehearsals and come to the theater. The piano was set up, and they learned the new routines as best they could until there were replacements for the eight who had been killed.

Just before the opening, the stage was illuminated. The orchestra was playing the last of the warm-up melodies for the audience to sing along to. My mother was standing in the wings, waiting for her curtain call. My father stepped out of the shadows and walked across the stage directly toward my mother. She said she felt her body freeze as he reached her. He stood for an eternal few seconds and then said to her, "I am scared, and I don't know if we will live or die from one day to the next. You are an Indian, I am an Indian—let us at least acknowledge each other in the time we have." With that, and without waiting for a reply, he crossed back over the stage. The orchestra played the first notes for the opening act, the signal was given, and the curtain went up. Enter baby Ramani.

Chapter 1

Collateral Damage, Ramani Rangan

Baby Gone

Although my mother was brought up Christian, she retained the rich and ancient Indian oral culture deeply embedded in her being. This tradition is a core influence that weaves like music through my own personality too. Mother spoke perfect English, with just a few quirks. She would, when excited or feeling things intensely, substitute a *w* for a "*v.*" So when she called someone "a viper," her favorite way to address people who she felt were cheating or being abusive, it would be pronounced as "a wiper."

My mother would tell her stories in the winter when we were huddled in the kitchen for warmth with a cup of tea, or on a summer's evening when it was beginning to cool off and we had eaten and were just sitting around. These stories could be told many times. The one I am going to relate now was told over and over, a hundred times easily. I never got tired or bored. It was like a wonderfully tasty meal, a fine wine, or a Mozart piece that could never be savored too often. Something precious and magical flowed out of it each time.

When my mother was about to tell a story, it was like she had tasted something that teased her to have more. Her body would settle into the sofa as though it were a flying carpet and we were off to an exciting adventure. I fancied that I could see the story welling up and taking possession, leading first with her heart and then her mind. It was always as if the story had been held as a deep secret never told before, and I was specially chosen by some invisible power to be privy to this unfolding. I was so tickled.

"When you were ready to be born," she began, "it was very dangerous in London. Your father arranged for me to give birth at a clinic in Workington in Cumberland in the north, away from the war. So we packed all the things I would need, and your father and I took the train. He had to leave me there and report back to the army to entertain troops.

"After you were born, your father thought it would be good to rest up and be safe for a short while before returning to London, so you and I moved to Blackpool on the northwest coast, where the war hadn't reached yet. We rented a room with a lovely lady who was so kind to us. She would bring me tea in the morning and hold you if I needed to do anything."

There was a lull in the bombing, and my father believed the rumor that the war would be over in six months, and then we could buy a house in London really cheap. He couldn't go himself, because he was still on duty, so we were to go eventually. But at the time we were still in Blackpool.

"One day, for your afternoon nap, I put you in your pram so you could be rocked to sleep by the movement. I left the house where we were staying and was on the high street."

My mother was still relating her story, and for me, everything else in the room had disappeared. I could imagine the street and the people walking by, the shops on her right, and the sun shining above and slightly behind her. Her tiny Indian frame made any person of her age look like a giant. Her black hair was tied back in a loose ponytail with a blue ribbon. She wore a three-piece maroon suit jacket with wide lapels, two large buttons, and shoulder pads cut to set them an inch out from the body. Her skirt fell a few inches below the knee. During the war, women's fashions were modeled after military uniforms. Because of her background in the theater, she had a slightly heavier touch with her makeup, especially her deep-red lipstick. The brown hue of her skin made everyone around her look either anemic or unwell.

Even though the bombs were not falling on Blackpool, each family was being profoundly affected, directly or indirectly, by the war. The tension and anxiety were palpable and could be felt throughout the body of England. My mother and her newborn were in the midst of it, being foreign and looking foreign. Everything foreign was "Them," either the enemy, or could be. Mind you, it was mid-September 1941. The war to end all wars in 1914–1918 was just part 1, and this was part 2. We were two years into it, and it was being waged with a vengeance.

My mother's story continued. "The wonderful smells coming from a bakery drew my attention. I really wanted something sweet. I parked you outside the shop window and put the foot brake on the pram. For two years, your father had been away most of the time. I was so young and afraid. You had become my only link to sanity." Many times at this point, my mother would close her eyes, looking for the visual images to appear, and I began to see them in my mind's eye.

"I walked into the bakery. While waiting in line, I looked out for you through the window, every few moments checking on you in your pram. I got a cake for myself and one for the landlady. When I got back to you, the pram cover was open, and you were gone.

"I went into shock. I was horrified. Where's my baby? Where's my baby? Oh my God! Someone had stolen you. You had been kidnapped.

"I searched for you frantically under the mattress. I pulled it out and looked underneath and under the pram and repeated this several times. My legs gave way, and I fell helplessly to the pavement. I started to scream, and someone helped me up and took me into the shop to sit on a chair.

"Someone went for the police, but I couldn't wait, and I leapt up and began to look for you everywhere, searching the streets. 'Have you seen my baby? Have you seen my baby?' I cried out to everyone I saw. Some people thought I was crazy and were frightened. Other people joined in the search. A police car began patrolling and questioning shop owners. Police officers who were on foot and in the area were mobilized.

"I was totally exhausted and out of my mind when, finally, a policeman told me that you had been found, and he would take me to you. Until I could hold you in my arms, my precious boy, I couldn't believe it. Finally, he led me into a shop where the owner had you in her arms, and I fell to my knees and put my arms around you.

"Do you realize how long it took to find you? It was the longest three hours in my life. Later, I learned that a woman whose own child died had gone mad with grief and sorrow. When she saw you sleeping in the pram, it must have made her want to hold her baby again. Maybe she needed to feel the warmth of her baby's body close to hers, and in a moment's impulse, she reached out and grabbed you. When she was with the police, she said she was shocked to find you in her arms. Do you know how they found you? They found you because you were a brown baby, and she was a white woman holding you." (This was unheard of in 1941.)

On every occasion that my mother retold this story, there was never a hint of anger toward the woman who took me. In fact, my mother felt sorry for the woman and for her loss. She was just so happy to get me back. She could not imagine what she would do if she ever lost me. Each re-telling of this story felt like a demonstration of love—my mother's love for me and for us together.

Safe in My Pushchair

Even after all these years of building and discarding thousands of generations of cells through the evolution of my body as it passes through the time and space of this mortal coil, as Shakespeare invites us to reflect, I remember looking down and seeing my three-year-old hands and the short sleeves of my gray jacket, revealing the lower part of my arms. I can close my eyes and see the light-chocolate color of my skin, fine fingernails ending perfectly rounded digits, so relaxed as my mother adjusted my shoulders and pulled down on sleeves trying to get the hand-me-down jacket to fit. It was as if my hands were not a part of me until I used them. As if they were tools of some kind that were close by so that they could voluntarily or involuntarily spring into action at any time. This vivid moment was my first acute awareness of my body.

I look up into my mother's dark Gujarati eyes, black eyebrows, and freshly applied bright red lipstick. She purses her lips together and looks into the damaged white-framed mirror. With a fine movement of her little finger's red painted nail, she takes a little of the lipstick away from the corners of her mouth. The smell of her lipstick is in my nostrils, mixed with airborne particles of light tan face powder and the alcohol-based scent she rubs on her wrist. She extends her wrist for me to smell and applies an extra dab to her neck. I see her hair as black as mine. Suddenly, the sound of the radio filling the room with our favorite show is extinguished. Silence attacks like a form of implosion. The electricity in the house has been turned off. We are in pitch black, and now everything has changed. In a second, we pass from harmony to chaos. Evil is on its way, and you can hear it. Bombers are coming from the east, over the British Channel, dropping their hell fire with explosions that rock the building so the loose ceiling plaster drops on my mother and on me. Things fall and break. Her screams mix with the screams of others in the house. The bombers move on to their next target. Terrified dogs regain their bark, and bells ring urgently, announcing fire engines and ambulances. It's funny how one totally unrelated observation can sit together with another in one's mind for decades . . . silence and devastation.

It is morning now, and I have been dressed to go out. My mother picks me up. In the light of day, her black hair has come alive with the reflections of ever-changing colors as she moves out of our room, into the passage, and out the door. No bombs now, just the sense of chaos. The only place of no chaos is in my pushchair, with a blanket over me, tucked in on the sides and a strap holding this all together. I feel the itch of my cap as the cold creates steam from my child's breath.

My mother was always nervous, and my child's radar picked up on her tension. I was told that I rarely smiled in public in those years. I recall jolts of the ups and downs of my pushchair as my mother maneuvered the sidewalk to the street, crossed, and then up the other side. It would be raining, as usual. I could hear the sound of my mother's wet shoe soles clip-clopping close to my ear. The brake would be applied, and I would look out from under the hood at people passing by while she went into the shop. She would look through the window at me every so often and lift her cheeks in a smile. After many ups and downs, turns, and several stops, it was home again. I can remember, on the way back, my mother speaking and not understanding what she was saying. My shoes would be removed at the door, and I can see myself being, once more, lifted up on the chair and my jacket and trousers being changed. Set down, I ran free along the corridor, met by the black-and-white house dog.

My Legs

I recently had the first of a series of sixteen physical therapy sessions for my legs. To be more precise, both knees. The history of my legs came to mind.

In a family album, there are pictures of me just three weeks old, lying on my mother's wildcat fur coat. She got it as a donation, probably from some British countess or duchess who wanted to feel as if she were part of the war effort. So sorry, wildcat. You were killed as though someone plucked a flower, but at least you are remembered in the picture. I am sitting up in a home-knitted off-white baby set, looking babyish with curly black hair, deep pools of unfocused eyes to the front. In another picture, I am lying on the same fur on my belly "in the altogether." There they are, the legs matching the rest of the perfect body, with very small toes—five on each foot, as my mother noted.

I first remember leg stuff when I was five years old, looking down at my legs vibrating as my shoes dragged on the wet sidewalk while I was in my pushchair. It was 1946, postwar London. We were living in a one-room rental in a boarding row house in Islington on Theberton Street. There were still bombed-out houses everywhere. Some had been leveled to the ground, and yet a burnt broken door remained, like a marker for those lost. Hills of bricks and torn mortar cleared from the roads and paths served as playground for scruffy, dirty-clothed children and encampment for the homeless. Ribs of wooden frames supporting interior walls were exposed. Streets were littered with pieces of broken glass that reflected back like countless jewels on the occasional clear day of sunshine, turning into stars as the street gas lamps of the night were lit. It was here that de-mobbed soldiers sought refuge. They were wearing ragged, torn, uniforms that hung off their body. Many were suffering from malnutrition after their time in enemy prisoner-of-war camps. They were all lost souls. Some were young in age, in their early twenties, now made old by their haunted spirits. Arms or legs were missing, phantom limbs evidenced only by a sleeve or trouser leg pinned up with safety pins.

In our room on the second floor, we felt protected from all of this. My mother had just bathed my baby sister, Charmaine, in an oval zinc bath with handles at each end and had laid her, wet, on a folded sheet on the bed. After she dried her, she massaged her legs with warm oil and sang Hindi songs, traditionally passed on from generation to generation by mothers for calming babies and young children. As she sang, her features seemed to change and embody another woman. I had never seen her mother or her grandmother, but I suspect they were both present in her expression. As I sat on a stool in the still slightly steamy room, she reminded me that she had massaged my legs in the same way

when I was a baby. With a smile directed within herself, she said that
I had long, long, beautiful legs and feet. When it came to Charmaine's
arms and legs, my mother's hands were fully encompassing. She rounded
the one hand that was oiled and held my baby sister's shoulder with the
other and ran her oiled hand up and down each limb, so it shone as the
oil covered her skin. Detailed touch was made for each finger and toe.
Whatever oil was left over on my mother's hands, she rubbed into her
own skin. I must have been enchanted by this, for I remember asking to
see her bathe my sister and oil her while singing the same songs, again
and again. In later years, as we remembered this together, she would
salivate as if she was eating up the memory. I still remember one of the
lullabies, "Jo, Jo Rai, Rai Jo." In the song, the mother is singing,

> You are beautiful, my baby.
> Please rest and feel safe.
> Please rest and feel safe.
> Baby, baby, beautiful baby.

During the war, my father was off entertaining troops. Afterwards
he was always away working, looking for work, or trying to recover from
the trauma of the war. I was, for all purposes, without a father. I missed
him. To fill the void, I latched onto the men of the household.

I liked to rest my elbows on my knees when I sat down on a step.
I remember seeing the man we called Uncle Burt doing just that. He
was the brother of the lady who ran the boardinghouse we lived in. I
copied him, as he held some kind of fascination for me. Since my father
was absent and Uncle Burt had no children, we adopted each other. I
would join him on the front steps of the house and relax, becoming still
and quiet just like him.

He was about five feet six, always wore a suit, except you could say
that this suit looked like it had gone to war. It started out as a gray poor
man's version of a herringbone three-piece with mottled specks. It was
now all dark gray-brown. Once it was well fit to a muscular man, but it
now hung on his body like an unkempt, unruly stray dog. Having been
torn and sewn many times, it was somehow perfect for the role that life
had cast for him. It was truly him. His face always appeared unclean,

even though I knew he washed it every day. It was either because of his job of cleaning chimneys or just because that is how some people look. His skin was stretched over his cheekbones as though it had been polished. He could have sat for one of Goya's paintings with his narrow face, piercing eyes, and wild thick, long eyebrows which hung down so far he had to look through them. He had long hair in his ears and small bushes peeking out of each nostril. Despite the residue of many painful injuries, he always looked comfortable in his old body. Sitting on the front house steps, he used his knees as a small table to balance his tin of tobacco on one and on the other an old rusty knife that he used to clean the burnt tobacco out of his pipe. The steps faced the street, so people would be walking by on the sidewalk, some carrying shopping from the grocer up the road. On this, a side street, only a few private cars passed by, maybe one or two a day. I tried to balance things on my knees when he wasn't around.

The next clear view is grazing my knee at seven years old. It bled like it wanted to give me a good reason to cry. I was a crier. My mother called me a sissy. She was a true molder of Indian machismo. Disappointed, she gave up and swung to the other side. To my embarrassment, I became her angel and was introduced to all her lady friends as such. At least she didn't dress me in girl clothes and really mess me up. It left a scar—the cut on my knee, that is—that I bear to this day. When I look at it, I feel younger . . . for a moment.

Of course, hopscotch and endless jumping and running made a typical boy of the times have to constantly pull up his socks. Especially since the elastic tops were always stretched to the point of uselessness. So I was always conscious of legs . . . Well, not the legs themselves. Not thinking, *These are my legs,* but the socks had to work with the legs to have the whole thing work, as it were. My legs could take me only so far. Even though they fulfilled a necessary function to propel my undirected, unlimited, sporadic young energy, they didn't defy the laws of gravity, as I wished they would do.

Since we are talking about legs, the legs referred to here include the area from the toes to just below the hips. So toes count. When I was nine and ten, we didn't have money to buy shoes for me, so I wore the cheapest sandals bought in the summer and repaired again and again.

On several winters, I wore sandals to school with plastic bags over my socks, but I got frostbite a few times. Once, the soles of my sandals wore out. So my mother cut two pieces of linoleum and stuck them over the holes. Her tenacity and ingenuity was heroic, but in the winter, when it was freezing or snowing, my feet still got wet and frostbitten. Sixty-three years later, I still have parts of my toes that have a compromised sensation of feeling in them.

A big day came for my legs. It was almost Christmas. There were just a few shopping days left until the twenty-fifth. I was twelve, and normally, ten was the age for this particular rite of passage to occur for a boy. Mother had promised me during the summer, because I had badgered her and sulked. The months went by . . . July, August, and September, my birthday, but no . . . By now, it had become nearly an abstraction. It had been so long. So when my mother called to me that we were going to get "them" now, I knew what she meant, but by then, I had lost all sense of excitement. We got to the shop, and she asked for a pair in my size. I had to go and try them on in a small kiosk with a mirror. When I put them on for the first time, I felt my heart jump. My mother asked me to come out and show her. After a few attempts we reached an agreement. Now, excitedly, I asked her if I could keep them on. I was given an affirmative, and on the way back, I walked as if floating out of the store, wearing my very first pair of long light-beige zip-fly corduroy trousers. I would never have to wear short pants again. Beautiful shoes, followed soon after with new soles. Two pairs. Just imagine . . . two pairs of shoes at the same time. That Christmas, my legs and my feet were very happy.

Backyard Tails

In the telling of my tale it is sometimes necessary to go back or forward in time, and then return to where we left off and continue. My memories are not linear. They are strands gathered into layers and woven together. In this case we return to the last years of the war when I was three and four years old.

Where we lived on Theberton Street in Islington, North London, there was a backyard. There were white rabbits with coffee and blackish patches, calm and soft. Sharing space with them was a very scary dark-brown bantam rooster with a floppy red crown and long shiny purple-black and red feathers for a tail. His movements, short and staccato, made him even more frightening. He was the supreme ruler over his harem of chickens who laid fresh eggs for the household. As eggs were on ration by the government, they were as good as gold. The animals all shared one smelly house constructed of a homemade wooden frame, chicken wire, and thin sheets of plywood to divide the rabbits from the chickens so they wouldn't fight. I loved the rabbits and would pick them up and stroke them despite my mother's protests. "They are dirty, and you will get a disease, and you'll get very sick." The chickens were a different story. They had to be cleaner. The logic here was that we ate their eggs, so they couldn't be that dirty, right?

We were just one of countless dark, grim streets of row houses occupied by the impoverished masses. Our house was located near the Angel, a district named after a sixteenth-century tavern and inn, said to be a rest stop for the horse-drawn carriages of the rich and elite who, when visiting the city of London, would change from their traveling clothes into attire more appropriate for high society. Who knows, maybe even to be received by their Royal Highnesses at Buckingham Palace.

At the time we lived there, the Angel was a Victorian public bar with ornate cut glass windows, varnished hardwood furnishings, torn leather seats, a dusty chandelier, and a special divided section called the Ladies Saloon. This was so a woman could sit and sip a lager or gin and tonic and be free of the approaches of drunken men. Any male companion would have to be invited by her.

The Angel was also the name of the underground station stop, which was over two hundred feet deep. It was used by hundreds of people each night, mostly women and children, as a place of safety from the nightly air raids of the Luftwaffe, the German Air Force. Bombs had devastated many parts of the area, leaving hills of rubble where houses had been. The threat was very real.

I remember that as soon as it began to get dark, everyone in the house would close all the shutters and then draw the curtains so it would be pitch-black outside and the German fighter plane pilots could not see their targets. I knew that it was time to close up for the blackout because the bantam rooster would begin to crow, joined by others in the neighborhood. Some dogs would follow suit, barking and howling until night fell.

We had a gaslight in the ceiling. To light it, my mother would move the small table from the wall to the center. She would stand on a chair and climb onto the table with a box of matches in her pocket. The gaslight made a hissing sound when she turned the little key on the side. She would wait a moment for the match's brightness to settle, bringing it closer till it met the gas flow. It would make a loud popping sound. She would shout, "Boom!," and we would both laugh.

When the sirens would begin to sound, my mother would turn the gaslight off. Then she would hold me close to her as we heard the growl of many airplanes flying overhead. The house would shake, and she would squeeze me closer so I could feel the rapid beat of her heart. Throughout the impact of exploding bombs and falling shrapnel breaking the slate tiles of the roof, she would sing all the songs she could remember, sometimes with tears in her eyes. One day when we were outside the German fighter planes were overhead, and my mother asked me to look up while Spitfires, the Royal Air Force planes, engaged them in a dogfight in mortal combat. There were other people around. They all cheered when one of the German planes spun out of control and went down in flames. My mother turned to me, shouting excitedly, "They got one! They got one!"

I was one of five children in the house of Mrs. Davis, along with her two girls and two boys. Also living with her were her two brothers, Uncle Burt and Uncle Arthur. There were other lodgers like us. There was an old man, Mr. Hart, who stayed in his room, and Uncle Frank, who was nearly always away visiting. There was also a lady we called Aunt Mary. She lived at the very top of the house with lots of cats. The largest by far was a ginger, red with stripes, who she called Tiger. One night Tiger disappeared, and she cried and was sad for a long time.

Sometimes it was my turn to get the eggs from the chicken house. I was given a basket with scrunched-up old newspapers and sent out into the backyard. The grownups would close the door to the house so the chickens would not get in, and I had to get by the bantam cock to get the eggs. He had spurs growing out of the back of his ankles, and he would charge me. So I would run as fast as I could, open the door to the chicken house, and slam the door shut before he could catch me. All the while, the grownups would be laughing behind the scenes. Those bastards! Getting the eggs and getting back was, for them, even funnier. I hope they had a contingency plan if I was in real danger.

My father, who was away entertaining troops, would come home to visit for one night after traveling for many hours on a train. His favorite chicken was Betty. He would go and visit her and collect her eggs himself. One day he was home, and we were sitting at the table with the Davis family, and soup was served. My father asked what kind of soup it was, and everyone got very quiet. He stood up and left the table. Later, I was told the soup was chicken soup, and the chicken was Betty! She had stopped laying.

Aunt Mary

Aunt Mary lived in what was obviously the attic, designed to store furniture and such. She behaved very differently than any of the other adults I was surrounded by and she spoke like a royal or a BBC announcer. I imagined that maybe she used to live in a palace, but had fallen on hard times. Her flame-red hair, once bright, was now invaded by silver, which she attempted to obscure with a hat that had been fashionable in the twenties. It was brown with folds, festooned with a bird's wing in muted colors of different shades, accented by one longer, slim, tapered, iridescent feather. When she was preparing to go out, a black net, which was folded on top of the hat, was rolled down and became a veil to cover her face.

The hat would be accompanied by a whole red fox wrap, which she wore around her neck. This she put on by first taking the middle of the body of the fox behind her neck and then wrapping it around to the front with its tail hanging down on the right side of her chest. The head had beady glass eyes. Its mouth served as a fastener. With one hand, she would take the spring-loaded jaw, press the top of it, and it would open. Into this she would stuff the base of the beautiful tail and let go, so it held fast.

I feared the signal from my mother to give Aunt Mary a hug when she was wearing it. She would bend down with her face a mask of makeup, and the fox's face would come nearer and nearer, till it was an inch away. At that age, it didn't matter if the fox was alive or dead. It was a fox, and I was terrified.

Favorite Sitting-Down Places

When was the last time you sat down and let everything be? I used to do that all the time. Like sitting on a step, on a bench, a rock, or a tree stump. I remember a few of the very first of these kinds of sit-ins when I was around four. They must have been my favorite places to just watch and feel, because I can remember them so vividly.

The one place was obvious—on my street. At some time of the day, especially on Saturdays, everyone, children and grownups alike, would sit on their front doorstep. I remember the warmth of the sun on the right side of my body, the distinct feel of it on the bare skin of my arms and legs. I would sit on the second step to the street level, place my sandaled feet on the first step and my elbows on my knees and cup my hands to cradle my face.

The second place was in Uncle Burt's stable. Uncle Burt was not a related uncle. He was the landlady's brother, but the children in the house were taught that all adults were to be called Uncle or Auntie no matter who they were. He was a chimney sweep. His business was within walking distance of our home. It was a dark, musky Victorian stable. You stepped through a door that was set into one of two large doors which were wide and high enough to exit and enter with a horse-drawn carriage. A passage opened up to a stall for his chestnut filly. She had wavy white markings running from the top center of her forehead between her ears, ending just above her nostrils, with hints of the same patterning on her light-brown body. Her mane and her tail were a darker brown. To my child-size self, she was a monster. Uncle Burt would remind me often when he babysat me not to ever stand behind her or on each side of her flank. I did get a few nibbles, which made me also respect her front and made Uncle Burt laugh. He taught me how to feed apple cores to her with an open palm. My hand was so small that she may have thought it was part of the apple, so I was quick to retrieve it back to the safety of my side. I remember nervously giggling on retrieving my hand, one of a very few communication sounds I made to people besides my mother. I didn't begin to speak, as a child of my age would normally do, until the war was over. Perhaps, in compensation, my emotional radar was highly developed and my awareness of my surroundings was acute.

The stable had a mascot in the form of a piebald Shetland pony who was more my style. He was closer to my size, quiet and friendly, and I loved to be close to him. I had my special brush to groom him. He didn't work like the chestnut, whose job was to pull Uncle Burt's work cart. Uncle Burt had purchased the piebald on a return visit to the place where he grew up, a coal mining town in Wales.

Uncle Burt joined his father working in the coal mines when he was himself just a lad of eight. He worked a twelve-hour shift helping ponies haul coal carts from the elevator cages that came up from a mile down below. While still underground, he had another eight hours of mucking stalls and feeding ponies. Then he would collapse, exhausted, sleeping with the ponies in the stalls deep below the surface, until he and the ponies would return to the work site for the next twelve-hour shift. Every third day, he was allowed to the surface to go home for twenty-four hours, only to repeat the same cycle, with the exception of Sunday. Because of their shared conditions and prolonged close proximity, he and the ponies grew attached to each other. He developed affection and concern for their well-being. After one year, he was sent farther down the coal mine to dig with his father, but he never forgot the ponies he had grown to love.

This lasted six more years until he and his family had to flee because there was a call for a general strike. The government brought in soldiers who started to shoot coal miners that were protesting in the streets. The next day, the miners continued the strike from inside their homes. The soldiers were ordered to drag the miners into the streets, where they were shot. Those who survived fled. He and his family escaped to London.

Uncle Burt put away a few coins every week for many years, and when he thought he had enough, he returned to the coalface in Wales where he had worked. There, he spotted a piebald pony designated to be slaughtered in the knacker's yard. His meat would be sold to France or possibly be used in tins of corned beef in England. His hide would make handbags, and his hooves would be boiled down to make carpenters glue. Uncle Burt went to the office and asked the foreman, "How much would you get for him from the knacker's yard?" They gave him a quote, and he offered more. He paid the piebald's ticket from Cardiff to London, where it was fed, housed well, and loved to boot.

When Uncle Burt was mucking the chestnut, she needed to be taken out of her enclosure. Smelling freedom, she would go a little crazy and try to get out of the stable. So Uncle Burt lifted me up six feet high off the pebbled floor to a ledge to sit and watch. It was so high up, but I was not scared because I knew that Uncle Burt knew everything— that is, everything in his world—and I was without question truly and completely safe. There was much to see as I sat up there in that dark, low-lit space of roughly fired brick walls with two tiny windows, cobwebs, and bedding and hay everywhere. There were well-worn harnesses, enough for several more horses and ponies, hanging on the walls and a full complement of blacksmith tools for shoeing and polishing brass. To the finer feminine eye of the time, it was a total disaster waiting to happen, and especially dangerous for a child of my age. That was why Uncle Burt never allowed my mother to peek into the back. Not even his sister was allowed. If I knew at the time what it would feel like to be a prince, I would describe it exactly this way—sitting in my favorite place in Uncle Burt's chimney sweep palace of horse, pony, and all the simple magic therein.

On certain days of the year, like Easter, Christmas, weddings, and neighborhood and regional contests, Uncle Burt would enter the chestnut and the piebald to compete and to show off. That was when the brass adornments on their harnesses were polished so fine you could see yourself in them because they were like small golden mirrors. The leather straps were shined. Even hooves were lacquered. Uncle Burt took his cart out of the shed into daylight to have the whole of our household scrub and polish, step back, and then scrub and polish again. Paint was touched up where needed, and cart and horses were bedecked with ribbons. In the end, the cart was gleaming, so that if it could see, it would not recognize its reflection as it proudly passed shop windows, with people all lined up along the streets clapping and cheering on. There I was, sitting on my mother's knee, and we were all dressed up in our finest, waving from the back of the cart. That was a more-than-special favorite place to sit. I ask, *Can anyone beat that?*

A Pipe Dream

I was sitting with Uncle Burt on the front doorstep of our row house in the first sunshine of the morning while he lit his pipe. The war ended in 1945. This was one year later. England remained devastated. Young men were just beginning to return, clothed in the unimaginable remnants of war.

Even at five years of age, I noticed their sunken faces, even more their sunken eyes. From where I sat, I could see them gathered in threes and fours on the corner, frozen in place, not moving for hours. Others stood alone. For the longest time, I thought it was normal for all men to have legs and/or arms missing, hardly compensated for by the medals pinned to their chest. The landlady of our house had a daughter who had married two years before, and her husband, Bernard, "Bernie," had gone off to war and was missing in action. He arrived unannounced one day, just standing at the doorstep, with all his limbs but not his spirit. Before he left for war he would smile a lot, tell jokes and pick me up, but when he returned, it was as though his face couldn't form that expression anymore. It felt like I was a stranger to him.

Smoking his pipe was a formulated nearly religious ritual for Uncle Burt. Every morning when I woke up, weather permitting, my mother knew that I was going to sit with him, and she dressed me for outside. In my younger-than-young mind, it was my job to be there and hold the space for him. I would come out on the doorstep and, without a word between us, sit down on the step with him and wait. This was one such morning. Later, I realized, he would only begin once we were together.

First, Uncle Burt would take his pipe pouch out of his old wrinkled suit jacket and open it very slowly as if it was a sacred book he was about to read from that could change the world forever. His pipe had a round meerschaum bowl which had taken on a deep-red burnt color from years of smoking use. The part that connected the bowl to the mouthpiece was a hardwood which shone with constant polishing. The mouthpiece was made of pearl-blonde Bakelite. He withdrew an old, broken bone-handle folding knife with a rusted blade and a spike with a beveled end from the same pouch. He unfolded the spike and began to scrape the inside of the pipe bowl, all the time humming a non-song with his mouth slightly open. This could go on for ten, even fifteen minutes.

From his time working in the coal mines in the Welsh pits, Uncle Burt's breathing was heavy and expelled from both his mouth and his nose at the same time as he hummed. That done, he put that knife in the pouch and that pouch back in the same pocket and then snorted, which he did on all his completions. It was then that he would first look for a split second at me and give me a smile, that same smile he would use when he calmed his chestnut mare as he slowly hitched her up to the cart when he went chimney sweeping. "Wuuuw!" he would call to her, and with the sound of his voice coming out of that smile, she knew she was safe and would comply.

Then from the other pocket of his jacket, he would take out a small dented cake tin that was at least twenty years old. Opening it released an aroma that touched many notes as it entered the nostrils. It was a combination of deep, earthy tobacco with a strong accent of cultured sweetness, honey that a relative in Wales would send to him especially for this purpose, and Irish whiskey. This would sit to "mature" in a secret place for months till it was just right for the next stage. Once it was mature, he would put his concocted recipe into a special box and press it slowly in a vise, making a turn every other day for a month or so, until it would become a block as hard as wood. This block was wrapped in a special rag and placed in the dented tin.

He would then set the tin down open on the step. Reaching into the pocket where the pipe pouch was and taking it out again, he would unfold the blade of the old knife and begin to shave off slices of the cured treasure into the palm of his hand. When just the right amount was ready, he would place the rest of the block back in the tin and close it. This tin would go back to its pocket home. Then he would rub the shavings between his very coarse and worn hands until the hardness submitted and became a soft ball, all the while releasing its fragrance of heavenly soma. This was then carefully pushed into the opening of the pipe bowl till it was snug but not tight. He would then stop and, for the first time, look up. Not at anything, just raising his eyes.

When all was placed just right, it was ready. A match would be struck. It was held vertically until the flame was wide. It was then held horizontally so the flame was the width of the pipe opening. With the flame above the tobacco, he would inhale, drawing it into the pipe. After repeating this several times, he would extinguish the match. The smoke would rise and engulf the world. It was like smoke rising from a sacred fire.

The stillness of these moments, Uncle Burt's meticulous preparation, and his devotion to this process created a sanctuary on the steps of our home. I was silent. Throughout all the time of the sacred preparation, I was silent, but now the silence was golden. Pure gold.

Uncle Frank

As mentioned before, Uncle Frank was a lodger in the house we lived in on Theberton Street from the time I was a baby until I was a young child. Like all the other grownups in the house, Uncle Frank wasn't a relative. He was a gentle giant of a man, at least six feet five. He had to stoop, then bow his head, when he entered rooms. All his movements were very slow and graceful. In his late seventies, a stroke rendered the left side of his face less animated than the right, and his eye on that side always watered.

In the beginning, he was the only person in the house who talked to us. His kindness broke the silence and the negative energy directed at me and my mother because we were Indians. He confided in us that he suffered from a genetic issue that made him have epileptic seizures. One of his parents had it and passed it down to him, and that was why he decided never to have children of his own. He said, "All children are my children."

He was what would be known nowadays as a strict vegan. He only ate raw food. He always took his meals alone as all the others in the household satisfied their appetite with meat for breakfast, lunch, and/or dinner. He said cow's milk was for calves, not for humans. The rest of the people in the house thought he was eccentric, defiantly different. My mother and I didn't. We thought everyone else was different. We loved him.

He would go off on long trips around the country, but before going, he would always come and ask my mother if he could put his hands on my head for blessing and healing. His hands were so big that my head would be covered right down to my chin. Closing his eyes, he would hold me for a minute or a little more. When he returned, he would always have a gift for me and all the other children in the household. As I grew older and could understand him, Uncle Frank would put his warm, very soft hands lightly on my shoulders and whisper words like, "Remember to chew your food well," or "Keep your head safe when you play." Other times, he would just look at me for a few seconds as if he was scanning me to see if I was all right. In these times, I felt as though there were communication between us, but not through words. Even though I was only five years old, I knew that there was something good going on. I just didn't know what it was, and I don't think my parents knew.

Mrs. Davis

In the beginning, Mrs. Davis, the landlady, was hostile to us. It was obvious she had never seen Indians before and took every opportunity to make things uncomfortable for us. She would cut off the electricity in our room at night, so my mother could not warm powdered milk and water to feed me. She generally ignored us. If it was up to her, she would not have had us in her house. When my mother first came to London with me as a baby in her arms, she was rejected everywhere she tried to find lodgings. Due to wartime curfew laws, no one was allowed to be out at night. A policeman found us wandering the streets. "Why are you not at home?"

My mother started to cry. "We arrived in London this morning, and no one will rent to us."

Knowing there was a room to let, he escorted us to Theberton Street. He knocked on the door, and Mrs. Davis answered. "I have no room," she said firmly.

The policeman, standing his ground, replied, "I know you have a room, and by law, you have to take them in."

She led us upstairs to a cold, dark room, said nothing, and left. My mother, exhausted, collapsed on the bed, and we fell asleep.

Mrs. Davis' husband was a merchant navy captain and had been lost at sea. She was left with four children and no means of supporting them. She opened up a lodging house and, in this way, secured a roof over her head and supported her children. Mrs. Davis was four feet ten, wiry, yet tough. She maintained a stern and icy expression at all times and always looked as though she were on the border of exhaustion. She ran her house military style and you knew you didn't want to break the rules.

One day, when I was just a few months old, there was a knock on our door. It was Mrs. Davis' oldest daughter. She asked if she could come in and play with me. Gradually, her younger sister would come to visit too, and the two of them would take me for walks in the pram. Eventually, they brought me down to the living room where their mother was. When I was hungry, the girls went into the kitchen, heated the milk, and for the first time, I was fed downstairs.

Soon after, I developed a bad cough, keeping the household awake. Late at night, there was a knock on the door. My mother opened the door, and Mrs. Davis walked straight into the room. With her sternest face, she gave my mother cough mixture and oil and gave her instructions on how to put the oil on my chest, wrap me well, and put me to bed. She returned with a cup of tea, which was obviously not for me. It was at this moment the ice melted, and I became the ambassador for a friendship to develop between them. It wasn't long before my mother was allocated household chores, and we left the confinement of our room to join the family in the dining room for all our meals. Mrs. Davis began to refer to my mother as "Dot."

This is how it came to pass that one day in the end of August, we were on a bus coach with a lot of people—my mother, Mrs. Davis and her brood, and a busload of strangers. They sang songs together, and some soloed, with the rest joining in on the chorus. It must have been more than a few hours because we stopped for lunch, and after two more hours, we were there. *There* was out in the country. This was the first time we had left the rubble, smoke, noise, and madness of London since we had arrived. To be out in the country with trees and hills, streams, and small paths was wondrous.

We shared a primitive cabin with Mrs. Davis and her children. As the first light of the morning broke, we were up and on our way, bumper to bumper in three horse-drawn carts on a winding cobbled road till we came to a field and stopped. Everybody jumped out. We were organized into groups, with the task of collecting flowers.

The flowers were green and grew profusely on creeping vines that were woven into tall wooden trestles. The grownups and older children climbed ladders to reach the flowers and throw them down. My job, along with other children of my age, was to gather them and put them in sacks.

We were there for a week, and we repeated this every day. Slowly, everybody began to relax. A cloud lifted, and there was a sense of happiness. For the first time, I got to learn to play with lots of different children. I was picked up many times by strangers who, by the end of the week, were friends. Each day, we stopped to have a picnic surrounded by a multitude of sacks full of the small aromatic flowers. In the evening, we all sat outside the cabins. A wood fire was lit, and we ate, and there was talk and singing and laughter.

Years later, I found out that the small flowers we picked and gathered were hops—hops for making beer. For working-class families, this was a way to be out in the country and have a working holiday, which we repeated several times over the years. The sense of being safe, away from the never-ending chaos, and experiencing the serenity for the first time that only nature can give was profound and brought us all closer together. As the years went by and the love grew among us, there was no doubt that we had become one big family.

Chapter 2

Warriors Behind the Mask, Ramani Rangan

Sonnee Rangan, the Voice of India

This feels like the right time to bring my dad into the picture. My dad, Ramsami Rangan, known as Sonnee, was born circa 1915 into an Orthodox Hindu, Tamil, South Indian family living under British Colonialism in Durban, South Africa. I say circa because my mother and I think he fibbed about his age out of vanity.

He had to leave his father's house because of the conflict they had when he rejected Orthodox Hinduism and embraced Puccini, Mozart, and Frank Sinatra. "That music of evil," his father insisted, "will lead you most certainly to your downfall." His father was staunchly against the British and anything associated with the "barbaric Western influence." So my dad, pained to leave his mother, moved to cosmopolitan Cape Town, where the middle and upper classes of all ethnic backgrounds mingled in exclusive nightclubs and country clubs. He formed a band and sang popular western songs to make a living, which introduced him into high society. He fell further in love with opera and began to study operatic voice. From there, he started one of the first recording studios in South Africa. As time went by, his operatic voice tutor recorded him on vinyl disc and sent it to an international competition in Rome. So the story goes, he won a scholarship to study opera as a tenor there at National Academy of St. Cecilia. That is how, in 1936, he found himself, for the first time, able to sit in a café or restaurant and talk and eat casually with fellow white students as an equal.

In June of 1940, Mussolini declared war on Britain. The secret police came to my dad's apartment and ransacked it. They confiscated all his belongings, but luckily, rumor had preceded them, and he had already hidden his money and valuables with his Roman friends. He was given thirty-six hours notice to be out of Italy as he was a colonial subject of the British Crown. He boarded a ship that docked in Belgium and, from there, continued on to England, where he sought refugee status. When he had left South Africa on his way to Italy, he had disembarked in the Congo and had contracted rheumatic fever. This left him with a heart murmur, so when he went to enlist to fight in the war, he was declared not fit to bear arms. To find some use for him, and because he could sing, he was recruited into the Entertainments National Service Association (ENSA) and sang for the troops throughout the war.

It was now 1943. The war raged on. I was two years old, and my mother was pregnant. There was no one to look after me, so my father took me on tour with him. I was told I was looked after by the "girls" in the chorus and slept in a traveling costume basket at night. I remember only the room filled with women, lots of strong lights and mirrors, and the smell of makeup powder. My mother lost the baby and then was pregnant again. Once more, my father took me on tour while he entertained troops. Some were U.S. military. It must have been the start of the secret buildup for the Allied invasion of Europe for D-Day. I was a year older and could remember more.

Once, I was crying for my mother, and so my father asked one of the dressers to bring me into the theater and take me to the Royal Box, which, in British traditional theaters, is situated on the first balcony to the extreme audience left. It is called the Royal Box because, as implied, this is where the royals would sit when attending a production. So it was my father's turn to perform. He walked on to the stage and stood at the center, waiting for the orchestra to start the intro to the song he was going to sing. The auditorium was packed full with soldiers, many eighteen and nineteen years old. The music started to rise from the orchestra pit, and at this moment, I started to cry for my dad. All the hundreds of pairs of eyes looked to the Royal Box, including my dad's. The conductor stopped the intro and started from the beginning, but I wouldn't stop crying. My father signaled the conductor to stop and, looking up at me, signaled my babysitter to bring me down to the side, offstage. While I was being brought down, my dad started to sing the song scheduled. I must have still been upset as my babysitter and I reached the side of the stage. Stopping the music again, my dad walked over to me and held me in his arms crying. He asked to have a chair placed on the center of the stage. He walked over and sat down with me on his lap. I remember being held tightly with his face close and his lips kissing me. He spoke to the conductor in whispers. You could have heard a pin drop. A new musical intro was started, and then my father sang, "When there are gray skies, I don't mind the gray skies, 'cause I have you, Sonny Boy."

I then stopped crying. This song, "Sonny Boy," was a very popular wartime song, and he was told afterward that there was not a dry eye in the theater.

On a third trip, I could walk by myself, and I was now declared the company mascot. My father and other performers decided that it was my turn to "hit the boards." So I was taught and rehearsed another popular song of the times. My father and the other artists must have had so much fun and some comic relief teaching me a routine to go with the song. I don't know how many times I performed it, but I know it was more than once. I was given the smallest straw hat and cane they could find and with a special little outfit of black-striped white jacket, white trousers that wardrobe sewed, and a pair of black shiny shoes, I was ready. They made a special adjustment, so I had my own spot. I would be offstage, stage left, waiting for my cue as the introduction of my song was being played. The whole company had assembled to cheer me on. When it was time, I strutted onstage in rhythm with the beat and started singing,

Shine on, shine on Harvest Moon, up in the sky,
I ain't had no lovin' since January, February, June, and July.
Snow time ain't no time to stay outdoors and spoon,
So shine on, shine on Harvest Moon for me and my gal.

I did a tap-and-shuffle dance, twiddled my hat and cane, sang on, and exited the stage, bringing the house down. I would go back on with my dad and take a bow. We would both sing the last two verses to the end in harmony, take another bow, and exit the stage. I still get flashes of the rehearsals, with the smell and feel of the straw hat on my head, and very bright lights in my face. Under those lights I could not see the audience, though I could hear the sound of them cheering and clapping.

Every time I saw a Yank, an American man in uniform, they would offer me something in a paper wrapper with a big boy blowing what looked like a balloon printed on it and ask me to say, "Have any gum chum?" When I said that, they would give me the wrapper, and I would have to unwrap and put the contents in my mouth. "Don't swallow! Just chew," they said. The flavor was always strawberry. The next lesson was how to blow a bubble. It was only then I realized the picture on the wrapper was not a balloon.

My mother told me that I loved my father so much that I was ecstatic when he would come to see us, traveling on troop trains, sometimes up to a day and a half each way, just to be with us for a few hours. When I knew he was going to leave, I would get so distressed that I would go into convulsions. So I had to be held down on the bed, and my eyes would roll up into their sockets. It would take several hours to quiet me enough that, totally exhausted, and insisting to have the picture of my father with me, I could finally fall asleep.

My father had grown up in the very dangerous world of South Africa in the 1920s. As a Sammy (the derogatory name for East Indians), he and his brother Krista had taught themselves a form of martial arts to protect not only themselves but the family home, as there were gangs that would try to break in and steal from, destroy, injure, and kill whole families. He told me they had built a barn especially to train. Part of their training was to have billy goats charge them and practice avoiding injury. This also included head-butting, although I can't imagine squaring off with a goat. Maybe it was small.

I tell this because it came in handy when he was in Britain after the war. There were people who were offended by just the sight of us. I had been out with him as a six or seven-year-old child in London when someone would say something that would anger him. He had learned from his experience to act first.

One day, we were on the top of a London bus, and there were four big men, each one bigger than my father, and they started to get very loud and look at us. I don't know what they said, but my father turned to me and ordered, "Just stay here, do you understand?" I had learned from the tone of his voice what he meant, and he meant exactly what he had said. So that is exactly what I did. He stood up. The bus was moving, and the top level of the double-decker, where we were, was swaying. He calmly walked over to the four men and spoke to them. One of them made a move to stand up, and within, literally, a few seconds, each one of the four men were either unconscious or wished they were. My father turned and walked back to where I was and sat down, not looking at me. Out of the corner of my eye, I could see that he was calm. After a few stops, we got off the bus, and he never mentioned the incident again. Many years later, after he passed away, I asked my mother if he had told her. She said he never spoke of this to her. I gather that in his world, this was a man's thing. Men took care of it.

He loved animals. I remember once, on the street where we lived, that he and I had just left the house and were walking down to the corner to catch a tram, when he suddenly stopped. He told me to hold onto the iron railings and gave me "the look." Seeing I had complied, he walked straight across the street. It was then I noticed a man with a horse and a cart. The man was whipping the horse. When my father reached him, he grabbed the whip out of his hand and began to whip the man. It must have been about a minute before he stopped and threw the whip down into a basement courtyard, where it could not be retrieved. The man was cowering. My father said to him in a stern voice, "If I ever see you do that again, you will seriously regret it." He then returned to where I was standing. In the meanwhile, while all this was happening, I had forgotten my instructions to hold on to the railings. Noticing this, my father said, very quietly, "I told you to hold on to the railing, didn't I?" I acknowledged him. He signaled me to hold on again and waited for me to comply. Then signaling to let go, we continued on in silence. Nothing was said about the incident. We waited till the tram came, clanging along the rails with an occasional set of sparks from the overhead electric wires. It stopped, and we got on.

These were not isolated incidents. I am sure now that the experiences of the war, being in so much danger, and seeing so much destruction and loss of life, left its mark on him. Many close friends and fellow artists were lost. It would seem obvious that people die at war, but it was still nearly impossible to comprehend. I sensed he felt they were not just killed, but murdered. Human beings he knew and had grown to love— in their innocence, unjustly destroyed. It had, in turn, destroyed a part of his heart, his spirit, and his singing voice. He had shown so much talent and promise. It was now broken, never to return. An operatic voice only has one chance. Age and war were the thieves that stole his. Five years of the horror of war aged him twenty. Like so many others, he was never the same again. I still have billboards and printed material from those times, with some of the places he performed. They all say, "Sonnee Rangan, the Voice of India."

Charmaine

While I was going back in time searching for clear images to come to the forefront of the stage of my mind, I realized that so many things that I wanted to remember were offstage, in the wings. (I used to work in the theater.) So I thought I would just let a picture of the past appear and see what happened. If I relaxed my demand for figures to come forward, the actors of times gone by might come into the spotlight by themselves, propelled by the natural magnetism of the flow of life wanting to be recognized. So here I wait, creating a blank space like onstage at the beginning of a theater production, with no back or side drops, furnishings, or props, just open stage before the actors come in for their very first rehearsal.

My sister, Charmaine, immediately appears in my mind's eye. More like my heart has eyes, and my heart's eye has opened. I experience a run of images of her, thoughts that have crossed my mind, and feelings from back when I must have been six going on seven and she was barely two years old. I could share with you what I am seeing and feeling, the museum I have constructed in the unlimited cyberspace of my consciousness. It overflows with exhibits, but that is not what I am after. There is an impulse to repeat the usual stories connected to her, but I manage to resist. Did I have to take all these years to give myself this permission? It seems so. Some places are just too delicate. Courage. I look at the empty stage again. So many plays want to be acted out, happy, romantic, sad and tragic, all fighting to crowd the limited space of my attention. I wait and stop waiting, just relax, and am present, eyes closed. I notice my breath. I become calm.

My mother was crying one day because my sister, in her pushchair, pointed to a peach on a stall and asked for it. Like children everywhere, she had her mind set and let my mother know it. The only problem was that my mother didn't have any money. Copper farthings, halfpennies and pennies were counted every day, sometimes twice. Occasionally, there would even be a silver sixpence. It was a couple of years after the war, and like everyone in England, we were still struggling, still on food rations. The amount of rations given was regulated by how many adults, children, and babies were in the household. Charmaine got extra powdered milk, and we both got what was called radio malt and cod liver oil. Radio malt was like a soft heavy caramel fortified with vitamins and was delivered as a huge and welcome spoonful. On the other hand, cod liver oil . . . No amount of orange and sweetener could disguise the disgusting liver-fishiness.

One Christmas, my father came home with a tin of baked beans with small cocktail sausages. I looked at the picture of the sausages on the label as my mother cooked up a few woody carrots and potatoes with purple eyes. The potatoes had been stored for more than a year somewhere by the government. They tasted bitter and old. My father ceremoniously opened the tin and heated the contents. A candle was lit, and Christmas songs were sung. There were enough sausages for my sister and me to get two each. What a feast!

One day I was on top of the roof of the air raid shelter in the backyard of the house on Theberton Street. I was told, "Never, never climb up there," but being a mischievous six-year-old, what more invitation did I need? Suddenly, a piercing scream came from the house, and for a moment, I froze. Then something must have triggered my instincts, because I was down off the roof in seconds and ran past the rooster without fear. The house was in chaos. I asked and asked, but was ignored. I heard fragments and words.

"Bitten,"

"Charmaine."

"Where is the dog?"

"What happened?"

I was desperate to find my mother. "Where is she?" I heard the ambulance's bell ringing and getting closer. I had heard that bell throughout the war, and it always scared me. Mrs. Davis's oldest son took me downstairs to the dining room. His mouth was moving, but I didn't hear a thing. He gave me a cup of tea and biscuits from a tin box. Then I began to understand. My mother had gone in the ambulance with my sister, and they were in the hospital. I was terrified and couldn't stop crying. I had never been without my mother or my father before. Mrs. Davis' eldest daughter was given the task to comfort me, and that night, I slept in the room with Mrs. Davis' two sons so I wouldn't be alone.

When I awoke, my mother was still not home. "When's my mummy coming home?"

"She'll be home soon."

Images of the day before were flashing in my mind. My sister had been attacked by the house dog. It was a guard dog in every sense of the word, trained to be vicious to protect in time of war, but was not expected to behave this way with members of the household. Mrs. Davis went to see my sister in the hospital. When she came back, she went downstairs in the coal cellar and came up with an axe. "Where's that dog. I'm going to kill it."

Nobody knew where it was, and eventually, she calmed down.

Charmaine had been bitten on the side of her face. They said it was not dangerous, and she was going to come home the next day. But then something happened. As a precaution, the doctors had given her a tetanus shot. She was allergic to it and went into convulsions. Charmaine was not responding to any treatment, and she developed a serious infection, so they administered a new drug—Streptomycin, a strong antibiotic. She was even more allergic to the antibiotic, and her condition worsened. I watched my mother plead with the doctors to stop the doses, but instead, they increased them. She felt that it was the treatment that was harming her daughter, but the doctors said, "We know best." This went on for three days. In this time, my mother was in agony watching her daughter suffer. Then Charmaine had a stroke, which paralyzed the whole left side of her two-year-old body. The doctors told my mother they were sorry.

When my father came back from tour and found out, he was stunned. Then he was overcome with anger and was looking for someone to blame. It took him a long time to calm down. I think the love he had for Charmaine was so strong that eventually, it overpowered his anger. He dedicated himself to her recovery. He was given compassionate leave from his job, and he spent every waking hour working with her until she could talk and walk again with the help of an iron brace on her leg.

Charmaine's Big Brother

The unhealthy environment we lived in was hindering Charmaine's recovery, so we petitioned for relocation. After many interviews, it was granted. When I was seven, we moved to a house near Regent's Park and the London Zoo. It was like coming out of a dark tunnel that never ends into the light of a sunny day. Charmaine did get back her strength and started to be her old self. Even though her stroke left her dragging her left leg, still in an iron brace, and using her right hand to do nearly everything, it didn't stop her from being a rogue. She would climb everything, especially if it was dangerous. I was commissioned to look after Charmaine when my mother was cooking, shopping, or cleaning the house—anytime she was busy and needed backup.

Charmaine was constantly dodging me. She would make it impossible to keep her from falling down, scraping her knee, hitting her head, or tearing her dress. Once, I found her on top of a five-inch wide ledge over the fireplace, laughing, with no visible way she could have gotten there. When we were outside, I had to be vigilant to keep her from escaping the confines of the front-yard fence. She had no concept of what traffic was or meant to her safety. She was forever getting me into trouble for not looking after her properly, or for complaining about all her antics and the ways she would tease me. "Mum, Mum, Charmaine's not listening to me. She's doing it again."

"You are her big brother. You're supposed to look after her. You know your sister's not well," my mother would remind me, which was frustrating because it happened several times a day. Or Charmaine would blame it on me. Whatever it was, I was always getting blamed.

I was called Roy, short for *Leroy*, and Charmaine called me Woy due to the lapse of control over her facial muscles. It was Woy this and Woy that. "Woy" could be repeated many times a minute for hours. "Woy! Woy, Woy, why is it raining? Woy! Woy, can you see me? I'm hiding, Woy." Even when I was totally present with whatever she was doing, she would still call out my name—"Wo'ee"—as if I were somewhere else.

Charmaine was at that age when children start to test what they can do, so she would, all of a sudden, hit me with all her might, and I would go and complain to my mother, "Charmaine hit me."

"You know she is not well," repeating the mantra of the day.

"Yes, Mum."

"You have to be kind to your sister, right?"

"Yes. But—"

"I am trusting you."

"Yes!"

"I know you love your sister."

"Yes."

"She is just a little girl, and she loves you."

Sometimes Charmaine would go to my mother and point to where she hurt herself. "Woy did this."

"But I didn't, Mummy. She's lying."

"You are her big brother . . ."

"Yes."

"Go out in the garden and play ball . . . not rough."

"OK."

"Charmaine!"

"Yes, Woy."

"Let's go outside and play ball."

"OK, Woy. Woy?"

"Yes."

"Am I good at playing ball?"

"Yes."

"Woy, Wewy good?"

"Yes, you are very, very good. Let's go." Now! Here it is. The screen is igniting with something. What I had forgotten was that she would never hold onto my hand when she was told to. I would try, and she would pull her hand away. I would complain to my mother but got no satisfaction. Perfect results were expected, and that was that. But when she decided, for whatever reason, she would reach out her hand for me to hold. It would, all of a sudden, be there, arm extended with fingers held straight in anticipation. I can remember not only seeing my hand with hers, but now, at this moment, I feel the sensation of her small right hand with mine covering it, four fingers visible outside my grip and her thumb pressing onto the side of my left hand. There it is—clear as clear can be. We are with my mother, and we are crossing the road toward the railroad bridge. It is summer, and we are going shopping. Right now, as I write, the stage in the theater of my mind is blacked out everywhere except in the center. Right in the perfect center, there is a small spotlight on our hands together. Holding! Perfect! I take a deep breath and place this new recollection in the temple I have built for Charmaine in my heart's mind. Now the gates are open, and there is space for more to come to the center of the stage.

Flowers for Charmaine

I had started to go to a Catholic school. We were not Catholics, but all the other schools in the area were filled with disenfranchised children from the war. Many were without parents, being looked after by a reluctant relative or living with one parent in poverty. For them, the only meal was the one at school or, possibly, one stolen off the counters of shops or street vendor displays. They were very hurt and very mean. Cruelty was a daily occurrence, so it was thought I had a better chance of survival in the environment of a Catholic discipline. It turned out that instead of getting beat up on the street we would get beat up by the teachers. They would pull our ears or hit our hands with a ruler till we couldn't write, and then report us for not writing. Receiving six swipes of a thick cane on the backside really, really hurt. It was compounded by the humiliation of knowing that the whole class had witnessed it. As soon as school was over, I ran the three miles back home so I could look after Charmaine.

In that time, Charmaine was growing and had to be fitted with a larger iron brace. She was seeing a physical therapist once a week. Sometimes she didn't want to go. She would cry and cry, insisting that she would not go unless I came along, which I did. When we first moved in, there was only a frail wooden fence surrounding the front garden. As our house was on a corner, it was a pee station for dogs. Understandably, my mother was paranoid about dogs being anywhere near Charmaine. It had become an obsession. So after many letters to the local council, finally, a brick wall was put up with a heavy metal gate that Charmaine couldn't open, which made it easier to keep her safe. It was a godsend. Having the wall up stilled my mother's mind a little, but she remained deeply wounded and blamed herself for the attack on my sister. In that time, Charmaine and I became very close, and I stopped seeing her as disabled, just my little sister.

The touring circus and fairground was in town, set up over at Hampstead Heath, north of us. So my father, my sister, and I took the underground train from Chalk Farm where we lived to Hampstead Heath Station, and then walked the rest of the way. My dad decided that it would be fun to try the bumper cars, so we all got in. The voice over the loudspeaker asked us to get ready and sit down. I looked up and saw the pole from our car reaching up and contacting a wire fence grid. The cars started to move as if by magic. I was sitting beside my dad, who had Charmaine in his lap. A few people bumped into us, and we into them. Then all of a sudden, someone crashed into us with a great big bump, and a few seconds later, Charmaine screamed. She had hit her head very badly. I was so shocked that I can't remember the rest of the day. She was taken to a doctor. The next day, I was told her head was hurt, the way adults talk to children when they don't know what to say. Later, I found out she had sustained a brain injury, making it swell, but I was not told this at the time. I was told not to worry and that they were keeping her in the hospital to make sure she was fine. I must have asked my mother every hour of the waking day how my sister was and when she was coming home.

Days passed into a week. I was told she was now OK and that she was in a recovery ward at the hospital. I asked if I could see her. My parents told me that only adults were allowed in, but I could come with them to where the hospital was, and I could buy flowers for her, and they would give them to her. I saved up my few pennies and bought her a small pony doll for my parents to take to her from me.

So each Sunday, we would take an underground train and then a bus to Hendon, get off, and walk to the florist. I would choose the flowers, and they would take the bouquet and leave me there at the florist. I was given a high stool to sit in a corner behind the front glass door so I could see my parents as they would cross the road and disappear through an arch. There, I would wait while they visited Charmaine. Each time they returned, I would ask, "How is she? When is she coming home?"

"She's doing well. She'll be home soon."

Weeks passed into months. Eighteen months. One day at school, during lunch break, my fellow students brought up the subject of their siblings. There was a competition of who had the best sibling. I was quiet for awhile, which was my way around other children. I hesitated because I hadn't seen her for such a long time. Then I found myself saying that I had a sister.

Someone said, "No you don't."

Then another boy said the same.

I insisted I did and said her name was Charmaine.

Then one voice blared out, "She's dead."

I stopped and waited and then said more forcefully, "No, she isn't dead."

A few voices chimed in, one on top of the other. "Yes she is. She's dead."

I had to suffer from lunchtime until school was out, and then I ran home as fast as I could, crying all the way. My father had come home early and was in his room when I burst into the house and ran to my mother's arms in the kitchen. "They are saying Charmaine is dead. I tried to tell them she's not, but they kept on saying it over and over again."

She was still holding me, but totally silent. There is a silence that comes from adults that creates a vacuum. A child feels it but doesn't know exactly what it means, just that it's awful.

My mother asked me to go with her up the four steps from the front of the apartment to the back and stand outside my father's room. She went inside and closed the door. Less than a minute went by, and then the door opened and my mother told me to go in to my father. I didn't understand why she stayed outside. My father walked past me and closed the door and sat me down. He looked ten years older, and his face was gray. He told me that my sister, my Charmaine, was dead. Everything went blank, and I didn't cry. After this, everything was a blur.

One Sunday a few weeks later, my mother and my father took me on the same train and then the same bus to Hendon. We got off and walked to the florist as we had done so many times before. I picked a bunch of flowers, and the florist wrapped them in cellophane with a ribbon as she always did. This time I left the florist and, holding my parents' hands, walked with them across the road through the arched gateway with the name "Hendon" and another word on the arch.

We walked past stone slabs and figures until there were no more stone slabs and figures, just sticks in the ground. We walked a little longer and turned to a piece of ground the size of a bed. It had its own stick with a number. My mother and my father stopped. They became very quiet. My father's eyes were watering. They whispered to me, "This is where your Charmaine is." With the flowers in my hand, I bent down and laid them on the earth by the stick. At last I got to give her my flowers in person.

Then something snapped. I had an overwhelming numbness, and from that moment on, the sense of separation from my parents was profound.

They were so caught up in their grief that it took a long time for the story to be revealed to me. Eventually, I found out that she had died eighteen months before. The pressure in her head was pushing against her brain and causing a hemorrhage. She died while being operated on. The way the children found out was that my mother had gone to my school and confided in the headmaster. He was supposed to let only my teacher know, but somehow the word had gotten out. My parents explained with remorse, "You were so close to your sister and loved her so much. We thought you were too young to tell you. We were afraid the shock would be too much."

Eighteen months. Every Sunday for eighteen months. I lay in bed many nights with the covers over my head going over and over what that meant. Eighteen months was fifty-two weeks in a year, plus twenty-four weeks in six months. That was seventy-two times I sat in the florist, believing my sister was recovering in the hospital, that she was getting my flowers to make her room look pretty, and she was going to come home to me. I began to speak to her in my mind, calling on her by name every night. Every night, for months, I cried myself to sleep. I asked myself what kind of people my parents were that they could lie to me for all this time.

They had kept me awake night after night arguing loudly, my father raising his voice and my mother crying. I had felt her tension and her bad temper over things that I had thought trivial. One day I was with them, and they were arguing in an elevator, blaming each other for something. Suddenly the pieces came together in my young mind, and I understood. They had been arguing over my sister.

My home and my world had been turned upside down. I was growing more and more nervous and already suffered from periodic attacks of hives. They nearly covered my entire body, incapacitating me for a week or two at a time. It became impossible for me to function at school. My mind would go blank, and when the teacher spoke, it was unintelligible to me. It sounded like a foreign language. Everything was puzzling and out of focus. Somehow I knew that life was not supposed to be like this. It felt as though I was an orphan and I was alone with these strange people who had made up their own world and imposed it on me. I began to think that if they could do this, they could be lying about Charmaine being dead. For several months, I believed they were hiding the truth and she was alive somewhere. I was afraid to confront them. Besides, they would just lie again. I strategized how I could find her. I had nowhere to turn and no one to turn to.

My father started to drink heavily, my mother stopped sleeping, and the arguments got worse. Then my mother started drinking too. It was now over two years since Charmaine died. The stick that had marked her grave was now replaced by a small headstone with her name and the dates of her birth and death. I finally understood the meaning of the word after Hendon on the arch over the entrance to the place where Charmaine was buried. It was "Cemetery."

As time went by, my crying grew less. Now it was a few times a week. It was different because I had accepted she was gone. On a Sunday, my parents would say, "We're going to see Charmaine."

I would say, "I don't want to go."

They would say, "You can't stay here by yourself."

"Well, I'll go visit my friend Dylan," I would say. The home changed into a house, and then a mausoleum as my mother became a shadow of her past self. My father stopped coming home except for a few times a month. He was becoming sick in his head, delusional, imagining things that were not there. At one point he was seriously paranoid. His body was deteriorating from the long term stress of going through the war, compounded by the drinking. He had difficulty walking and had to rely on a cane.

I look back and realize I saw myself as Charmaine's protector, and my parents were not. For many years I felt that she died because I didn't do my job. That she died because I wasn't there, wherever "there" is. This feeling lasted till I became a father for the first time. Holding my newborn baby girl in my arms, I was scared that she might die and it would be my fault. Then one night something changed and it was healed. That feeling that I had carried for my sister all those years evaporated.

The simplest things can bring hearts together. One day I found some of Charmaine's building blocks that had been used to build up and level out the draining board near the sink. By then, I must have been about twelve years old. I took the blocks out and saw the pictures of alphabet letters with animals on them. They were faded, but still there. I showed my mother, and we both held the small blocks in our hands. There in our small kitchen, for the first time, my mother and I cried together for our Charmaine.

Uncle Frank and Spirit

Just after I found out about Charmaine's death, Uncle Frank appeared unannounced. The last time we had seen him was just before we moved from Theberton Street. We would get little bits of information about him from Mrs. Davis, the landlady. It turned out that he was well known as a healer, and for over fifty years, he visited many places throughout England, Scotland, and Ireland, performing his spiritual clearing and "laying on of hands," as it was called. I was told he never took money, saying, "It is a gift from God that is passed through me to others." He survived over the years solely by donations. This served all his humble needs. He was always hosted wherever he went with great love and affection.

From his perfect timing, I believe he knew I was in pain over the loss of my sister. In his usual way, speaking softly, he asked if he could do a healing. My parents allowed him because they didn't know how to refuse, but I needed him. If a child can know true love, I felt it for my Uncle Frank. As he put his hands on me, I became still in my mind, and I felt some of my burden relieved. He whispered something in my ear that sounded like, "Beyond life there is life." I wasn't sure if I had actually heard it or felt he said it.

As he was preparing to leave, in a very calm and matter-of-fact way, he said, "I am tired, very tired. I will be leaving this body in ten days." He paused, closed his eyes, and then continued, "This will happen on Wednesday, July the twenty-second, at 3:00 p.m. I have asked friends to congregate and pray for me and give witness to my passing. I want you to come."

I felt he especially emphasized for me to be there. I didn't question what he was predicting. The way he said it made it seem normal to me. My parents didn't believe in that kind of thing and didn't reinforce it, so the twenty-second came and went.

Some months later, my mother and I were once more visiting Theberton Street, where we had lived with Uncle Frank. A few of his close friends were there, collecting the rest of his belongings. My mother was somewhere speaking to Mrs. Davis and I was in the living room, when Uncle Frank's friends walked into the room. He must have mentioned me to them, because they knew about things that had happened in my life. It was comforting. The impression I got, not spoken but implied, was that I had been expected at Uncle Frank's transition from this life. They told me there were ten or more people from all over the British Isles who attended, including themselves. As the time he had allotted, 3:00 p.m., approached, he blessed everyone and closed his eyes. At exactly 3:00 p.m. on that very Wednesday, July 22, he took his last breath.

The story doesn't stop there. The warmth of his person is still indescribable for me. I never lost the sense of his presence. Of course, I was distracted during my teenage years, which made it difficult to notice, but he—or, if you like, his spirit—continued to come in and out of my life, especially when I was in trouble.

Once, when I was in my twenties, I was visiting my mother. She was still living on Regent's Park Road. I had been in the house a few days and needed to get out and stretch my legs. My mother was taking a nap, and as it was a bright, sunny day, I stepped out and decided to walk to Primrose Hill, less than five minutes away. It was around one in the afternoon when I reached the corner outside a pub across from the gate entrance to the Hill. Suddenly, crashing out of the pub was a group of about twenty men in their mid-twenties and early thirties. There was the smell of high-level tension in the air and very loud, angry rhetoric. There I was, right in the middle of it. The group divided into two. The larger were locals, tough working class, inclined to solve conflict with violence. In the other smaller group were middle-class men in business suits. One of the men in the smaller group tried to calm the situation down. There was an aggressive reply from a heavyset man in the larger group, and he stepped forward and took a stance. This was all happening within a few seconds. In the next split second, he charged and landed a vicious blow in the face of the man who tried to calm everything down. As soon as this registered, all hell broke out. I was right in the middle of people punching and kicking.

At the point when everyone was engaged, the sound of all this action seemed to mute. All was silent—even all the background noises of cars, birds from Primrose Hill, everything. It was then I felt a large hand on both of my shoulders come from behind and press me to the ground. I went from standing to sitting in a flash. I landed in a half lotus yoga pose, which normally was impossible for me to achieve. All around me, bottles were flying. Heavy beer glasses were being hammered into people's faces and heads. Out of the corner of my eye, I saw a man sink the broken end of a bottle into someone's face. A big man picked up a smaller man and took him over to the iron fence that surrounded the Hill and hung him on one of the spiked railings. All this time, I was sitting quietly, seemingly invisible, like I was in a different dimension, a different time occupying the same space.

I must have been sitting there for ten to twelve seconds. Everything seemed to be happening in slow and at the same time fast motion. Those hands on my shoulders . . . I recognized them. I had felt that sensation many times before. Then that doubt came involuntarily into my mind, and suddenly, the sounds of conflict rushed back in. It was at that time that I became visible and as I moved, a hand came down and grabbed my shirt. It was the hand of one of the men. As he pulled on my shirt, it seemed as though I was being lifted up to a standing position without his assistance. Out of the corner of my eye, I saw a car start up, ready to leave. At that very moment, someone else grabbed the back of my Levi jeans at the top of my right leg, at the pocket. I found myself running beside the car as it began to accelerate. The car speeded up and left me behind, but now I was about two hundred yards away from the fight. I was running in the opposite direction of home. If I turned around, I would be walking back into danger, so I took a side road. Still running and now mentally numb, I managed to get home and through the door. After half an hour, I stopped shaking. I expected to see a rip on my shirt, but there was nothing to be found. However, my new Levis, built to endure, were torn exactly where I had been grabbed, from pocket to knee. Tough denim that lasts for years had ripped so I could escape. But for this, I am sure I would have become a victim of that barbaric killing zone. On further contemplation, I am convinced the two large hands that pushed me to the ground into that yoga pose were the hands of the spirit of Uncle Frank. This would not be the last time he interceded. Many other incidents occurred, all involving extreme danger, all solved by some strange physical or unusual circumstance, and all with the signature of Uncle Frank's guiding protection.

Chapter 3

Rite of Passage, Ramani Rangan

My Mother's Curry

When I was just ten years of age, I became aware that the best smell in the neighborhood was my mother's cooking. I had been eating Indian food since I was a baby, if you include my mother's milk, and never thought about it until that one day.

This is how my mother made curry in our house. It was religiously prepared on a Saturday. By Wednesday, we were already anticipating our rescue from the bland consumption of something, either with toast or potatoes. Curry is made up mainly of a blend of six to eight exotic spices. The balance of each determines the flavor of the food. The kitchen becomes a temple of aromas as both hands and all five senses are engaged in grinding and blending leaf and seed into a particular personal mix. Each province in India, each village, and each home has its unique signature. If you consider that there are currently 638,000 villages . . . well! The mandatory ingredients in our mix were cloves, cinnamon, ginger, coriander, turmeric, bay leaf, and chili.

On Saturdays, after my mother and I cleaned the house, we would walk to Camden Market. It was beautiful and sunny on this particular day. We were walking down Gloucester Avenue with folded carrier bags, as we came to Camden Canal and passed through a gated entrance. We walked down the two flights of steps and then along the canal path, passing under several archways until we could hear the bustle of people on their way to shop. Then up onto the street level, where we walked a short distance to be greeted by the cries of vendors selling their fruits and vegetables.

The market was packed with mostly women wheeling their shopping carts like small chariots, pushing them into the back of people's legs. This was the strategy to intimidate their way to the front of the stall where they would find the potatoes and onions necessary for their family's lunch. Looking for the best bargain, my mother hooded her eyes like a hawk, and the battle was on.

We successfully maneuvered this stage of the hunt, and it was then on to the butcher. We had already made our choice beforehand from our three usual options—lamb, chicken, or beef. That was the period when I ate red meat. A short visit to the grocery store for rice, a can of tomatoes, and other things needed for the weekend and the following week completed our shopping.

With a full bag in each hand, we walked home. I helped my mother put things in the kitchen cabinet in their right place, and then she sent me out to play. She gave me her usual direction. I was not to go farther than Betty's house, which was about fifty feet down the avenue.

Dylan, my mate, was out. He was a Welsh boy, shy like me. My mother said she would call me when the curry was finished and we were to eat, but she never ever had a chance, because as I was playing, all of a sudden, the tantalizing aroma of her curry reached my nostrils. I dropped everything and shouted to Dylan as I was already on my way, "I got to go now." I ran to my gate and swung it open and swung it back without latching it and leaped through the front door. There I was, greeted by the beaming face of my mother, who looked as if she had found Shangri-La and was about to show me. "How did you know the food was ready? I hadn't called you," she said.

"I could smell it down the road," I said.

"So that's the perfect place to play, then," she answered.

I sat down to a table that was already laid out. The saucepans were brought in from the kitchen with the curry and the rice. The lids were lifted, and the whole of the room was full of magic. First the rice was put on the plate, and then the curry on top. By this time, my salivation was out of control. My mother sat down opposite me, and we both exchanged a knowing smile and took our first mouthful. It was wonderful. At that very moment, I felt that I belonged. And not only that, but I belonged to a very special family—an Indian family.

On the Hill with Primroses

You wouldn't think of London as open and full of nature, but we were lucky. We lived just up the road from a hill and a beautiful park. I was nearly a teen. The boys were all a few years older and a few inches taller than me. I wanted to be a part of what they were doing, to be noticed in a good way, but the bad way was predominant. If they felt like it, they would throw stones, milk bottles, zinc staples fired from a catapult, or launch lead-weighted, point-sharpened arrows from whittled-down birch branches formed into very powerful bows. There were street wars between gangs that now mimicked the violence of growing up at war with Germany and the horror that their fathers and brothers brought back and played out in drunken rages. Some said the lucky ones were lying unmarked in a foreign field, their unimaginable suffering now over. Loss and grief was etched on the faces of these boys who carried too much pain, too much heartache, making them too old for their age. Primrose Hill came to be my sanctuary from the insanity surrounding me.

Our house was on the corner of Gloucester Avenue, and our street address, Regent's Park Road. To get to Primrose Hill, I had to walk three blocks past shops, pubs, and restaurants. There were always people about, fetching stuff from the grocers, stamps for letters, bread from the bakery, or fish and chips wrapped in butcher's paper and then newspaper to keep it piping hot. Like every neighborhood, we had the off license where beer, alcoholic drinks, and cigarettes were available for purchase. The bookseller, the stationery, the chemist, and the post office were all housed in a Victorian corner building with tiled walls, cut glass, finely carved mahogany furnishings, and high ceilings. Besides getting prescriptions filled, my mother and I would go once a month to pay the gas and electric bills with a money order. Banking and checks came later in our house, along with the refrigerator and television. It was 1953 in London, and rationing for all food—like eggs, cheese, sugar, salt, and fresh fruits and vegetables—was now over. The last to go was meat from the butcher.

The shops were all on the street level, with apartments above. As you walked past, the shops looked clean and bright with shiny paint and windows displaying the newest products and fashions. Each day floors were swept and mopped, even the front pavement. Then the soapy water left over from the job of cleaning the floors inside the premises was splashed outside and, with a stiff brush, swept to the curb. But if you looked up one floor past the bright signs, which I was always doing, you could see extensive damage from shrapnel and explosions—gifts from the war. Some windows were still boarded up. Others had not been cleaned for many years. Exposed bricks and ledges had become home to wild bushes and tribes of sparrows. It was obvious that beneath the surface, chaos was lurking and things were still not right.

As a child of twelve, and even at an earlier age, I sensed the air was full of breaths not taken, nervous chain smoking, tremors and twitches. People would stop for no visible reason as if they needed to look at a map in the sky or inside themselves. Women as well as men were blind drunk, walking as though they were on a ship rolling on a stormy sea going nowhere. They staggered down Regent's Park Road or stumbled out of the Prince of Wales pub across the street from us at night. I had been afraid of them for a long time, but now I made space on the pavement and went my way as they spoke to imaginary friends or family members or ghosts of people they had lost. I was surrounded by erratic behavior. Even the sober, internalizing their losses with invisible strings attached to the momentum of responding to the passing of time, only appeared to function, placing one foot in front of the other, one breath following the next. "Hello." Chat. Chat. Chat. "Bye now." An exchange of quickly disappearing smiles and hand gestures. Life goes on . . . cup of tea . . . walk the dog. In the silence of empty shells, spirits permanently drifting just outside of reach, they floated. After so much had been ravaged by the unspeakable carnage of war, that which was lost, was now gone forever—irretrievable. Many, not quite alcoholic, kept the amount imbibed to a permanent level just under the horizon of obvious numbness, so they could recapture the imaginary feeling of being in control. As if being out of control was a thing of the past. It seemed that they all—alcoholics, drunkards, and controlled drinkers— had given up on finding themselves. Sometimes I wondered if they were just waiting, passing time, for Death to take them to join the honored dead. The sober mocked the un-sober, but they themselves, in many cases, had members of their family in the same situation. They too had lost all and were now in some way orphaned, knocked off their path, numbed by a less-visible obsession or addiction.

I remember soldiers back from war searching for their loved ones, even after so many years. Tattered pictures which had been carried through mud and filth were pulled from pockets.

"Have you seen her, my wife?"

"My daughter, my sister, my brother, uncle, father . . .?"

Occasionally, there were miraculous reunions.

There were many still walking around missing limbs left at home and in foreign lands. They had been teamed up at recovery centers. One with one eye and one totally blind walked two in step, sighting the other in permanent darkness, feeling the edge of the sidewalk with the end of a white stick. Tap, tap, tap. Dampened exchange of words with arms linked. The blind one wearing a trench coat over civvies smiles, but not the eyes. Later, I imagined that the sighted one maybe owed the blind one his life, maybe the other way around. Maybe they were brothers, or just now, a bridge of love bound them to the earth. Stark is an understatement, but there isn't a word to be found, so let this be sufficient.

All this would be soon forgotten in just those few minutes after the walk up Primrose Hill, climbing to the top where I could feel the wind blowing and see the birds hovering at my height. Far in the background, I could peer over the London Zoo to Central London. Being up there was like flying. The many-colored kites with dragon tails fluttered in the wind, declaring their freedom of expression. Then it took just a run down the Hill to a path, crossing the road, past the calls of the animals of the London Zoo to enter Regent's Park. First, was a field of neatly mowed grass fringed on one side by hundred-year-old trees. My favorites were the horse chestnut, silver birch, and weeping willow. Ahead, there was a Chinese garden with a bridge crossing over a narrow man-made waterway. Cascading along the banks, thousands of beautiful flowers waved gently in the breeze in a profusion of choreographed colors and shapes. Farther on, there was a boating pond with ducks and waterfowl squabbling, then agreeing, and then squabbling again. Past that was the inner circle, including the Regent's Park Open Air Theater, summer cafés where afternoon tea, scones, and clotted cream could be enjoyed, restaurants where the menu offered light meals and a glass of wine, and kiosks for ice cream, to pacify the junior members of society. If that weren't enough, more magic was to come. Deep in the center of the inner circle, I was transported into another world—Queen Mary's Gardens. This was a sanctuary for approximately twelve thousand roses of eighty-five singular varieties in company with other bordering flowers like delphiniums and begonias. In season, the fragrance was mind altering. The whole park was about three miles from one end to the other. When I was tired and needed to rest, I could find a tree with shade and lie down, feeling more safe than I did at home or anywhere else. It was my world away from *their* world.

It is an unfortunate fact of life that some things in a child's world are so marked by travesty that he grows up faster than he ought to. You don't know this at the time. You see your mother crying again for the hundredth time for no reason, and no words from you can reach or comfort her. You feel the disturbance. It is apparent, but not understood by you. This question mark is hammered in so many times that it becomes embedded, and you prematurely age, so your childhood is lost. Infiltrated, embroiled. You stand in the dark passageway of your cold apartment and find yourself frozen beyond thought, because you know that she is devastatingly unhappy and has been for what feels like forever. You know it is many things, but the giant monster is the loss of your sister. You can't move, the cushion of energy from her pain is pushing against you to stay away. She doesn't know you notice all, feel all, but understand nothing. She may see you looking at her fumble for a few coins from her purse and, without looking up, ask you to go and get something, a pack of Woodbine or Navy Cut, the cheapest cigarettes. Maybe the request was for onions or potatoes, even if there were onions and potatoes in the kitchen.

It took awhile, but I learned to not ask or question. I would just go out and take my time to come back. Sometimes the sadness in me and in her took over, and I forgot what I was sent out to buy and returned home empty-handed, with no repercussions, as my mother had retreated back inside with no signal to engage. Women neighbors would come over and talk in low whispers about sad things that I didn't understand. This was before tissues, so handkerchiefs were taken from hidden places on the person who was visiting and lifted to their faces to cover their eyes and wipe tears. Sometimes my mother would slump to the floor sobbing, and whoever was in her room would help her up.

But when I was in Regent's Park, all of that fell away. As soon as I walked past the gates, I entered a world that dropped all history—mine, my mother's, my father's, and my sister Charmaine's. It wasn't a conscious choice—it just happened, like a reflex, spontaneously. My feet found the gravel, I turned, and started to walk slowly. For one, two, sometimes three, four hours, I was free, just walking—looking, feeling, seeing. From the outside of the zoo, I could greet my animal friends. Some I could see, and others I could only hear. The giraffes, Brumas the polar bear, Guy the Gorilla, exotic birds, elephants, camels, peacocks wandering around freely, and in the petting zoo, goats, sheep, giant tortoises, and rabbits. They felt like my family. Sitting with an ice cream cone under a chestnut tree, I watched people watch other people playing cricket and soccer or strolling with children in pushchairs. Pollinating butterflies and bees who were busy doing their work among all the flowers saw no difference between the noble, prized roses and the humble, wild primrose. Dogs on the leash sniffed on a scent and pulled to discover more. Flocks of sparrows and crows animated the sky as they looked for safety and a place to forage. This was the perfect way in these moments to be in the world. Did you know that on a hot, sunny day when you eat your ice cream under a tree, because it is cooler, the ice cream takes longer to melt, so you don't lose any or very little? It was in these instances I forgot time, placement, the order of things, and returning. Returning home. Returning to other people's past. In this place, this refuge, returning didn't exist. Leaving the primroses was not possible in this world, my world. In these moments and moments like these, I had disappeared, and there were only my animal friends, in the wild and in the zoo, gardens with the promise of unlimited adventures and primroses on the Hill.

The Children's Hospital

In that time, my father was working for Disney U.K. They were producing their famous characters in latex with bendable wire inside so they could be twisted into different shapes. After he had worked there for three months, his boss would come and pick him up in a big black car early in the morning and bring him back in the evening. He told me that he had invented a way of increasing production three times faster than before and with a better product. I even got up early one day, took the day off from school, and went with him and his boss into work. Very few people at that time had cars. I had seen Queen Elizabeth II in a big car, so I was very excited.

One Christmas Eve, I must have been ten or eleven, the front door opened, and my father started bringing in large plastic bags full of Disney dolls. There was Mickey, Minnie, Goofy, Pluto, Prince Charming, Snow White, and some others. When he finished, most of the dining room was full. On Christmas day, after we had opened presents and had breakfast, a taxi came to the door. He asked me to help him pack the taxi with as many dolls as we could. In the end, I was sitting in the front on the floor next to the taxi driver, in the spot where the luggage was usually stored. There was an enormous bag of dolls on my lap, so I could barely see out the window. We drove for what seemed to be a long time through light snow. We finally stopped, and as we started to unload, I could see we were outside a children's hospital in London.

Some people from the hospital came out to help us into the elevator. The doors opened to a ward full of sick children. A few were on oxygen, some had their heads shaved, most were in bed, and others were in a plastic tent. My father disappeared and a few minutes later reappeared with a clown face and a large sparkly cone hat. He started to talk to the children. Nurses and other people dressed in white appeared and joined him. He told me to take some toys out of one of the plastic bags and put them on a trolley. He went to each child and began to sing them a Christmas carol. I handed him a toy, and he gave it to them. We were there for more than two hours visiting other children in other wards. He sang many Christmas carols, some more than once, until all children had been sung to and given a toy. What was left was put under a Christmas tree in the lobby.

I don't remember my father saying why we were we doing this, but we returned each Christmas for several years. Later, my mother told me that my father had arranged with the Disney director for all rejects to be saved and given to him. Throughout the year, my father would stay after work and repair or repaint them so they would look perfect for the sick children. She explained that it was at that very hospital where my sister, Charmaine, had died. So that is why he visited and sang to the children each year and why his eyes were full of tears each time in the taxi on the way back home. She told me that he wept with her and said, "I never got to sing to my Charmaine before she died." There is much we have to learn about what it takes to be a father and a man.

Mr. Varney

Mr. Varney owned the house we lived in. We were in the ground-floor apartment, with a friendly married couple upstairs. For a few years, a man who escaped from Hungary during the Soviet occupation lived down in the basement. It was very dark and damp down there, and I was afraid of it because of ghosts and things. That was before he moved in. Now I was afraid of him. He would have nightmares and scream. Sometimes he ran up the stairs to our floor, and my mother would get scared too. He would say he was sorry, but it didn't help. Then one day, he came up carrying a knife. He was having a flashback and didn't intend to harm us, but to be on the safe side, my father took some old chairs and a few tables and blocked the staircase so he couldn't come up. He understood. Later, he had an arranged marriage with a woman from Hungary, and she came to live with him. I liked her. She had long blonde hair and smiled even when she was talking about things that weren't funny. They had a child. He still had bad nightmares that scared his wife. Eventually, after a few years, they left. We left the chairs and tables in the staircase. I don't know why.

Back to Mr. Varney. Though he was the owner, he never came to the house in twenty-two years, except for once when his son died. Looking out the kitchen window, you could see the bridge over the railway, which we would cross to catch the bus or take the underground. When you walked over the bridge, just before it ended, there on the left was a tiny shop. It looked like it was part of the bridge. When you entered, you could see that the floor hung over the railroad tracks. The whole shop shook when a train went by, and that was every minute. Mr. Varney owned the shop. That is where he could always be found.

He was about five feet, an inch taller than my mother, round and heavy, with eyes that were pushed close by the size of his cheeks. He was always looking down, showing no expression whatsoever, oblivious to all except the function of his shop. He must have changed his clothes, but there was no evidence, as his trousers and his vest were always baggy, and his shirt was so off-white it could have been dirty.

My mother, born in India, was very strict that children—that meant me—never spoke ill of any adult, or child for that matter. Mr. Varney was a perfect target for childish ridicule, but my mother's Indian protocol and home-bred superstitions had taught me better, and my lips were sealed. I had to jump through hoops to stay on top of her many taboos, and I never knew when I was breaking one. On the other hand, my father, born in South Africa, had a whole other set of rules I had to dodge and weave through. I should have gotten a degree on my twenty-first birthday, just for life experience with them.

It was my job to take the rent to Mr. Varney in his shop. We had a rent book with all the amounts and dates that had already been paid. First, I would have to walk halfway over the bridge to make sure his shop was open, because he didn't keep a regular schedule, especially, my mother told me, after his wife died. I would then walk back to the house and get the money and the book. Each time I was instructed by my mother to go straight there and have my hand in the pocket where the money was at all times.

The interior of the shop was very dark, so all the items on the walls looked to me as though they were glued together in a collage. The counter had glass on the top, and underneath, all the items looked as though they had not been rearranged since the shop first opened. He never spoke to me, just took the money and the book and disappeared into the back room. I always wondered how it was possible that there was enough space to even have a back room.

Mr. Varney would hand me the book without looking up, and I would leave. I never told my mother that I was nervous a few days before the end of the month, terrified to go there and step past the front door into that shop hanging over the railroad tracks. This was, by far, the scariest shop in the world with the scariest man I had ever met. After recently seeing the movie, *The Hobbit*, he came to mind. He would fit in easily as a dwarf warrior or a background drinker at the tavern in the Shire.

The Magic Apple

Straight over from Mr. Varney's shop on the bridge was a greengrocer. The front of the shop was no wider than two standard doors put side to side going back thirty feet. The grocer had small stalls on each side of the opening, with fruit on one side and vegetables on the other.

It was summer. I was twelve and on my way over the bridge to visit a friend when I passed his shop and saw an apple and took it. He caught me with the evidence in my hand and sternly directed me into the shop and told me to go to the back and wait while he served people. I was shaken and surprised to find the apple in my hand. It happened in seconds, without conscious awareness. I was really frightened. Would he call the police? What would my mother and my father say?

He ignored me for over an hour, as there were many customers to attend to. The flow stopped. He came to me and, without saying a word, looked deeply into my eyes. He turned and began to fill an empty orange box with vegetables and fruit. When it was overflowing, he signaled to me to follow him out of the shop, onto the pavement, and pointed to a large tenement building that was down the hill, on the other side of the main road. "I want you to take this box to a lady who lives on the second floor. Here is the list, the prices, and the address of her apartment. Can you do this?"

I nodded and answered yes.

"She will give you money. Put it in this envelope and bring it back here to me." I was afraid to look at him. "Are you sure you can do this?" he asked again.

I said, "Yes."

I was totally confused and I had no idea where this was all going, but I knew I had to do it. I had stopped shaking, which helped. I followed his instructions, delivered the box, got the money, and returned and gave it to him. By then, he had filled three more orders, and I delivered them too. He then gave me the apple that I had taken and asked me if I wanted a job each Saturday. I would be paid a small amount and get a box of fruit and vegetables to take home. I was still in a daze on my way home and sat for a while looking at the apple. I didn't tell my mother that I had stolen the apple, but I did tell her that I had my first job. I worked for him for two years, till he closed the shop down. I learned a stunning and valuable lesson that day.

Nathan Samuels

When we moved to Regent's Park, I thought we were the only family of color in the neighborhood, and probably one of less than a hundred others throughout a population of over 7.7 million in the

Greater London area. Within a few months, we found out that we were not the only ones. There was an African man who lived across the road. He was in his seventies. I was nine years old at the time. It turned out that he rarely left his apartment and it was his Welsh wife who shopped and took care of outside business. Theirs was a mixed-race marriage. I can't recall ever seeing Mr. and Mrs. Samuels out together.

One day I saw him across the road walking with a purpose. Our eyes met. I could tell by his glance I was seen, measured, and noted. A few months passed, and one day, his wife knocked on our door. My mother must have spoken with her at some point before. She was introduced to me as Mrs. Samuels, and I was sent out of the room. The next day, my mother and I went across the road to their apartment to visit. Mrs. Samuels had gone to Wales because of a sickness in her family. Apparently, Mr. Samuels never accompanied her on her visits there. Mr. Samuels was feeling poorly, and she wanted us to keep an eye on him.

Over the next few years, he visited us a dozen times or so, and we visited him. He struck me as a very private person. As we became used to each other, he began to relax. He was especially pleased when my father was home, so they could talk about what men talked about at the time. A lot was to do with politics and how men of color were being treated. They were both boxing fans, I think because at the time, black fighters, then known as coloreds, like Floyd Patterson, Joe Louis, and Sonny Liston, were winning international fame. Men of color were identifying with them. It gave them a sense of pride under the enormous weight of racism. Both loved jazz and big band music, so the portable record player was taken out, and they would listen, sipping a whiskey and water while I had a fizzy drink. My mother always took her first chance to leave the room so the men could find comfort in each other's company. She didn't ask me to leave as she usually did. She hoped that something would rub off on me that she knew I needed and that, as a woman, she couldn't offer.

None of the houses I knew had closets. We all had wardrobes. Mine was falling apart. It had been bought at a time when everything in postwar England was of very poor quality. Mr. Samuels had a wardrobe that he wanted to get rid of. He invited me and my mother over to his flat and showed it to us. My young eyes thought it was beautiful.

The wood was real, and you could see the grains showing beneath the mahogany varnish. The door was already open, and I could see slide-out shelves on one side and on the other side a bronze bar to hang suits and coats. It was about three quarters the size of my old wardrobe, which made me feel that it somehow fit me perfectly. Mr. Samuels got out some string to tie around the door so it would stay shut, as it had lost its key a long time ago. As he closed the door, I saw the full-length mirror on the inside. It felt like a miracle.

We managed to get it down the stairs and across the road, while Mr. Samuels looked out for traffic. All the time, I was praying that it would not somehow fall apart. It creaked and groaned a little up the three steps, the one step at the front door, rest, up the four more steps to my room till we set it down and turned on the light. It was shuffled into a corner, making a triangle facing out.

To be honest, I wanted my mother and Mr. Samuels to leave straightaway. It was a few long minutes as my mother and I took turns thanking him several times before they were gone. I sat on my bed and just stared at it. Eventually, I got up and inspected the veneer, running my hand over it. I looked at the sides and could see they were made from two pieces of the same wood joined together, so the grains were mirror images of each other. I took off my shoes and carefully stepped inside, not wanting the bottom to break. It didn't even give with my weight. I could stand up. I opened and closed the door several times to see the change of my reflection in the full-length mirror. This was big, really big. That it had come from Mr. Samuels, a man, seemed to mean something—that I was being recognized as a male by another male. It was very new for me, and I felt expanded and welcomed into a world that I didn't have words or concepts for. I spent a few hours putting all my clothes in and then rearranging them to get them just right. Then finally, I sat down in my wardrobe like it was a cave—my cave. I stayed there until my mother called me three times to come down for tea. I usually went out on the street and played, but when I had finished, I ran up to my room, opened my bedroom door, and closed it behind me. Somehow, I felt as though I had changed from an older child to a young man.

Mrs. Samuels would come over every so often, and I was beginning to be old enough to believe I knew everything. Sometimes when my mother and Mrs. Samuels were talking, she would say something to my mother that I felt was wrong. One day, I opened my mouth and questioned Mrs. Samuels. Everything went cold. "Never, never question an adult," my mother said later, scolding me.

"But . . . but—"

"No buts. Respect your elders."

"But she was wrong," I pleaded.

"I know," my mother said, "but that doesn't give you the right to say anything. You are a child—" She saw a look on my face. "You are young, and don't think you know everything."

Every time after that, when Mrs. Samuels came over and said silly things, I held my tongue.

He was not a conversationalist, Mr. Samuels. He had a dry humor that I didn't really get. He would smile or softly laugh at his own remarks, which seemed to be just for him. It was as though he was sharing from the inside, once in a while cracking the door to the soul. We didn't chat. Our conversation was minimal, always direct and warm. I was comfortable with him, and I could be myself.

One day, I was visiting Mr. Samuels, and he took out a book. The book was a history from the point of view of Africans about their Diaspora around the world, including Africans in the Americas. He sat me down to read the book and then left the room. For several weeks, I went over to his apartment, and each time, he handed me another book on African history from a set, all with the same binding. That is when I learned about slavery and its horrors in all the colonial countries. Also about the people who helped slaves in the USA when they journeyed north on the Underground Railroad. There were chapters on the secret coded messages that slaves would use to communicate with each other unbeknownst to their masters. These were hidden in songs or sign language. I learned about the caste system of discrimination within the black community based on how light or dark skinned you were. I read about the plight of Australian Aboriginals and people in Fiji and Borneo and other islands in the Pacific. Mr. Samuels sat with me and showed me one book in particular. He emphasized that there had been ancient African kingdoms and empires with untold riches that traded for thousands of years with other countries as well as India. He told me about Timbuktu, one of the hundreds of centers of learning, culture, and commerce on the African continent. This, he said, was the largest continent, consisting of over fifty countries. He mentioned the Queen of Sheba and told me that Egypt was part of Africa. These were large, oversized, heavy books, illustrated with etchings. They were at least sixty to seventy years old, printed in times when it was extremely dangerous to possess them. Mr. Samuels gave me the impression that they were still controversial. For some reason, he didn't show my mother or my father these books. I think he saw something in me that was special, something that I couldn't see in myself at the time. These afternoons with Mr. Samuels stayed with me, and I knew he was telling me something about himself and what it meant to be a black man in a white world.

Things were what they were in my world, and the mountains and valleys of that time were just landscapes in the mist, until one day I came home from riding my bicycle. Mrs. Samuels was visiting. I went to my room, and I heard her leave, and then it was suppertime. We listened to the radio with a cuppa tea, and then to bed. On Saturday morning, my mother told me that she had not seen Mr. Samuels. It turned out that Mrs. Samuels had left on Thursday to visit her family in Wales, which was a long train ride, and she would be away for a week. My mother said that Mr. Samuels was going to come over on Friday morning for breakfast, and it was now Saturday. She asked me if I had seen him. I hadn't, so she decided we should go over and check on him.

We knocked on the door, but there was no answer. Mother tended to get worried easily and get nervous. She called the landlord. He opened the street door, and we all went up and knocked on the apartment door and called out his name. There was no response, so the landlord opened that door but didn't go in. He was scared. I turned to my mother, and she wouldn't take another step. She told me to go in and look through every room. There I stood, a child of twelve, and this big grown man, the landlord, was paralyzed on the spot. At that time, I thought landlords were really lords, as in—important, brave, and rich people. Well, that way of seeing landlords changed that day.

My mother urged me again to go in, so I did. I walked into the dark apartment. All the blinds were drawn. I called out, "Mr. Samuels . . . Mr. Samuels . . . it's me." I eventually got to the kitchen, and there he was, with his back to me. I walked up toward his right side, and just before him, I knew that he was not moving. I gently moved a little forward so I could see his profile. He was sitting there on the chair with his eyes closed. I had never seen a person like this, so I went back to my mother and told her what I had seen. She was shaking, and the landlord was gone. She asked me to tell her in more detail. Had I touched him? I hadn't, so she told me I had to go in again and touch him. The thought of it terrified me, and it felt like a nightmare. I hesitated, but she insisted. So I went in again and went right up to him and touched his shoulder and then his cheek. He was as cold as marble. Then strangely enough, I became quiet inside and calm. I went back and told my mother, and she held my hand tight as we crossed the road back home.

What happened after that was vague. I remember hearing that Mrs. Samuels came back early, and she didn't leave her house, and I didn't see her for a long time. I was told that his body had to be "reorganized." They had to break his bones to get him to fit in the coffin because of rigor mortis. Why I was given these details, I still don't know. In all the deaths that had occurred affecting my young life, it was the habit of my mother and my father to "protect me" by keeping me from the service, burial, and reception, and not to even talk about it. This case was no exception. Many years later, I found out from others that Mr. Samuels had been a hero and a civil rights activist in Nigeria. He had served in the Allied Merchant Navy during the war. Two of the ships he was on had been sunk by submarines, and he was cast out to sea in a small lifeboat for many days before being rescued. I was told that many people traveled from Africa and from other countries to attend his funeral, and there were lots of speeches and tears.

I remember him on Martin Luther King's day. Mr. Nathan Samuels is still my hero. He was the first man, besides my father, whose very presence called forth the aura and the mystery of manhood. To this day, I am still learning the lessons that he taught me so many years ago.

Chapter 4

Tribe Dance, Ramani Rangan

Kitchen Adventures

I would watch the beads of condensation on the inside of the kitchen window begin to collect and start to run down, inviting other drops to follow suit, as I waited for my mother, wherever she was on the other side of our apartment. She would have to hurry through the kitchen door so as not to let the heat out. The only way to warm the apartment was with coal, and we didn't have money for that. Our sole source of heat was the oven.

It was the height of winter in London. The smog was so thick that when you opened the front door, you could not see the front gate only ten feet away. In the house, it was very cold and damp—so much so that there was one room across from the kitchen that we never used. It had mold and mildew all over the walls. The kitchen was the savior. Imagine a sink and a small counter, a food cupboard, a gas stove, and just enough space for two chairs. That was our kitchen. It had two doors, one to the hallway, the other to the dining room, with both opening inward, so it took a special maneuver not to lock them together by their handles.

My mother would come in and simultaneously, while filling the kettle, propose, "Should we have a good cup of tea?" The tea she used was Brooke Bond, packaged so it had to be measured. On the outside, there was a stamp. She collected the stamps, which went into a book, to save up and get a gift for the house, usually for Christmas. Water on. Empty teapot close to the heat for pre-warming. Measure tea leaves. Wait for kettle whistle to blow. Rest a few moments so the boiling water does not bruise the leaves. Pour. Replace lid, brewing time exactly four minutes. Perfect. Cup and sugar to the ready. Next, my job was to bring in the milk from the dining room as it was as cold as any refrigerator in the winter. All that was necessary for completion was placed to the ready on the flip-down door of the cupboard. The chairs were adjusted so as to be even closer to the warmth emitting from the open door of the oven. I had my special place. Above my head was the gas meter. To have gas for the gas stove, one would need to feed the meter with coins, and it would be dispensed for one's use, like the electricity meter. Sometimes there were no coins, hence, no tea. So we had to go to a very cold bedroom, placing all the coats we had on top of the blankets of one of the beds, and huddle to get warm.

When the ritual of the making of the tea was complete and the aroma of the brew had permeated everything, including one's mind, the tea was poured. Two teaspoons of sugar were added with a touch of milk, stirred, and then there was a breath. I was finished with everything I needed to do, and my mother's duties were complete. She would very carefully put her feet on the bottom of the inside of the oven, and I would follow. Sipping on our lovely cup of tea, with our feet getting toasty warm, we began to talk about all kinds of things that no one else could ever understand, because it was just for us.

My First Bike and Independence Day

My father was home on Saturday when he wasn't working, so it must have been one of those Saturdays. The sun was shining as I sat on the low wall to the right of our front door. It was my perch, the space I had claimed that was only mine. From here, I had a front-row seat to watch what played out in my theater across the road at the Prince of Wales pub. In the morning, the pub owners and the staff would be visited by trucks, called lorries in England. They unloaded a full range of alcoholic beverages and the necessary food supplies for a daily rotating menu, designed to accommodate the palate of local patrons. Everything was tidied, cleaned and polished to immaculate brilliance. The stage was set for my matinee.

Lunchtime at the pub was a daily ritual attended mostly by laborers and workingmen with skills such as house painting, carpentry, plumbing, and all things mechanical. The opening scene was signaled by the sounding of the noonday bell. Curtains were drawn. Sandwich boards were placed outside, announcing the menu specials of the day. In anticipation, the actors of this very long-running play would swarm to the front door, standing at the ready. From my perspective, I could view the setup as if I were backstage while the choir of an opera waited for their cue to go onstage. The doors opened, and the merry men and women of Gloucester Avenue rushed in for the Pint, each one loyal to their particular brand of ale, beer, or bitter.

I watched them putting their orders in and then standing in groups inside and outside or in the small beer garden at the side of the building, talking about what men have talked about for thousands of years. Now I was the audience for the two and a half hours of entertainment. I would have other things to do in the house, but I would return to my place of power and could easily catch up where I left off. The ten-minute bell for ordering the last round would sound. Laughs and cheers would fade and the groups would start to thin out until the last players disappeared from the stage. Curtains down, end of scene 1.

Then there was a long break as the stage manager and the stagehands prepared for the evening performance. The light outside would dim as the sun set into the evening. The lights inside would go on, and music would begin to play. The bell would ring. Within half an hour, the scene was packed with all the occupants imbibing their beverages, generally limited to a couple of pints to ease the strain of the labor of the day. Inside, smoke from cigarettes, cigars, and pipes mimicked the same intensity as a London winter smog. The final bell tolled, the last call. The guests were ushered out and the doors were closed for the night. It was only on a Friday and Saturday night that a few remained. The staggerers, the singing criers, the high-volume speakers, the arguers, the vomiters, the red-faced smilers, and the looking-for-a-fight fighters would tumble out into the street, sometimes lingering for hours. Mostly, the performers didn't change, and the performance was the same.

But I digress. We are back on my wall to the right of the front door steps. It is still Saturday morning, and the sun is shining. My father tells me, "Get ready. We're going out." As usual, I am not told where to or what for. It's one of those adult secrets, things they do to their children, thinking they will enjoy the surprise. But in reality, it's torture.

So what was it this time? We passed the pub, crossed the Victorian iron bridge that spanned over ten train tracks below, and walked down the hill to Chalk Farm. Then we turned right and passed the roundhouse, a brick building that was big enough for a train engine to enter, get fixed, turn around, and leave again. Next we turned left onto Malden Road, following the route I usually took to get to my school. That route would take me through two gang areas and dogs trained to bite children each weekday. Luckily, today, my father steered us in a different direction. We turned right before that, and I breathed more easily. After walking and talking for a while, the sound of bustling shoppers welcomed us to Kentish Town's main street. Like determined hunters on a safari, solemn stone-faced women were stalking the cheapest game to satisfy their list. They were in a hurry as Saturday was just a half day. We passed shop after shop. Where were we going?

Then suddenly, my father turned and opened a high glass door, and we were in the palace of bicycles. The overhead lights sparkled on hundreds of shining metal wheel rims, spokes, gloss-painted frames and bells, reflectors, and lamps. The whole back wall was mirrored, doubling everything. I walked the rows from one end to the other while each bike stood at attention for my royal inspection. In the daze of an altered state of mind, I managed to pick out my bike from a selection in the lower price range I was expected to choose from. I found one with a light-blue frame and large deep drop handlebars. It had a bell. It smelled of new rubber tires and chain oil. We were a perfect match. I was in love. OK, it was good my father didn't tell me beforehand, because I would have been sick with excitement.

What has this to do with the Prince of Wales pub across the street? Suddenly I was free. I could get on my bike and leave the theater of the pub and the drama of my life behind. I was master of my own ship on two wheels. Every day I rode around my neighborhood. On Sundays, I would even ride through Primrose Hill, past the London Zoo, through Regent's Park to Oxford Street, on to Trafalgar Square and up the mall to the Buckingham Palace. I was twelve years old, and that day that I first got on my bike and rode away from the family stuff, the neighborhood gang madness and the Prince of Wales was, for me, my very own Independence Day.

Famous Moments

One evening, when I was thirteen, there was a knock on the front door. Who could it possibly be? Through the glass panels, I could see a dark man's figure under the light from our hallway against the blackness of a late fall night. I opened it, and in front of me was an Indian. From his features, I gathered he was from the South. I knew this because my own father's family originally came from Tamil Nadu, a state hugging the eastern coast of South India. From the kitchen, my mother asked who it was. I didn't know how to say he was an Indian, which was a very rare sighting in the part of London where we lived. I stood aside and let him in the passage and ushered him into the dining room next to the kitchen. I had not answered my mother yet. You could say I was speechless.

My mother opened the door between the kitchen and the dining room to see this strange man still standing there, obviously cold from his night walk. My mother looked at me with her eagle eye, hesitated, and then smiled and, not looking at him directly, asked him to sit down. As with all those who passed through our doors, he was offered a cup of tea. The kitchen door was left open so my mother could still converse with him. He said that he was the London agent for Asian film extras and that he was short of Indian males for a film production. As I was tall for my age, I fit the general description. Would my mother let me work for three days on a movie that was being made in Elstree Studios? I, of course, was immediately in love with the idea, but my mother, in all her wisdom, asked so many questions that by the time the third cup of tea was offered, I thought he would get angry and just leave. He mentioned the amount I would get paid per day, and it was the equivalent of her three days' work. He said he would pick me up and bring me back and make sure I was safe. Just when I was about to throw a tantrum, which was never done in my household, she saved the day and agreed. I was to be ready at 5:00 a.m. and would be back by 7:00 p.m.

I was going to school at the time, so my mother and I plotted a plausible excuse that I had a very bad cold and cough. As it was a three-day casting call, and it was only Wednesday, it would have to be a prolonged cold. She said she would call the school office and tell them the sad story. When it came to lying, adults had their own standards. It was hammered into me that lying was very bad . . . if I did it. For this time, I thought it was just great. I went to bed at 8:30 p.m. so I could be fresh in the morning, but I was so excited I didn't fall asleep until 2:00

a.m. I managed to get up in the morning and be dressed and ready on time. He came a few minutes to five, and we stepped out into the frosty night and headed for the Underground.

We took the Northern line north, straight to the end station. Then we got on a special bus, which was full of Indians, and we were driven to the studios. I thought of all the times I had been in the cinema and dreamed of being on the screen, and now it was about to happen. We passed through the gates into the studio lot. Our names were called out, and we were given a card, which was good for a free breakfast, lunch, and tea. The agent instructed me not to wander around, listen to the assistant and to the director, and follow him when it was time to go to the soundstage. He had asked me to wear a bright shirt. I went quickly through wardrobe and then makeup to have my face dusted over with a powder, then moisturizer, and finally sprinkled with oil so it looked as though I was perspiring. I realized that the other film extras knew the ropes, so I followed them to the cafeteria, and there I saw more film extras all dressed up in bright summer clothes, some with hats and some with torn shirts. There must have been another film being made, because some were dressed in late eighteenth century European costume. I was overwhelmed with excitement and wonder. The food was free, so I had eggs and bacon, baked beans, toast, and tea. The agent came in, and we were led to one of the large buildings resembling an airplane hangar from outside. We passed through two doors into pitch black, and I could sense that we were behind a large film set. I was told to stay where I was, with ten other extras, and slowly my eyes started to adapt to the faint light.

It was now 8:30 a.m., and I was eager to start. I could hear people speaking, talking about things that were too technical for me to understand. I saw big lights mounted on a six-foot pole on wheels being pushed around. Through the slits between the set, I saw just enough to make me even more excited, and a little nervous, but not enough to dull the anticipation. After a very long half hour, a man with headphones holding a clipboard waved us past the back to the front. I was ushered into a tropical scene with bamboo huts, coconut trees, a boat tied up to an artificial dock, and tropical flowers.

We spent the whole morning shouting and acting as though we were gambling, stopping and starting and stopping again till lunchtime. We were served Indian food and I remember thinking, *If this is what working is, I'm all for it.* Afterward, we were taken to another location within the set, this time with white buildings and walls, tall palm trees, and a cobbled street with a few live donkeys hitched up to carts. This time we were asked to sit around and look as though we were talking. Four of us sat at a table chatting for about thirty minutes when the studio called us on a loudspeaker and told us that we were going to start shooting in ten minutes. The actors took their positions. I got a lesson that day in how arduous it was for them, saying their lines over and over again, and portraying the same feelings so that the camera could capture all the different angles necessary. After two hours, the actors left, and we were asked to do one more scene before breaking for the evening. This time we were asked to walk around as though we were on our way somewhere.

Hollywood had been my steady diet from early childhood, starting with the memory of standing with my mother in a line with hundreds of other families, waiting to get tickets to see Walt Disney's *Jack and the Beanstalk*, starring Mickey Mouse, no less. My mother often took me with her to the cinema. Sometimes there was stuff on that silver screen I didn't understand. She seemed to love whatever was going on, and I loved being with her, and that was enough. There were always two movies, starting with a full-length B movie, the news—remember, no TV—and sometimes a cartoon. Then when the lights went up, my mother would give me money to run and buy us each an ice cream cup from an usher holding a tray and walking up and down the aisles. Now satisfied, we would settle in for the main feature. As I grew old enough to be trusted to go to the cinema by myself, I got to see Francis the Talking Mule, the Dead End Kids, Chaplin, Bud Abbott and Lou Costello, Laurel and Hardy, Tarzan, Sabu the Elephant Boy, Flash Gordon, and too many more to even mention.

I did extra work for the next six years. I was in films such as Robert Mitchum and Rita Hayworth's *Fire Down Below*, and another called *Bhowani Junction*, with Ava Gardner and Stewart Granger. You can imagine my elation when I came face-to-face with icons I had only seen before on the big screen. Seeing them convincingly portray a character and come out of role so many times taught me a lot about life. I took away from this experience that I am not a set of roles played out for each person I meet, but *me*, like each and every one of us, a unique gift of humanity. It helped me to identify an authentic self, a point of reference. To this day, I still have the movie bug. I love movies. Not just for the famous stars or the story line, but for the art. The art of moviemaking. Not that a movie can be perfect—there isn't such a thing, but there are perfect moments. Some movies I see over and over again, and each time, it is a whole new movie for me. So back there on that cold night with the knock on the door, the dark Indian man gave me a precious gift of a lifetime. This gift is still being revealed each time I sit in a dark theater, relax, and wait for the first projected movement on the blank silver screen or settle down in front of the television in the comfort of my home.

Making Things from Scratch

When it came to food, my family made things from scratch with just a few exceptions. The main reason was economy—the lack of economy, that is. The first step in the preparation of all meals was to take out the cutting board and the knife. The blade of the knife had been bent a few times. The handle was of a common pedigree with the varnish long rubbed away. Dark food stuff in the crevices was now so embedded that it missed the critical eye of the main washer of all things, my mother. Onions were the first to come under the chop, followed by garlic. A solemn rite performed by a dignitary would not come close to the ritual of chopping the onions and garlic in our house. Were soup to be the menu of the day, potatoes, carrots, turnips, and cabbage would be similarly sacrificed with sacred intent. The largest aluminum pot on the gas stove would be filled with water. Add a little salt, bay leaves, and a handful of lentils and rice, and it was more than fit for our table.

My favorite, which by now might be evident, was when my mother was cooking curry. Her first task was the melting of the margarine into our medium-sized saucepan. Next, the onions and garlic were lightly sautéed and then pushed to the side. The saucepan would be tipped a little to get the melted marge to collect in the opposite corner, where the curry would be mixed into a paste and gently fried. At the perfect moment, the saucepan would be returned to flat, and the spices would be mixed in with the onions and garlic. Careful never to let it burn! Thousands of years of India would rise up and fill the room with the aroma of pungent spices. Cut-up chicken would be added, and then the tomatoes and then the salt, all brought to the boil. The lid was placed on top, gas turned down to simmer, and wait. Of course, curry without rice would be like fish without chips. If you are familiar with the English, that could be considered heresy!

My mother, like most Indian women, had been taught by her mother to use her fingers as measuring tools and calculator. She would take her thumb and, using the plump part of the inside of the little finger as one unit, count down to the next phalange, past the crease, as one, two, and three. Then she would do the same to the ring finger, and on to the next digit. Thus, there were twelve plump counts, and if needed, twelve lines. That was just the one hand. In this way, minutes, hours, days, weeks, months, amounts and quantities could be calculated for innumerable matters. She measured the amount of water needed to cover rice by placing her index finger into the water so it came up to the first crease. By this method, it would be perfectly light and fluffy every time. How many days till it was time to pay the rent, send off bills, when the milkman came, and how many bottles—the functionality of this finger system seemed to be unending.

But it was really my dad who inspired me to cook. He was like a magician in the kitchen. He would come home and tell me and my mother to go upstairs to the living room, as he was going to make food for dinner. He would signal us to leave by closing the door to the kitchen. After half an hour, he would invite us back into the dining room, and there would be the most amazing artistic presentation, with the curry as the centerpiece. If there were a cucumber or tomato about, it would become a sculpture for garnish. It would taste like it had taken hours to prepare, always different and delicious. When I first tried to get a look into the kitchen, he shooed me away. This went on for many months, and I became more and more curious. One day, while he was in the kitchen culinary conjuring, the door was left a few inches ajar (I think, on purpose). He saw me peeking. Faking an annoyance, he ushered me in and, after scolding me, instructed me to sit and be quiet. With that, he started to hand down his skills to me. His method of cooking was very unique, passed down from his grandmother, who was Tamil from South India. For example, he would cook with oil or butter. His spice blend had more heat, more ginger, black pepper, coriander leaves, and clove and was more pungent than my mother's Northern style. His spices would brown first in the oil, followed by the onions and garlic, which were more coarsely cut. He used only fresh tomatoes, never sauce. He bruised the bay leaves between his fingers to bring out the fragrance. There was a different blend for each kind of meat or fish to bring out its unique flavor. Sometimes he might add a carrot or a potato or small dumplings that were so light and fluffy they nearly melted in your mouth. His curries were always dry, and he never tasted—he cooked by smell. His rice was always a beautiful turmeric yellow, and a cinnamon stick or cardamom or a few cloves were added as a complement. He never measured the rice or the water, but it was always perfect. He would hand-make chapatis (Indian flatbreads) with whole wheat flour. They would be served with butter. He used to travel long distances by bus or the London Underground just to gather his ingredients, which included chutneys and pickles of many flavors, like mango and lime. This was his way of bringing India into our home. He had an instinctive connection to the process of making food that had a feeling of sacredness and gratitude and transformed our kitchen into a temple. This was an essential secret ingredient he passed on to me.

Our shared time in the kitchen must have prompted him to consider other necessary additions to my training. First lesson, he took a button off my shirt, sewed it on, took it off again, and then it was my turn to sew it back on. Next was darning socks, then ironing shirts and trousers so the creases were perfect. This was followed by the correct way to polish shoes, tie a tie, stand, shake hands, and open doors for adults, as well as how to behave in the company of girls and women. Those days, it was a sign of respect to hold a door open for a woman, especially women who were pregnant and/or with children. In buses and trains, he taught me to give my seat to the old and the handicapped, to give them time, and to assist them to get off and on. I learned to wait till I was asked a question and sense when it was appropriate to ask or give an opinion. Each Saturday, there would be a test of the last lesson and a new one given.

Finally, one Saturday, he sat me down and laid the table formally for four, surrounding each plate with utensils, glasses, and serviette. Nothing I had seen in my house before. He must have borrowed them from work. I was told to remember the placement, and then he took it all away and asked me to lay the table as he had done. It took a while, but I finally got it—like all the other lessons, I practiced during the week. The next Saturday, he explained how each utensil was used and why it was placed so. He showed me how to correctly hold and use the silverware and the serviette and what each glass was for. I was told that on the next Saturday, I would be tested. So I was. Nervous, but not showing it, I completed the table and explained to the satisfaction of my father that I had grasped the fundamentals. He congratulated me.

My mother had not said a word about this training to me or to my father, at least not while I was present, but she witnessed this last test. He told me that as a real gentleman, I should not expect other people to do the things for me that I could do for myself. He went on to say that I should teach myself everything that society expects a woman to do, with the exception of childbirth. That made my mother's eyebrows lift, but he wasn't finished. He asked me to stand up and take a step back from the table. There were a few long seconds of pause, and he then added, "Now forget all this and be yourself."

I was shocked. What did he mean?

My mother protested, but he didn't answer. She knew better not to continue as he was as stubborn as she was.

He invited us both out to eat at the Ceylon, the only Indian restaurant near us at the time. It was wonderful to get his recognition and have him spend so much time with me. From then on, I loved to cook for myself and for my mother and me. It took a while to understand what my father meant by "Now forget it and be yourself." His lesson was that the knowledge you acquire is not who you are. This became part of the essence of who I am, surviving all these years. I've tried to pass on this wisdom to the grandchildren he never met.

An Ultimatum

It is here I need to tell you about things that were percolating and then came to a boil. As the threads of life interweave, complexities arise. Things are not all lineal.

Amid the foreground of all the craziness of wartime and post-wartime, moments of harmony were rare in my home. After the tragedy of my sister's death, all hell broke out in the form of heated arguments that would escalate and result many times in violence. It rose to such a pitch that my parents would wake me during the night, drunk and screaming at each other. Sometimes they would fetch me and place me in the middle to listen and decide who was right and who was wrong. This was not easy, but there was worse. I went downstairs, and my father had stormed out, and my mother was on the floor with the stench of whiskey on her breath and one of her teeth on the other side of the kitchen. My father was living a double life. He could be away for weeks. I never knew when he would come home and they would repeat these horrific scenes.

The whole of my life was being affected. I was constantly in fear. I was having nightmares and was paranoid about going to sleep, because I imagined there was something in the room that was going to attack me. School was useless. I did not understand anything that was being said, and eventually, the teacher put me in the back of the class and forgot me. The more violent children in the school must have sensed my vulnerability and picked on me. In one case, a child pushed me to the ground, jumped on my head, and knocked out two of my teeth. Once, they surrounded me and took my pants down, to see what color I was "down there." They laughed at me and left me naked on the street. Another time my mother came to pick me up and several of the other mothers noticed that my neck was dark and asked, "How do you ever know if your child is clean?" My mother took me home in haste and scrubbed my neck until it bled. There were more incidents.

I was desperate, still in mourning for the loss of my sister, and had a deep sense of being betrayed by the people who I was supposed to trust. By this time, I must have been mentally out of balance and seriously overstressed. I was at the lowest point of my life. Then one final episode between my parents tipped the scale. Now, at thirteen, I decided it had to stop. That is when I started to plan to kill my father.

Many nights I lay in bed imagining how I would accomplish this. Would I sneak up at nighttime? Would I wait till he was drunk? Would I do it while he slept? Then something changed. All these thoughts dissipated, and my mind flipped. I decided I was not going to kill him—I was going to confront him. This was the father that was highly trained in the martial arts and was out of balance from grief and alcohol abuse. I felt at the time that he was insane, extremely dangerous, and capable of killing me. With all the violence I had witnessed, he had never laid a hand on me. This could be the exception, and the consequences lethal. Realizing the full impact of my planned action, I became resolute, and all fear dropped away. Somehow calmness flooded over me. I set the scene in my mind. He was coming home on Friday night and sleeping over. I would approach him on Saturday morning.

Friday night I slept well, the first time in a very long time. Saturday was a bright summer morning. He was in the living room, my mother in the kitchen, and I was ready. I said to him that I needed to talk and asked him to come with me to the front garden. My voice was steady, and I was not shaking. I had strategized that on a Saturday, people were off work, and there would be many walking by, which I hoped would be a deterrent for any violence toward me. I escorted him to the spot I chose, close to the street at the front gate on the grass. I said to him, "The violence has to stop . . . because if it doesn't, I will kill you. I know that you are a great fighter, and you could easily kill me . . . but you have to sleep . . . or one night you will be drunk, and in the dark, I will get you. So the violence has to stop . . . now."

I felt as if it was another person saying these words. I was now no more than a few feet from him, so only he could hear and not the people passing by. I looked in his eyes to see his reaction. The man before me was totally different. He was not looking at me but a little off to the side and up into the place where we go to search for answers. The skin of his entire face was drawn tight, his complexion a shade lighter and ash-like. His nostrils were opened wide, flared, as though he were trying to get more oxygen into his body.

I left him there and went inside, looking for my mother. Finding her, I told her that I was not going to tolerate any more violence in the house. Did she understand? She began to blame my father, but I stopped her and said, "You have been playing this cat-and-mouse game too long. When he wants to leave, you block his way out of the house. You know his buttons, and you push them. I won't have it."

She didn't say anything.

"I have told him that this ends it. That is the end. No more. Finish."

I went to my room, got my jacket, some pocket money, and left. I walked and walked. My mind was blank, the sun was shining on me, and I heard the sound of my own footsteps on the pavestones. I was thirteen years of age. It had been going on for five torturous years. I had stood up for peace in my world. I had faced up to what was stealing my life away. I challenged the craziness, and it worked. My father never lifted his hand in anger again. Never.

The Resurrection of My Mother

Throughout this period, my mother was still not sleeping and was still nighttime drinking. Somehow she managed to get herself together to work. I understand she was liked and that she communicated in a balanced and friendly way with her coworkers, but when she came home, she was like a ghost. Her eyes would glaze over. When she spoke to me, it was in short sentences, and only about practical matters. After making and eating supper, she would stand at the kitchen window for hours, searching for the phantoms of the past that would never appear. She cried for all those she had lost. One day she cried and cried for her grandmother, as if to call her forth to comfort her.

In the beginning, I tried to engage her, but she didn't respond. She ate like a bird and became so thin that I wondered if she was going to die. My mother went from deep grief, to numbness, then to anger against God. "God doesn't exist, because if he exists, how could he take my Charmaine away from me?" She had lost all sense of hope. She had fought like a warrior for Charmaine through so many devastating setbacks, against all odds, trying to keep her alive. My mother had already lost three babies before Charmaine, two stillborn and one that died on its third month. The total impact of all of this pushed her over the edge, and she became insane. She started talking to herself and started swearing. She would rock back and forward, and during the night, she would go in and out of all the rooms in the house. I can only guess who she was looking for. My father was no longer living in our house, and now it was just the two of us. I had to think like an adult. I felt that if I didn't do something and do it quickly, I would lose her.

I had discovered a church called St. Dominic's. It was a beautiful large church with twelve stained glass windows and pictures and statues of saints. It was a place where I felt safe. One Saturday, my mother broke down and, throwing herself on the floor, started to scream and curse God and say there wasn't a God. I began to feel desperate, and then St. Dominic's Church came into my mind, and I knew that somehow I had to get her there. I told her to put her coat on—we were going out. I did not say where. She resisted, but I wouldn't give up. I struggled with her, and eventually, she conceded. Besides work, she had not left the house for over a year. I did all the shopping and all that was needed for the house to function.

As we left the house, her body was limp, but she was standing. So I started to walk her in the direction of the church one and a half miles away. We crossed the first few streets smoothly. She was in a daze. When we started on a street with an incline, she stopped and insisted on knowing where we were going. I told her, "To St. Dominic's Church." She fell to the ground and started to wail and cry and shout the things that I had heard so many times before. People were walking by and staring at us, but I didn't care. I picked her up. Still protesting, partly walking and partly carrying her, we were able to make some progress. We must have gone through this falling down, refusing to go farther, crying, and screaming more than twenty times before we reached the massive doors of the church. Here she started swinging at me. So, to avoid her blows, I had to stand back and then step back in to hold her. She dropped to the steps, and we repeated this several times till we were both exhausted. I won the battle and walked her into the church.

Its immense interior enveloped us as if we were mice coming out of our hole. It was empty. Our footsteps echoed as I steered her to a bench where we could finally sit down. Now she started to sob. I was still and just sat next to her for the hour we were there, before walking home in total silence.

The next Saturday came around, and when I felt the time was right, I took my mother's coat off the hook and held it for her to put on. She hesitated, but made the completion, and we walked side by side to St. Dominic's, went in, and sat down in the same place on the bench for about the same amount of time. My mother looked at me to signal that she wanted to leave, and we did.

The next time, she took my arm, and we walked slowly. Several times later, I was in my own world in the church, thinking about something, when I saw her light a candle. She stayed with it for a few moments and then walked to the door. I followed, and we went home. Then one day, she got up from the bench, lit a candle, and started to walk all the way around the church. I saw her stop. It was by a statue. I joined her. She was looking up at the brown face of a saint. She got down on her knees, closed her eyes, and I left her there and went back to the bench. I heard her ask for help with the loss of her child, to forgive her sins, and to take her prayers to God.

During the week, I did some research and found out that the statue was of a man named Martin de Porres, and that he was part African and a native of Peru. I realized he had not been proclaimed a saint yet, that was to come in the future. He was known as the patron of people of mixed ethnicities and those who worked with the sick and the orphans. Many miracles were attributed to him, and he was said to have the blessings of levitation and appearing in two places at the same time.

I told my mother what I learned. The next time, she went to church by herself and came home with a small statue of Martin de Porres, a relic of his garment, and a print of a painting of him. The print she kept in her handbag, and the statue in her room next to her picture of Charmaine. She prayed to him each night and began to sleep again. She stopped drinking. Before long, she was smiling and had moments of being her old feisty self, the self that included me in her world. I found a women's counseling organization to visit with my mother. With my support and guidance, my mother sought for a separation from my father. I was thirteen, it was relatively calm in the house, and now I could get on with my life.

Chapter 5

Awakening, Ramani Rangan

My First Suit

All the things I had experienced to this point left me stunned. I had
retreated into my own world. I was lost as far as my scholastic involvement
went, and everything seemed to sail over my head. The only thing I
did well in was art and, oddly enough, religious studies. I was slow and
quiet, as if I was in a permanent daze, and didn't fit in anywhere. All
the other children and the world around me seemed to be moving fast.
Obviously, what they were teaching wasn't sinking in, so at fourteen, I
had to repeat the year before. After fifteen, you had to choose between
vocational school and high school. I had heard of the malicious things
kids did to each other in the higher-level schools, and quite frankly, I
was scared for my life. It was so bad that teachers were getting attacked,
and they had no control. I knew I would be a target. So I decided to
exit the world of one school room, corridors, and playground and enter
the unknown territory of adults. I left school three months before my
fifteenth birthday.

After going to the labor exchange and a few interviews that never
amounted to anything, I got one job where I had to give two weeks'
notice. I was there two weeks. Figure it out. The job was welding iron
fire escape ladders for buildings. The noise was so loud it was painful,
my ears ached, and the smell of noxious fumes was overpowering. I
spent the rest of that summer driving around with someone who wanted
company while he delivered stuff in a van. My birthday came and went,
and then Christmas and New Year's. I spent a few weeks laying wooden
railroad ties with mostly Irish laborers and a few weeks painting walls
inside a government building.

Then in the fall, around my sixteenth birthday, my mother, seeing
my plight, contacted my father, related my situation, and said, "Your son
needs help. He needs a good job with a future." During and just after the
Second World War, when we had lived in Islington, there was a theater
called Collin's Music Hall where my father used to perform as a singer.
As I understand it, Lew Grade, who later became Sir Lew Grade, and
then Lord Grade, was the theater manager of Collin's at the time. He
was also a talent agent. Lew Grade and my dad were friends. He called
in a favor to get me an interview. Lew Grade was a founding executive

of Associated Television Ltd., ATV, the first commercial television station serving live and film weekend programming to Greater London. As usual, my father told me to be ready on the following Saturday but gave me no clue as to where we were going and why. As usual, I didn't feel it was my place to ask.

Everything always seemed to happen on a sunny Saturday, and this was no exception. After I finished cleaning the house and shopping and got dressed in my best, my father and I walked down the hill to the bus terminal and got on a 68 bus. We climbed up to the top deck and took the fifteen-minute ride to Camden Town High Street, passing bustling crowds to the end. I found myself standing outside a long wall of blanked-out multi-windows. Having no idea what to expect, I was pleased my father opened the door, for I never would have. Inside were suits, jackets, and counters with shirts and ties, three rows to each side of me, twenty rows deep. I had never been in a place like this, just for men. All the employees were male, and there was an aura of mature and comfortable man-ness. We were approached by one of them. My father worked in a nightclub in the heart of London and met a lot of people, from those of most questionable backgrounds to those in high society. The man who greeted him and assisted us was one of his nighttime connections. All my necessary measurements were taken, including the inside leg, which was uncomfortable. We walked the rows, pulling out suits, holding them up to me, putting them back or leaving them out still on their hangers. Those chosen were hung on the racks facing out. From these, many were selected, and I was instructed to try them on in a small room in the back of the store and then come out and model. There were hmm's and ha's, shaking of heads, and a full range of other expressions. After trying on about twenty suits, we narrowed it down to four and accessories. At this point, my father invited me for the first time to express my opinion about what I wanted to wear, a new realm where my word was given a man's consideration.

The quality of the suits was magical for me—the feel, cut, and colors. I had never seen anything like them before. We settled on three suits with a commentary from my father about what made them work. This was the first time he mentioned the color of my skin. I looked in the long mirror and saw a very different person in front of me. I was looking at a person that belonged to another world.

All the suits were of Italian design. One was a pinstripe midnight-blue, one was a dark tan sharkskin wool, and another was double-breasted with a waistcoat (vest). In 1957 London, menswear was uniformly dark, ranging from black to dark gray. These were different. The material I had worn up till then was coarse and heavy to hold out the cold and dampness of the English weather, but these were made from cloth that was soft to the touch and had a sheen that picked up the light when I moved. The effect was very subtle, but made the suits seem as if they were alive. A camel-hair coat like my father's, with leather buttons that reached to my shins, was also chosen in the same manner as the suits. After several ties were added, my father handed over large notes of money, the likes of which I had only seen counted by tellers in banks. We left with my suits of wonder on our way to buy other stuff to match, including shoes, socks, cufflinks, and a tie pin.

My father explained to me that we had just exited an upscale gentlemen's consignment establishment (secondhand shop) with garments likely to have graced the wardrobes of British aristocracy, and even royalty. I don't know if this was at all true, but it just as well could have been, because I felt like a king. I spent most of the rest of Saturday trying them on over and over again. My mother had to admire me countless times. When it was finally time for dinner and my mother reminded me that the food was getting cold, I ceremoniously laid them side by side. A jacket with a chosen shirt inside with tie on top, trousers lined up on their natural crease, and shoes on the floor.

Early the following Monday, my father and I once again took the 68 bus past Camden Town to the center of London. We entered an impressive building and took the elevator up to the administrative offices on the fifth floor. There, we were told to wait by a beautiful woman who looked like a movie star. She had big eyes and yellow-blonde hair piled up on her head a good five inches. She wore a perfume that was a little invasive and intimidating for my delicate young mind. Eventually, we were ushered into a large office by a tall man wearing his version of one of my suits. At this point, I was getting an inkling that something big was happening, but I didn't know quite what. Considering my father, it would be something out of the ordinary.

My father spoke, and then the man asked me a few questions that I can't remember. Maybe nerves, you think? He picked up the phone, spoke for a minute (perhaps to Lew Grade), and told me I had the job. I started the next day working in the mailing room as a mail boy, delivering to all the secretaries who sat outside the offices on two floors. It took a while, but gradually, things started to fall into place, and I was drawn out of the winter of my mind into the spring of unlimited opportunities.

Using Whatcha Got

I was now in an honorable job, and one month had passed. Arriving just before 9:30 a.m., I would walk to the entrance, easily twenty feet high and flanked by regal stone columns, built to impress the general public. Above this was a ten-foot sign bearing the ATV House logo, which was a stylized eye. ATV (Associated Television Ltd.) was an independent commercial station that offered another option besides the state-owned BBC. They were introducing exciting, modern, creative film series, comedies, quiz shows, variety productions, documentaries, sports, nature, and shows for children. Hollywood movies and film series agreeable to the British palate were imported, adding a whole new dimension. Westerns were especially treasured. The movie stars of films became part of the family through the television screen in the average home.

Just walking up to the ATV building and having passersby notice that I was about to push on the swinging doors to go in made me feel like I was famous. I had been fulfilling my duties as a mail boy, sorting out mail and making deliveries to the offices on two floors, duplicating papers (that's what copying was called then), and every other thing that went along with the least prestigious job in the company.

But wait! I was told in the interview for the job that I would also be working as a call boy in their studios on Saturdays and Sundays on live shows. Video came later. It was explained to me that I couldn't get paid an official wage because of some regulations, but I would be given compensation in the form of generous expenses to cover three meals and transport for each day, which would show up in my wages. They even had profit sharing—unheard of in the day. So it came to pass that after a month I was put on the studio schedule. Now I would have to be up at 7:00 a.m. It took an hour and a bit to get to Wood Green Studios or Hackney Empire, both old theaters from the late 1800s that the company had converted for television use. You can bet that walking through the stage door, especially in the evening before we would go on the air, was the all-time best booster for a seventeen-into-eighteen-year-old ego, since there was always a large crowd of fans looking to see who you were.

As a call boy there were hundreds of things to remember and to do, from the hours of rehearsals to the performances. When I was working on *Saturday Spectacular*, which had acts, singing, and dancing with live music, I was not only responsible for having all the performers in their place on time to "go on," I was also responsible for making sure that every member of the eighteen-piece orchestra was ready too. More times than not, I would have to find members of the orchestra in the local pubs just before the show started. Mostly, it was the same musicians I would have to herd back to the studio. Needless to say, they had more than one way to warm up. Small glasses were filled with a liquid that could be dispensed for a small fee, strong enough to use as rocket fuel. Sometimes they would come back with me, but when I wasn't looking, they would sneak out again. Not only that, they would go to a different pub than the one I had originally found them in. Three gentlemen of the wind section were the worst. One was a saxophone player, another was a trumpet player, and the third one—what did he play? So the stage manager would count heads, it wouldn't tally, and I would get yelled at. Ten minutes before the ten-second countdown, I would be running like the wind to find the, by-now-red-faced middle-aged men in their wrinkled black evening suits and bow ties. There they would be, completing their ritual of ordering three whiskeys and lining them up on the counter. After pleading with them to come so I could keep my job, they would calmly and ritualistically down their three drams. Then, and only then, accompanied by my frantic encouragement, would I get them to the stage door, through the wall of fans, into the passageway, up two small flights of stairs, past the soundproof stage door, onto the stage, and finally, up the three steps onto the rostrum to their section. This would leave just thirty seconds for them to sit, turn their sheet music to the right place, and blow some warmth into their mouthpiece. Then, Jack Parnell, the band leader, would raise his baton in readiness for the audio signal on his headset to cue him to start.

Throughout the next three years, I worked forty hours at the office and, on an average, twenty-four hours at the studios. I know now, from what befell most of the boys-to-men in my depressed neighborhood, that the studios saved me from taking a really bad path to nowhere and projected me into a world of magic.

So what about the title "Using Whatcha Got"? We, my fellow mail boys/call boys, got up to a lot of stuff. A lot of stuff. Not criminal, but fun. How to meet girls was one of the subjects. Not just meet them, but how to impress them in what we thought might be a clever and sophisticated way. We discussed strategies at lunchtime, and one day, we had the most brilliant idea. We had noticed on the top floor, in an out-of-the-way corner, that there was a designated "put everything you don't know what to do with it" room. On further investigation, we also noticed it was unlocked sometimes, and there were some old, broken camera units, audio stuff with microphones, and a mixture of meters and technical junk with lots of very important cables. We had no idea what most of it was for.

We found out the door was open on Wednesdays, so we started to take large empty bags into work, and at lunchtime, one of us would sneak into the room and fill up the bags with the equipment. We would walk to Waterloo Bridge, which was five minutes away, arrange and set up the broken old stuff so it looked like it was functional, and, with our company photo IDs pinned to our coat collar, stop girls on the bridge and interview them as if it all worked and we were the real thing. We told them that we were shooting a documentary at the Marquee Nightclub, and if they wanted, we could arrange for them to be in it. With widened eyes and a matter-of-fact demeanor, we acquired their telephone numbers.

I had an agreement with the backdoor bouncer at the Marquee to get in at less-than-half price with a few friends on Fridays and an occasional Saturday, when I wasn't scheduled to work in the studio. Some of the girls turned up. We would say we had to reschedule the documentary but invite them to stay for a drink. It worked. Those were the days when you got to speak to a girl, and maybe get a dance, a kiss, and a cuddle, and you thought you had uncovered a Spanish treasure. Over the next few years, we learned through trial and error, mostly error, that we needed more than just "using whatcha got" to impress the girls. Thank God, that's another story.

Man to Man

I was nineteen, it was 1960, and I was in my third year working in the mailing room at ATV. I was still a step-and-fetch-it for the administrational offices Monday through Friday, and a callboy most weekends, another more glamorous version of step-and-fetch-it. We, the mail boys, had taken the job with the expectation of becoming a cameraman, studio manager, or even a director at some point. Television was so new then, and I felt a young man's pride and ego, tickled to be dressed in a suit and tie, walking into ATV House in the center of London. This was sufficient in the beginning, but now after three years, I was still in the same place while others in my position had left the mailroom and had moved on to jobs in the studios.

As I went around delivering mail, I would speak to the secretaries of the heads of departments. One of them was really attractive and knew it. She was a flirt and, for some reason, liked speaking to me. In conversation, I brought up that I had been passed over many times for promotion. I confided my sense that it was because of being an Indian. She paused, as if she were taking in what I had shared. "Come and see me tomorrow," she said. I spent the rest of the day and the evening imagining the two of us together in many scenarios. I was chewing over how to ask her out. I thought she was hinting at that. Ah! The hopes of youth!

The next morning, as soon as the mail was sorted and I was ready for rounds, I inconspicuously rushed to her office. She was pleased to see me. My heart was trying to leave the confinements of my body by pounding its way out. She leaned forward—men can faint too—and whispered that she had arranged a meeting with the top director of the company, Lew Grade. I mean top. I was to see him that very day, that afternoon. I became so nervous that I started to perspire noticeably. I told her I couldn't. All her beauty, all her attractiveness, disappeared in my mind as she spent over ten minutes encouraging me. "You can do it, and you should do it. He will listen to you." She coached me, saying I had to be straight and tell it as it was.

I was on automatic pilot for the rest of the day as I rehearsed my lines. I knew I was dying. I knew that I was heading for the edge of a cliff. I speculated that I would be fired on the spot and saw myself being thrown out the window of his eighth-floor office. I arrived early, and while waiting, I had the distinct feeling of floating above my body. I could not feel myself whatsoever. When it was time, I was ushered past my secretary friend to the executive secretary, who looked close to seventy, dark, crinkled, and never smiled. She pointed the way with merely the gesture of a glance. It was now or never, and never seemed the better choice. But I found myself walking in anyway.

His office occupied the whole top floor. He seemed a small figure behind his huge desk at the other end of the hundred-foot room. Without looking up, I appeared in his peripheral vision, and he signaled to me to walk closer. I was pulled forward by the magnetism of the invitation and found myself stopping at about twenty feet from him. One hour later, actually only three seconds later, he looked up at me, and I stared at him. A soft voice coming out of this deity figure asked, "What can I do for you?"

It was then I felt the shackles of my race, being a stranger in a strange land, and the self-imposed prison of limited thinking. Simultaneously, there arose in me an intangible feeling of centeredness. I spoke as if I was asking for my liberty, as if I was a baby too long in the womb, turned, low, and ready. "I have been working here for three years," the words came out. They were words that I had not rehearsed and tones in my voice that I had never noticed before—deep and emerging from my body like that of a man speaking to another man. "Others have been promoted over me. This is unfair."

He put the telephone back down on its cradle and looked at my shoes and then scanned me from my used men's clothing store suit to my black head of hair, shining with too much Old Spice hair cream.

"I feel that if there isn't a future for me here, it would be a waste of my time and yours." Yes! That came out of my mouth. A young man had just put all his cards on the table, and it was me. It was the truth, and there it was.

He lifted his index finger and motioned for me to wait. He picked up the telephone and made a thirty-second call in his soft voice so I couldn't hear what he was saying and then put the telephone down again. "Thank you," he said. "Thank you," he repeated. It was then I noticed a ten-inch Cuban cigar resting on its landing place. He picked it up and, looking at it, said, "I will make some more calls." There was the slightest body movement, and I knew the interview was over.

I thanked him and left his office. His executive secretary looked up as I walked by and gave the smallest of warm smiles. My friend, the Enchantress, who arranged the meeting, looked up as I walked by and, with the slightest change in her professional mask, projected a sparkle of the eyes toward me. I had faced the monster and survived.

It was not long before I started to get job offers in the studios. I had won my freedom, and it was now up to me to do the best with it. Note: I eventually asked the Enchantress out. She said she liked me, but I couldn't afford her taste. Somehow, the way she said it didn't make me feel rejected. In fact, I was relieved, because if she said yes, I would have had to meet my own expectations of what her expectations were. Now that would have been really scary.

Valiant Purpose

I decided to take a break from ATV and go on a mission. I would hitchhike to Marseilles, France. There I would find a ship going to South Africa and work my passage. I hoped to solve a longstanding dispute that my father had with the confiscation of our family properties.

My father had told me that the climate of British colonial rule in South Africa in the 1930s was highly suppressive and extremely racist.

All nonwhites were treated as inferior. Blacks were at the bottom, then Coloreds, and then Indians. This hierarchy was already in place at the time, and Apartheid, which would be instituted later in 1948, just made it official. One of my father's brothers was in the Indian Civil Rights Movement, a splinter faction of the Natal Indian Congress, originally founded by Mahatma Gandhi, collaborating with Nelson Mandela's African National Congress. He was discovered and had to leave with his other brothers and hide in the countryside. My father's name appeared along with all of his brothers' on the Most Wanted blacklist. It didn't matter that he was in England and too young at the time to be involved.

According to my father, the brother in question was captured and tortured. He died a year later of his injuries. Even though the family knew nothing of his activities, all of their properties were seized without notice in the middle of the night. They had a hundred-acre farm and a couple of laundry businesses. Everyone was thrown out into the street, including the women, elders, and children. Somehow my Aunt Barbie was separated from her mother and family. At thirteen, she found herself without a home and with only the clothes on her back. After several days, she ran into a family member. He told her that he had also lost everything, and because he too was blacklisted, he had to leave the province to find a job. He took her to a factory and got her work. She continued living on the street until, eventually, she got a little room. She fended for herself till she was in her twenties. Then she met a soft-spoken man, Uncle Norman, and they fell for each other and married. With no education and no way to improve herself, she continued working in the factory for the next thirty years. (This, she related to me much later when I met her for the first time.)

When my father found out about the desperate situation of the family, he wanted to go back. His mother pleaded with him not to return, for she feared he would be arrested, tortured, and possibly killed. As I was growing up, my father was always attempting, through South African lawyers, to get compensation for the loss of his family's properties. It was painful for him, and somehow in my young man's mind, I was going to spring into action, go there, solve this, and run up the family flag. I thought I could make my father happy and lift our family out of mediocrity.

I was excited as I got on the ferry in Dover, overloaded with a humongous backpack and an overstuffed suitcase. Imagine, these were the days of no wheels on luggage. Now that we have them, I often wonder why it took five thousand five hundred years of wheels to put them on luggage. Just asking. I was the white knight in shining armor— brown knight, in my case. The quest was clear and noble. There was extra excitement because I had not told my father. What better way to impress him than to kill the dragon that was in his path?

It was late September, and there was a British chill in the air as I found a place to put down my load and look out over the waters. It was clear enough to see the French coast. Or was it just my enthusiasm that had created a mirage, a phantom land? That moment, as we pulled up anchor, with the sound of the engines straining to find their synchronized pulse in the water, I felt the first movement of departure. I stood on deck among people of all ages, with salty air blowing in my face. I smelled burning diesel, mixed with old-ship rusting metal, blended with the aroma of tens of cups of hot tea. I was off on a quest toward a valiant purpose.

The dragon I was looking for didn't appear. It was the time of the Algerian War, and bombs were exploding throughout Paris. I couldn't get back to my hostel before curfew, so I took refuge under a bridge. I woke up to see the police dragging three bodies from the Seine. Reaching Marseilles, I was arrested for eating breakfast with a knife that was an inch too long. After a day of inquiry, I was set free minus all possessions, with only my passport, my travelers' checks, the clothes on my back, and my empty backpack. I attempted several times to gain passage on a ship to South Africa, but no one would take me. I reluctantly came to the conclusion that this was not going to work. I couldn't save my mother and my father or relieve their struggle. Greatly saddened, I returned to London and my job at ATV. Many years later my father did receive compensation, but by then, it was just a token, dwindled by lawyers' fees.

Theater Magic

Soon after, I was laid off from work. That I was laid off was my own fault. I was so clumsy, still in a daze, my mind not synchronized with the outside world. Even with the extraordinary help of Lew Grade, who I suspect had a guardian angel allocated to look out for me, they had to let me go in the end. They were more than generous and gave me three month's severance pay, plus my yearly bonus.

It was winter. I went to the Labor Exchange, and I failed every interview they sent me to. My financial situation was getting desperate. I had worn a hole in one of my only dress shoes and was repairing it using leftover linoleum pieces, when the lady upstairs asked me to come up to their apartment. Her husband had a favor to ask of me. This was very rare. I went up and saw that he was sitting down on the edge of a chair with a hospital back brace supporting him from his tailbone to his armpits. He told me that he was in great pain. He had a part-time job working as a stagehand in the West End theaters of Downtown London. He was scheduled to go in that night, and it was already two in the afternoon. He asked me if I would go in for him as he couldn't get hold of his boss and it was important that they were not short a man for this production.

Having had experience in the television studios and having been backstage with my mother and my father many times as a child, I agreed. I never hesitated then. I just reacted with a yes or a no, and this was one of the yes times. The bus I normally took downtown happened to stop within a few minutes of the Aldwych Theater. My upstairs neighbor had not told me what the production was. I found the stage door, asked for the stagehand foreman, and told him who I was filling in for and that I had worked for ATV and was used to backstage. With a slight frown of disbelief, he led me upstairs, stage left, where he showed me the rigging for the counter weight system that lowered and lifted the backdrops and lighting rails for the scenery. The twelve-inch-by-eight-inch, ten-pound iron weights were fitted to a platform and were secured in a vertical shaft that had guiding rails. When one pulled on the rope system, the counterweight being balanced equaled the weight of the backdrop and thus made it easy to lower and lift, like an elevator. These individual counterweight guide rail systems attached to the stage's left side wall and stretched the depth of the floor side by side from front stage to backstage, with possibly fifty vertical systems. In a normal production, for scene changes, there were lighting lamps and front, middle, and backdrops. There were also special effects drops and side drops, which added a sense of depth to the scene. Side drops were necessary to hide standing lamps and things that were happening offstage which could be otherwise seen by the audience on the far sides of the front rows and front balconies.

The foreman showed me the running order of each of the scenes. The stage manager would turn on the red light to signal me to "Standby," and the green to signal "Go," to move into action to lower or lift the drop. From my vantage point, I could walk from one end of the gangway to the other. This allowed me to see the two front rows of the audience taking their seats on my side. I could also look down and see the actors assembling, some on stage and a few just behind the opening curtain. Groups of dressers for quick changes, stagehands, and assistants to the stage manager were readying themselves for the opening scene. The last touches were being made—arranging wigs, straightening costumes, and checking makeup in handheld mirrors.

The auditorium was now full, and I could hear the buzz of anticipation from the audience and the whispering of the actors backstage. I still didn't know which production we were doing, as the foreman never mentioned it, and I, nervously excited, forgot to ask. A bell rang announcing the last call to be seated. The smell of painted canvas, heat from the stage lamps, mixed with old hemp ropes, greased iron rails, and the makeup of the readied performers, reached my nostrils and touched off childhood memories of long ago. Mind you, I had never ever done anything that came close to this before.

It turned out that my first signal came near the end of the fourth act. I lowered and lifted the scene change drops under the supervision of the foreman. Confident that I could do the rest by myself, the foreman left and went down to stage level. I watched the signal lights like a hawk and successfully completed my part. It wasn't until my last signal near the end that I realized for the first time that this production was Shakespeare's *The Two Gentlemen of Verona*.

ACT 5
SCENE 4
VALENTINE
How use doth breed a habit in a man!
This shadowy desert, unfrequented woods,
I better brook than flourishing peopled towns;
Here can I sit alone, unseen of any,
And to the nightingale's complaining notes
Tune my distresses and record my woes

And I was hooked. At the time, I didn't understand the plot or the language, but I was moved, and there was no going back. I had experienced something that I could not explain. It would take more than a lifetime to understand. I saw the whole engine of this world being played out on the stage, as though I were in a temple, and truth was being laid out in a code for each individual present to make a spiritual jump, if the ego were willing. In the theater, our role in time and space is transformed, so we become a simple witness. Our truth, both visible and hidden, is related to us so we can relate to others and, in doing so, discover empathy for our shared human struggle. In the dark, in a crowd of pure strangers, we are individually vertical, but horizontally one tribe that is greater than each and every one present.

This heightened exchange of energy was now over. The last curtain was down. All had left. The lights were turned off. I was gripped by the piercing silence that remained. As I left for home through the stage door, with a cash reward in my pocket, I knew this was going to be my livelihood. The night air seemed different, more welcoming, a feeling which would return countless evenings after working performances in many theaters over the years.

The next day, I went to the NATTKE (National Association of Theatrical Television and Kine Employees) union office and signed on. It wasn't easy to become a member. It was the old story. If you have a job, you can become a member, but you have to be a member to get a job. It's who you know and not what you know. But that day, the doors of serendipity opened, and the ancient muse blessed me. A call of desperation came through from a theater. "Can you go straight over to the Adelphi? They need a stagehand right away!" I got a membership card on the spot.

The Adelphi Theater took me on permanently as a stagehand in the evenings. Later, they needed a day man. That meant coming in at 9:00 a.m. and sweeping, mopping the stage, and a few other duties, then returning at night for the stagehand job. Soon there was a need for a full-time stage electrician, which meant changing lightbulbs, checking a few theater switchboards and fuse boxes during the day, and, in the evening, working directly with lighting on the stage. Then there was an opening for a lighting board console operator. The two who were working the lighting board took a liking to me. They needed to train somebody quickly to cover and they chose me.

It was the most challenging job I ever had. Mind you, this was 1960, the dawn of computer hardware. At the time, our lighting system was a one of a kind, first ever crossover computing hardware contraption. Believe it or not, it was a converted Hammond B2, a 1950s electric church organ, designed by my two ingenious mentors to handle the demands of the show *Maggie May*. This show was technically groundbreaking for the time, with revolving stage sets and two motorized floating platforms. The organ was set up so the keys were wired to a lamp or groups of lights above and on the stage. The switches above the keyboard and to the left and right were programmed in sequence for each scene. Every individual lamp had a preset level of brightness to allow for multiple combinations. There were only twelve computerized preprogrammed possibilities, but one scene could have more than twelve changes. I could use only eight at a time, as I needed to use the other four to program the next scene. So I had to be on top of three things at the same time. One was what was happening at that moment on the stage. The other was the following sequence in the same scene. The third was to reprogram for later sequences in the same scene or in the next scene. Each sequence could demand a whole new setting of brightness or use of any or all the lamps. But wait, there was more! The foot pedals for the bass notes of the organ had been modified to operate motors on the lamps that controlled their direction or changed their color. The composition for this old organ was ever changing and demanded that I be on my toes and nimble with my fingers for the show to go smoothly. Needless to say, there was hardly time for a scratch, and yawning was not advised.

We worked in a very small space with just enough room for the organ console, the wires, the panels, the operator, and one more person to stand pressed against the door to help with some of the quick changes. The only window was very small, facing the stage. I felt like I was an astronaut in a space capsule on the way to the moon. My two lighting comrades in arms had set up a coded system for the running order of the show. They taught me the code when they began to trust me. This happened quickly with the incentive that if I could operate the lights alone, one of them could take a day off. The logic in having a secret code was that the theater management could not fire us to get a friend in, which had happened in the past and could again.

I loved the job and the challenge. I worked on *Maggie May* for a year. I developed a knack for improvising and could quickly cover up mistakes on the stage. The word got out, and I was invited to work in other London theaters including the Talk of the Town, the Prince of Wales, the Cambridge, the Savoy, the London Palladium, and the Shaftesbury Theater. This was 1960, and in the West End, the heart of London's theater district, I was the first and only Indian who was working backstage in any position. I shared this distinction with the first Persian.

Footnote: I recently looked up the meaning of the word *theater*. It comes from Greek *theatron*, akin to Greek *thauma*, "miracle," as in an extraordinary event manifesting divine intervention in human affairs. Theatrical performances originally took place in temples. Greek gods and muses were called upon to reveal themselves, channeled through priests and those dedicated to the temple. Later, actors in the amphitheater attempted to invoke the Divine. The intent was to teach personal, social, and spiritual morals. I believe the Divine is still invoked in the theaters of today.

What's Not Reported

I have noticed over the years that newspapers, radio, television, and online news bulletins report in the same way. What we get are headlines, repeated over and over. All of history is like that—only the chess pieces are visible, and the struggle of the rest of humanity is not even on the board. We are less than pawns, our destiny decided by the players of the game. Looking back, there have been countless examples of things that I experienced that deserved to be reported and paid attention to, but were not.

While I was still nineteen, living in my mother's house, I was out with some friends on a Saturday evening hanging out and walking around aimlessly on Camden High Street. About five Irishmen stepped out of Moody's Drinking House. They were obviously well lubricated, but just laughing and talking, not doing anything harmful. A police van pulled up, and six or seven London Bobbies rushed out and began to violently attack them, slamming them to the ground. Then with bloody noses and torn lips, they were stuffed into the van and driven away. This assault had happened so quickly. I was in shock.

One of my Irish friends explained to me what had just taken place. The Irishmen arrested were laborers who did the jobs that the English didn't want to do—for a low wage and often under dangerous conditions. These men had left Ireland for the big city like so many around the world still do. They lived, crowded, in one room and sent most of their earnings to their families back in Ireland. He said they, himself included, were openly despised by the British police, who had a quota of Irishmen they were supposed to arrest each weekend. They would be locked up until Monday, where they would be brought to court to be legally processed by England's "equal" justice system. I must have had a look of disbelief on my face, for my friend invited me to go to the local court Monday morning to sit, watch, and listen from the benches reserved for the public.

So I did just that. The first one on the dock was one of the very same Irishmen arrested on that Friday. He looked awful—I mean really bad. He still had blood and bruises on his face, perhaps some new ones. His already-shabby clothes were now torn, so one of his jacket sleeves was hanging. The buttons on his jacket and his shirt were gone. It looked as though he had been brutalized. His case number was called out, and he was asked to verify his name and address. A policeman said that the man had attacked him and had violently resisted arrest. I knew this was absolutely not true. After the policeman finished his statement, the

Irishman was asked if he had anything to say in his own defense. He said that he had just come out of the pub, and was standing around with his friends talking, when he and his friends were beaten to the ground, pushed into a police van, and dragged around on the floor of the police station. He was kicked and hit and was not allowed to even wash or go to the toilet. He had to relieve himself in the cell and was beaten again.

"The Court finds you guilty. Pay fifteen pounds." Then he was led out of the courtroom.

That morning, I counted eighteen Irishmen, obviously from other arrests, being processed in the same manner. In the evening, I met up with my Irish friend who had invited me to witness what was going on for myself. I related my experience to him and told him he was right. He added that this was happening throughout the whole of England.

Similarly, later, Caribbean Islanders were recruited from Jamaica and Trinidad to come over to do the menial and labor-intensive, low-paying jobs. In the beginning, they were treated quite well. Things changed when the economy got bad. Prejudice set in and it became dangerous for them. Of course, not all people treated them badly, but many did. I remember them being friendly, laughing, happy people. When the racism started, they stopped laughing in public, and their numbers started to fill the jails. There were race riots and gangs roaming the streets looking for dark faces. The worst were the Nottinghill race riots of 1958. I learned very quickly that they couldn't distinguish the difference between the Islanders and Indians, like me.

Then there was "Paki-bashing" by gangs of skinheads, and I was an obvious target. At this point, it became necessary to keep a low profile, go straight to work, come home, and stay inside at night. I could hear them roaming the streets outside my house, and I would turn off the lights so they couldn't see in. I was afraid for myself and terrified for my mother's safety. After all these years and many later incidents later, I still have to sit facing the front door when I am in a public place like a restaurant. With few exceptions, I never go to a place on Friday or Saturday where alcohol is being served. The riots were covered by the media, but as a sensation, not as a terrorizing experience.

Within each of us are headlines, our own version of reality, minus a full picture of diverse perspectives. I believe the dire circumstance of our world situation is calling upon us to be aware of the suffering that is created by seeing people as the Other, the Enemy. Each one of us is a unique story in history. We are all individuals and deserve to be acknowledged as such, no matter our ethnicity, gender, or station in life.

One of my greatest heroes reminds me of this. Mahatma Gandhi. The peoples of the whole subcontinent of India were treated as less than human by their English masters over many hundreds of years, to the point that many Indians believed it themselves. One little thin man changed the course of history by freeing India from the most powerful colonial ruler the world has ever seen. This, he accomplished solely through the dynamic action of nonviolence. Each one of us has the ability to move into action and make new headlines just as he did. We have an imperative to be awake—if not for ourselves, then for the next generations. What are we not seeing or paying attention to, and where does it lead?

Charlie

I made my breakfast on Saturdays for myself, until at fifteen, I met Charlie. How I met him is lost to time and my powers of total recall. He was a year older than me. We had a symbiotic relationship. He was over six feet and had a chip on his shoulder, so nobody challenged him, which in the street culture was an everyday occurrence. At the time, I was, as my mother told me on several occasions, a sissy. I didn't want to hurt anyone. The fact that if I didn't defend myself I would get hurt, for some reason, didn't make a connection. Charlie became my defender. I had my own personal superhero, and he had . . . me? I was the only young Indian male for miles. I was different and I was quirky. Maybe that was the visible representation of how he felt inside. Or not. Who knows? The main thing is it worked, and it worked for five years.

He always came to my house. In fact, in all the time I knew him, I visited his family only a few times. His house was graced with a constant stream of visitors. He liked coming to us because it gave him more space and some peace of mind. Like me, Charlie painted and was creative in many ways, but he never allowed me to go into his room where he lived or let me see his work. He told me directly that not even his mother was allowed in. Charlie was a loner like I was. Our differences were many, but there was an intangible quality that drew us together, and it was perfect.

Saturday breakfast . . . Oh yes! That's what we were talking about. He would come over on Saturday mornings around nine, and we would make the English breakfast. I mean two eggs, two sausages, mushrooms, tomatoes, and baked beans from the can. Did I miss bacon . . . heresy! All this fried in so much butter that it would now be considered a mortal sin. Of course, one slice of toast with more butter for mopping up the egg yolk, and another slice under the baked beans was absolutely mandatory. In the first years, it was tea with milk and two sugars. We graduated to coffee and cream with brown sugar lumps. As mentioned, my kitchen was small. Somehow we fit, growing out of our clothes, but not out of our ritual. Now that I think of it, if boys-to-men must have a rite of passage, then this was, I can imagine, the best one in our city jungle of London.

We eventually went our different ways. I was nineteen, and it was time for me to get serious and not put off my involuntary responsibility to the gene pool. It was time to approach manhood. I was fumbling my way. Luckily enough, some friends set me up with a blind date—Julia. She was shy, and this helped, as I was visibly hesitant, not knowing how to enter the flight path to land in the ritual of flirtation. Our relationship of two years was one of the calmest of my many serious relationship orbits. She was down-to-earth, had a love of music that came in the form of playing vinyl on a turntable, and enjoyed just sitting and talking. I was still living at home during this time, and we had set up Thursday as the night I stayed over. Sometimes we would get together on the weekends. I found out, as it wasn't ever said, that Julia was in love with me. I, however, did not have the emotional capacity to even know where that feeling resided.

Charlie, on the other hand, fell in love. He had been missing from my life for about six months when one Saturday, as I was making breakfast, there was a knock. I was in the slow frying bacon stage, which gave me time to answer. I opened the front door, and there was Charlie. He had always been tall, but he appeared even taller and now had evolved from the young man I knew to a man. I was very pleased to see him. A lot of images of our shared time together flashed into my mind as I welcomed him into our little kitchen. He seemed more serious than usual. Noticing him respond to the aromas being produced, I asked if he wanted to eat. He nodded. I doubled all the ingredients to include him. He fell into step, rolling up his sleeves and washing and slicing the mushrooms as I captained the chef duties. This helped to open him up a fraction. Before fifteen minutes had passed, we were eating in the dining room and beginning to get beyond the estrangement that time can create. We started to laugh about some funny or strange situations we shared in the past.

When he finished eating, he leaned back and told me that he had met a woman. He described his feelings for her without actually saying he loved her. This was implied. He asked me what I thought about marrying her. I asked about her, and he revealed that she was twenty years older than him and from Argentina. I didn't react straightaway but asked what his parents thought of it all, and he said they didn't like it. They had protested strongly against dating a non-British woman of her age and said he needed to get out in the world first and date other women, focus on studying, etc. I didn't say it, but I agreed with them, not about the mixing of culture, but about the age difference, and that it was too soon to marry. We arranged for me to meet her during the week. It felt rushed. I think he didn't want to wait, as if the opportunity would escape him.

When he left, I walked over to Primrose Hill. It was my deep thinking and contemplation place of power. I had great concerns for Charlie.

I met them in the local pub. Charlie introduced her to me as Luisa. She was very pretty and petite, with features that were noticeably symmetrical and deep, and dark eyes that seemed to have a slightly watery effect. Her skin was dark like mine. I found myself wanting to make her feel safe. She was obviously nervous and sat bolt upright in her formal red outfit as if she had been asked to pose for an official picture. She spoke softly with a South American accent, but her English was so well articulated that it was easy for me to understand her. I think she had rehearsed. There was small talk, and by the time I left, I felt she had warmed to me and me to her. She seemed to be a very sincere person, but my mind kept on reverting to her age and Charlie's age, and other differences. She was a practicing Catholic, and Charlie was several times removed from any tangible belief system.

Over the next month, we met a few times. On one of these days, he came over without Luisa, and I plucked up the courage to ask him about the age difference. I felt I had to take the chance. He did not get angry, which was the last thing I wanted. Instead, he told me that he had made up his mind, and that was what he was going to do. Luisa and I became even more relaxed with each other. On several occasions, she visited my mother, who treated her as a daughter and made her feel at home—a touch of empathy which also seemed healing for my mother in her many struggles and losses.

One Saturday afternoon, on a beautiful summer day, Charlie, Luisa, and I were people watching in Camden Market. As we were walking back, Luisa stopped, became very serious, and then faced me and told me they had set the date for the wedding. The ceremony was going to be in church in two weeks' time. She said she was very nervous, that she was so far away from her country and family, and that she wanted me to escort her down the aisle and give her away. She explained that I was dark like her father, and that she felt that we were like family, the closest she could get. I was honored to be asked.

So on the day, I was dressed in a dark-blue pinstriped suit and a muted diagonally striped tie, a matching handkerchief, a white carnation with a few sprigs of green in my left lapel, and polished black shoes. My mother gave me a final inspection but did not attend, for some reason I can't remember. The organist began to play and fill the church with music. The signal was given, and Luisa and I walked down the aisle with her arm tight into my side. I felt very proud and protective of her. I knew she could feel my support, and her nervousness dissipated, and she began to carry herself with more confidence. At the altar, she turned to me and smiled while I stepped back.

Afterward, waiting for a few minutes for the car to return, she thanked me for giving her away. They disappeared in the interior of the back of the car and drove off. On returning from their honeymoon, they became very private. After a few weeks, without a word, Charlie and Luisa left for Argentina, and I never saw or heard from them again.

It was obvious that I had defined an important part of my life by my relationship with Charlie. There was a sense that was deeper than sadness, a loss, and a grief. The next Saturday, I made our usual breakfast, sat in the dining room, turned on the radio, and ate by myself. I cleaned up the dishes and went over to see Julia and was quiet all day into the evening and night. I have thought of Charlie many times over the years, even trying to see if I could trace him in the age of the Internet, but . . .

Chapter 6

Chaos, Creativity and Revolution, Ramani Rangan

The Slow and the Fast

When I was in between theater productions, I loved to travel around Europe, especially France, Spain, and Italy. I was drawn to slower, smaller towns with their focus on working to live and not living to work. To sit somewhere near the town's open market and eat a selection of local cheeses, with a slice from a tomato bigger than the size of your fist, olives, fresh bread, and a liter of the local wine was pure heaven. Cobblestone paving stretched over the whole surface of the town square, with its shade trees, benches, small cafés, and narrow streets dating back hundreds of years. Churches looked down like giant sentinels in carved armor of stone, there to protect the vulnerable innocent from the world of evil. People gathered in outside seating, chatting, while children played nearby. The occasional word could be heard above the hum of the few discerning shoppers choosing bunches of beautiful flowers from a stall, in their mind's eye already placed in the vase just so. If any place I visited had this to offer, I would always be enveloped by an overwhelming sense of release and calm.

This was totally missing from my London life, which I would have traded in a heartbeat. I was enjoying what people did throughout the ages, being in the sunshine of this perfect moment—shopping, eating, talking, laughing, and loving. But life goes on, and my budgeted spending would eventually run out. I was madly in love with the theater, and summer was over, so it was back to London and the stage.

There was an opening at the Shaftesbury. They needed an assistant to the property master, so I came in as they started rehearsals, which is always magical. It turned out that the property master was an aspiring drummer and was secretly taking his musician's license with the hope of fulfilling his dream of playing on luxury cruise ships. So one day, he announced he had his musician's union card and a place in a band with a cruise ship line, and he sailed off. The company hired another person, but that didn't work out. Within a few weeks, I took over and became, at twenty-two years of age, the property master of the American hit show *How to Succeed in Business Without Really Trying*, performed at one of London's oldest and most famous theaters.

The star of the show was Warren Berlinger. He was dynamic and humble at the same time. He treated me with an American ease that was respectful and friendly and quite different from the British formality I was used to. Then there was Billy De Wolfe. He played the CEO of the company in the show. He was a very tall man with a large presence. He had a dry sense of humor, and I couldn't always tell if he was joking. He would tease his fellow cast members by changing his performance every time. Just slightly, a little thing, but enough to have them cracking up backstage. A warm, kind man.

My job was to make sure that all props were in good condition and at the right place at the right time. Props are basically everything that can be moved in a scene, except the furniture or what hangs on the wall. An example would be what is on the table, but not the table. The whole process—from starting on an empty stage, the first rehearsals, scenery setup, lighting, costume call, orchestra and dress rehearsals, and then opening night—was my addiction. Even today, I'm like a child, enthralled with wonder when I step onto a stage.

The cast members drew me in, and by the end of the production, I felt that I was part of their family. Once, I was out to eat with a friend, and Warren was there. He paid for our bill. Another time, I was dressed in my finest to go out after the show, and the entire cast formed a catwalk with rows on either side of me and clapped. I said, "What's going on?" Warren said, "You're such a classy dresser. You should be in the show!" Kindnesses like these made me feel at home.

Meanwhile, out in the world, the incidents of Paki-bashing and skinhead racist violence continued. It was bad in London. Gangs were targeting people who looked like me. I stopped accepting invitations from my friends to go out after the show for a drink or a meal. Attacks were reported on public transport, so sometimes I would walk ten miles home. The show ended late at night, and leaving the theater in the dark was frightening. When the show closed, I was offered an opportunity to tour with the company for double wages and all expenses. The cities they were planning to go to were having race riots. Every day on television, there were images of people being attacked and vandalism and fires to property of colored people. So I turned them down. I left England and its race relationship dilemma and went traveling to Europe just to feel that I could emotionally breathe.

All Roads Lead to Copenhagen

One of the cast members in the show said he was going to Rome and had contacts in the film industry and could get me a job as a film extra or doing small parts. The studios were on a roll, making biblical epics, and they were a huge success across the globe. In the evenings, I hung out on the main drag and started to make connections with a mixed group of straights and gays—beautiful, intelligent women, artists, poets, musicians, and playboys. I began to realize that being an Indian was a bit of a novelty, and it was chic to be seen with me.

One day, while sitting out with my new tribe, I noticed a well-kept used Alpha Romeo sports car. The same car seemed to be driven solo by different young men, with a different driver every half hour or so. I pointed this out to the people I was with, and they explained to me that there were twelve of them and they had scraped money together to buy this status symbol to impress film agents, talent scouts, and anybody else who could open the film studio gates to them. At the time, Rome was like Hollywood, and everybody who thought they had talent was streaming into town with the hope of breaking into movies. Behind the scenes, wannabes were crowding together in slum rooms, but sharing one expensive set of clothes, enshrined in plastic until it was needed for an audition or interview.

After three weeks, my theater friend had not turned up. I had seen all the tourist sights, and the night scene was getting boring. The Romans I was hanging out with had deeper pockets than mine, and it was challenging my budget. It was the summer and getting hot, so I was looking for a place I could cool off. I remembered I had an uncle who had moved to Denmark. Going through my ragged address book, I found his telephone number. I called him and asked if I could come and visit. He sounded very enthusiastic, and so I pulled all my things together, made my reservations for the train journey, and said my good-byes with promises of keeping in touch.

That evening, I boarded my train to Denmark via Paris. The trip would take thirty-six hours. It was wonderful, crossing over rivers and presenting views of countryside, mountains, and valleys. We stopped in small villages and towns. Getting off to stretch my legs, I had time to smell the air, occasionally walk the town, and purchase a few things from family-owned shops that caught my fancy. I could become part of the scenery, people-watch, and enjoy a nibble, no doubt of some outrageous local indulgence with something to wash it down.

Paris is eternal, but it's a sprawl. You need three lifetimes to begin to see it all. So I went straight for the place I loved the best—the largest and oldest flea market in Paris, and possibly the largest in the world. It has a long name, so better recognized by the metro stop, Clignancourt. I spent four hours wandering around this huge, exciting menagerie of items and colors. In the evening, I boarded my final train to Copenhagen with presents for my uncle and his family. I arrived around 8:00 p.m. the following day.

I was excited to see my uncle after so many years. We had spent a lot of time together when he lived with us in London. I hailed a taxi. By now, it had begun to get dark, so I was relieved to arrive at his door. I was very tired, as I had slept only a few hours. I was looking forward to lying in a bed, fully horizontal, which wasn't jiggling up and down and back and forth. I put my two suitcases down by my side, checked the address number one more time, and knocked on the door. There was no answer. I repeated this a few times, and eventually, the door opened, but only by a third. It was my uncle.

"Hi," I said with a broad smile. I expected him to open the door fully, but he stood his ground. "You remember? We spoke two days ago about me visiting?"

He looked at me and said, "I'm so sorry. Some very serious things have come up." He added reluctantly, "I'll have to ask you to find another place to stay."

I will leave it up to your imagination, but everything—I mean everything—came crashing in on me. After all the traveling, I was thoroughly exhausted. I managed to flag down a taxi and asked to be taken to an inexpensive hotel. The taxi driver spoke very good English and asked me where I had come from. I finished the short version of my story. When we arrived at the hotel, he declined my tip sympathetically. I checked in, went downstairs to the bar, and ordered a rum and soda with lime. My body was still vibrating from the hours in the train, and I thought a walk would be good. Get some fresh air, stretch out my limbs, and shake off the frustration that was beginning to circulate in my mind and pass on to my body. So I went out to discover Copenhagen.

Illumination came mostly from streetlamps, as opposed to the blinding neon advertising signs I was used to in London. I marveled at the trolley cars, their rails picking up the light with occasional sparks from the overhead electric wires. The streets were filled with bicyclists of all ages, passing by on both sides of the street. I noticed the most beautiful women—tall, soft, chiseled faces, with long golden-blonde hair. They were on black bicycles that looked like remnants from the twenties, and they rode them like Amazons on a chariot with an expression of "I know who I am, and where I am going."

I walked a little more, but my tiredness took over. So I decided that all could wait for the morning, after a good night's sleep. I walked back toward the hotel, but where had it gone? I looked around in all the places I thought it might be. I searched in my pockets. Surely, I had taken a card, but no. I searched and searched and searched, with no luck. By now I was in a kind of daze, past any other thought than "I need to lie down." It was late, and after one more try, I found myself passing by the train station where I had arrived earlier. On the corner, a restaurant was just closing and locking up for the night. They had left the tables and chairs outside, chained to each other. I sat on one just to take the weight off my legs. As I glanced down, the space underneath the tables started to seem inviting . . .

I was awoken about nine in the morning by the man who was unlocking the chains. He politely asked me to leave. I looked around for a place I could get a cup of coffee and a cake, and there in front of me, across the road a little bit and up on the left, was my hotel.

It seemed easy to meet people in Copenhagen. It was 1963, and wherever I went, I felt strangely included. This was very different from what I was experiencing in London at the time. I loved it. I could go to any bar, café, sit out in a park or on a bench in a walking street, and I would get into a conversation and find myself invited to meet up with some of their friends or go to a party. If a woman was interested in me, she would let me know. I found out that every enquiry wasn't because of a sexual attraction but could be just curiosity. As I got used to how people treated me, I began to respond differently, and the process that I had apparently cultivated in my London surroundings melted away. I realized that I had created a "way of being." I had created a strategy to be the life of the party, tell jokes, lighten the atmosphere, and be alert, if things got too serious, to prevent violence from erupting. In reflection, it was a necessary survival technique, but not necessary here.

I met a few women that I got on well with. One time, I started a conversation with a woman. She didn't agree with my point of view and wanted to convince me I was wrong. We ended up back at her home. I have never been very good at making an advance, so I was surprised when she asked me in. It was about 11:00 p.m., and everyone in the house was asleep. We drank coffee and discussed some more. She said she was tired and showed me to a spare bedroom and left me there to sleep on my own. In a way, I was relieved that I didn't have to go through the preliminary wrestling of male-female engagement. She woke me in the morning with a smile. I was shown to the bathroom and given a spare toothbrush for visitors. When I came out, I was greeted by the family—her father, mother, sister, and brother all smiling at me. I was invited to sit and have some breakfast. I shyly answered a few questions about who I was and where I came from. Her parents went off to work, her siblings left for school, and she took me to where I recognized my surroundings. We said a warm good-bye, and that was that. I had never had a man-to-woman experience like that before, and I consider myself very lucky that this was not the last one.

One day, I had been walking up and down the main walking street in Copenhagen for a few hours with a friend, stopping a few times for coffee and sitting and people watching, when we decided to go sit on the steps at the front of the City Hall. We were there for a few minutes when two women came and sat near us and began a conversation. One of them said she was an artist and wrote poetry. Her name was Ania. I found her intense and interesting. We all went for a coffee. The others left, and it was just us. After a few days, we became inseparable. Far from anything that was on my mind, we were to be in each other's life for a long time.

All's Well That Ends Well

Backtrack with me, if you will, to Rome. I was sitting outside in a plaza sipping a coffee and people watching, when I noticed a man of about forty sitting at the next table. We began to talk, and I could tell from his accent he was from the United States, somewhere in the Deep South. He was flamboyant and had exaggerated feminine mannerisms. He told me his name was Maxie. I'm a person who tends to appreciate people who live outside the box, and Maxie was just that kind of person. We became friends. As we were both connoisseurs of cuisine, we had some fun reviewing restaurants, visiting bakeries to find the best bread, and trying to taste-test every dessert in town. Over time, he related to me that he was from old money. When he was sixteen, his family found out that he was gay. They sent him to a doctor to be "cured." He was barred from appearing at all family functions. He was ostracized by his fellow students and friends and treated as though he didn't exist. When he was twenty-one, his family opened up a bank account in his name, giving him a generous allowance once a month for the rest of his life under the condition that he reside permanently outside, not only the state, but the country. He had traveled around the world and had not found a place he could call home. He had just learned that his father had died. He was in a period of reflection and sadness. When I first met him, I got the impression he was isolated. By the time I left Rome, I was glad to see he had started to be part of a circle of friends.

Fast forward. I had now left Denmark and returned to London. I sent for Ania, and we settled into a beautiful apartment in Chelsea. I was working at the London Palladium on lighting. I had connected with old friends and made some new ones, mostly from the theater. Ania and I were planning our wedding. Her parents and my mother had not given any indication they were going to attend. So we were both looking at different possibilities for how to fill those crucial empty seats. I had not seen my mother in months. We'd had some very serious disagreements about my choice of partner. I had lost my dad by this time, but if he had been alive, he would have smoothed out the conflict. It didn't look like Ania's family would come over from Denmark, given the distance.

It was lunchtime. We had just finished rehearsals, and I was standing at the stage door with a few of my mates when I heard a familiar voice call my name. "Who could that be? I know that voice." I turned around. Out of a completely different world emerged Maxie. It didn't compute. The look on my face morphed from astonishment to a smile. The obvious question was, "What on Earth are you doing in London?"

Maxie, lifting both his arms up to heaven, asked, "Where else should I be?"

"How did you find me?" I asked.

He said he had heard from a friend that I had left Denmark and gone back to London. He knew I worked in the theater, and it would be easy to find a "crazy Indian" like me. It was.

Of course, he came to stay with us. Ania had heard his story so many times from me it seemed as though she had been the one who met him in Rome. There was immediate affection between them as if they were old friends. We sat down, and he wanted to know everything. "Who is this wonderful woman in your life? What happened to Denmark? I can't wait to meet your family."

We filled him in on our wedding arrangements. He wanted to know the details. We told him we were going to be married in a town hall. He said we were such a beautiful couple, and with a name like mine, we should be married in a palace, not a town hall. I was going by my first name at the time, Leroy, French for "the king." He asked who would be my best man, and without hesitation, I said, "You." He began to cry.

We had invited everyone to join us for lunch on the day of the wedding before going to the town hall. I had planned this with hopes that the someone who had known me longest in my life would show up, and she did. My mother appeared in a wheelchair, pushed by my half-sister. I was so pleased to see them both. I wanted so much for her to be a part of this. I could tell by the look on her face that she was relieved. Before long, she was talking to everyone.

Just when I thought I had gotten my breath back, Ania screamed as if the restaurant were on fire. She ran to the door and was embraced by her father and her mother, who had come all the way from Denmark. Her father shook my hand with tears rolling down his cheeks. Her mother was obviously pleased to be with us. As we all went to sit down and everyone was introduced, warmth circulated through my body, and I experienced a sense that all was complete.

It was a short ceremony, and like all good things, it was over in no time. I looked over and saw my mother, and Ania looked over and saw her mother and her father. Maxie was there, dressed in his wonderful

Italian suit, standing next to me. The justice of the peace called upon the best man and the ring bearer. "Are you Thomas Clements?"

Maxie, standing to his full height and with a loud, commanding voice, replied, "I, sir, am Thomas Maxwell Clements," emphasizing "Maxwell" so it wouldn't be lost to posterity. You could see by the expression on his face that he was the proudest man in the world.

One of my friends, Sandra, had insisted on doing the reception for us. I knew that she was married, but I hadn't yet met her husband. I understood he was a professor at a prestigious college. The family and all the guests arrived at Sandra's house, and she had made it so beautiful. We hadn't lifted a finger—flowers and all, she had done it. We had a few drinks and mixed, and then Sandra called my name and came over and said she would like me to meet her husband. The husband she presented to us was a very distinguished woman, who ceremoniously congratulated me and Ania and said in Spanish, "Mi casa es tu casa." I blanked out for a moment as the picture I held in my mind fractured. I recovered quickly and, hoping my hesitation had not been noticed, reached out to hug her husband. She lunged forward with an outstretched hand. I got the signal—too soon for a hug.

We sat round the table and enjoyed a sumptuous meal and many toasts. Then it was time to put the music on and dance. Our theater and non-theater guests blended perfectly as the evening progressed. After many more glasses of wine, Sandra's husband insisted on dancing with Ania's mother, cheek to cheek. I quickly cut in and rescued her. All's well that ends well.

The Royal Theater

Ania and I were now living in Copenhagen. She was in her eighth month of pregnancy, and I had only managed to find part-time jobs. I had just transferred my union membership from England, and I took Ania with me to the union office in downtown Copenhagen.

It was a sunny late August midday when we arrived. I didn't speak Danish yet. I was getting by with English, as most Danes spoke it very well. There were two men behind the counter eating their lunch. I asked them to look up my membership, and they said to come back after lunch.

"My wife has a doctor's appointment, and this is the only time we have," I replied.

They said they couldn't help me and turned away.

I asked them to lean forward and look over the counter. They looked puzzled. I pointed in the direction of Ania's big pregnant belly and said in a matter-of-fact tone, "I need to be able to feed this child."

The spirit of motherhood seemed to press a start button, and they stood to attention and began to quickly look in a file cabinet and turn a few piles of papers over on their desk.

One of the men sheepishly told me there weren't any job vacancies, but there was a hesitation in his voice.

"I'll take anything," I said and maneuvered Ania so her stomach was more visible to their gaze.

"Well! There is a need for a lighting stage man, but it is at the Royal Danish Opera House in Copenhagen, and you don't speak Danish. You wouldn't get the job."

My father-to-be valiant knight stepped in, and I stood my ground. "I want to go in for the interview anyway," came deep from my chest. There was only one conclusion. I was going. They signed the papers, called the theater office, and set up my appointment in two days' time. This would be on the first of September.

The Royal Theater had been pointed out to me when I first arrived as a tourist. I was definitely impressed, but actually finding the stage door and walking in was a whole other story. At the time, it was overwhelming. I found myself in a maze of people hurrying about in a rushed chaos. I showed my papers at the front reception and was directed up the stairs to the theater manager's office, where I sat and waited. The longer I sat, the more nervous I became about not speaking Danish.

A woman walked by, looked at me, and asked, "Are you the father-to-be in need of a job?" she asked with a hint of warmth. I replied, "Yes." She looked me up and down, taking her time, smiled again, and continued with her original task. A few minutes later, she signaled that I could go in.

Inside, sitting behind an untidy old desk, was a heavyset man who looked as though he had formed himself over the years to fit and overspill his high-back chair. He motioned for me to sit down. "So why do you want to work here?" He answered his own question. "Your wife is pregnant." He seemed sure of his position in life. I think he was enjoying the role I had given him.

"I have worked in all departments of London's West End theaters, except stage management." I went through a short history, adding that I had transferred my union membership.

He had a partly finished cob of corn on a plate in front of him. "You are an Indian, yes?"

I concurred.

He picked up the cob and began to imitate a cartoon character, rapidly eating it in a machinelike action. "Indians love corn," he said, putting it down with an exhaling laughing sound, as if this were funny.

I didn't answer. It happened so fast I didn't have time to react.

"I'm sorry," he declared abruptly, changing his facial expression as if he was readying himself to tackle the next piece of paper in the pile on his desk.

I made a move to stand, and at that moment, the woman who had spoken to me outside, walked in. She added a few papers to his pile. "His wife is due anytime now. He looks like a good man. Give him the job," she said nonchalantly.

"I can't. He doesn't speak Danish."

She answered again, matter-of-factly, "He will learn." Facing me, she asked, "Are you a quick learner?"

I answered with a swallowed "Yes."

She didn't move. She stood as if she was dug in and was taking root. "Give him a chance. If he doesn't work out, you can fire him." With that, she walked toward the door, slowed, and half turned.

"Can you start on Monday?" he asked, as if the words were being forced out of his mouth.

The woman changed the subject before he had a chance to think it over. "You want coffee?" she asked him. He stood up and stretched out his hand.

I reciprocated with a half smile, walked out as fast as I could, and floated home to tell Ania.

For some reason, I wasn't nervous when I turned up for the first day at the Old Stage at the Royal Danish Opera House, Copenhagen. Within a week, our first child was born, and I became a father. It took a few tough months of being teased as I struggled to learn the language, before I got the hang of reading the signals between my fellow workers. They all spoke English very well. With their help, I began to fit in and was able to complete my duties smoothly. During the theater season, the repertoire changed evening to evening—some opera, some ballet, some play. The plays were always in Danish. So I had a constant repetition of association to a visual cue. After a while, I started to dream in Danish and then realized, to my surprise, that I was speaking Danish fluently.

Work schedule was two days on and one day off. A typical day started at 8:30 a.m. There were production rehearsals before the opening of the season. New productions had new scenery, staging, and lighting. Each day the theater set from the night before had to come down, and the new one had to go up. Sometimes we had all-day rehearsals and had to set up last minute. Elaborate operas like Faust or Boris Godunov might have to be taken down so the stage could be prepared for a night of ballet.

I loved rehearsals with full orchestra. Powerful music, sculpted by the composer, was being arranged to meet the heart and ear of the conductor, then communicated to the audience through the artistry of the musicians. The process was magical. I learned that classical music scores were a vehicle for the attempt to transmit the essence of pure emotion, not just dots and lines on a sheet of paper or sound and vibration.

My job was lighting. My favorite was working the spotlight. It was unusual to end the day before thirteen or more hours had gone by. Over the three years I was there, I could be exhausted from the day's workload, but just before the performance started and the curtain went up, I snapped to attention, sharp as a razor. I loved my job. Something intangible awoke and created a metamorphosis for the parts of me that had been cocooned due to the rigors of my childhood. Some performances moved me deeply. I always found my eyes tearing up in the last act of Puccini's *Madame Butterfly*, as she sings the aria "Un

Bel Di Vedremo" ("One Fine Day We Will See") even after witnessing thirty performances. *La boheme* and *Tosca* spoke to social justice and the plight of those most vulnerable, paralleling much that I had witnessed as a child. Mozart was something very different. His story line was secondary to the effect his music had on me. Where Puccini touched the emotional, Mozart touched a feeling of wonder and power. In *Cosi fan tutte*, the opening of the aria, "Per Pieta," is so fragile and disarming that Mozart's ability to embody a living, breathing person on the stage borders on the metaphysical. Each season would bring voice, movement, and storytelling from around the world and Denmark's most talented. I saw Rudolf Nureyev eating beef tartare with a raw egg in the canteen. During his performance, when he was offstage, he would totally collapse on the floor in exhaustion. When it was within a few seconds of his cue, he would stand up and, holding a proud pose, leap onto the stage with such energy and freshness that his performance was breathtaking.

Working in the theater is dangerous. Backstage between scenes, sets including large mobile equipment are being changed, "drops" are going up and coming down, heavy lamps are being moved. All this while dozens of singers, stage extras, stagehands, electricians, dressers, makeup, and stage management are rushing to complete tasks in nearly pitch black. I have seen many bad accidents and experienced some myself that plague me still. One such accident happened to a stagehand working on the counterweight system above the stage. He was waiting for his cue to lift a backdrop. He got distracted for a second, and the counterweight he was working with struck him on the side of his head. This knocked him out, and before I could respond, he toppled into the railing opening and fell forty feet headfirst to the bottom of the shaft. We continued working as the ambulance came and took him away. He was out for two months and seemed distant and disoriented when he returned.

The sets and the equipment were sometimes massive and had to be stored away. We had industrial elevators large enough to fit four midsize cars. I had some stage lamps and scenery that needed to go down to storage, so we had filled the elevator up, and someone pushed the button to close the heavy doors without warning us. The same man was standing between the elevator and the landing when the double-gate door closed on him crushing his chest. He never returned to work, and no one would talk about him when I asked.

I myself was at Covent Garden Opera House in London, up on the landing above the stage, moving a very heavy 1000 watt lamp. It was dark, and someone had left the six-inch-by-six-inch door open to an electrical outlet on the floor. I didn't see it, and my right foot sank in up to my kneecap, which was pushed up several inches. At the same time, the lamp fell forward and was hanging by its cable over the side of the safety barrier. It was directly hanging over the heads of an offstage group of singers. If I let go, the lamp would fall and kill at least one person. If I held on, I would have to wait till the scene was over. I held on even though I was in excruciating pain for the twenty minutes it took for the scene to end and someone to see me. My knee took a long time to heal, and it still gives me problems.

In another accident, I was taking a tall frame canvas sidepiece across an alley to its storage space when a strong freak wind caught it like a sail and twisted my upper body from my lower. This tore the muscles in my lower back, and I collapsed to the floor. I was given a prognosis of 50 percent disability and told I would be an invalid in ten years' time. I stubbornly refused to accept this, and with a lot of painkillers and effort, I was on my way to recovery within three weeks.

Once, in an opera at the Royal Danish Theater, the singer portraying Faust was lying down on a couch. He started to breathe so heavily that it could be heard by the audience. A rattling sound started to come from his throat, and I ran over to tell the stage manager that he was sick. The stage manager took a look and froze. "We have to bring down the curtain," I said, but he wouldn't. The woman singing a duet with him knew there was something wrong, but continued to sing. The audience also knew that something was wrong. A very long few minutes went by, until finally, the curtain was lowered. He was taken away, the audience was informed that the singer was unwell, and they would be given a credit ticket to the next performance of their choice. The next day, we found out that he had died onstage.

On a brighter note, it was not unusual to see King Frederick IX of Denmark, father to the present monarch, sneak into the theater by a side door. He would wait until the theater lights were dimmed and quietly slip into the royal box. With the faintest of lights, he would open his sheet music to that night's performance and follow the music score. He was an ardent student of classical music and was himself a competent conductor. Eventually, he would be noticed by some in the audience, but it was an unspoken agreement to act as though he wasn't there.

I was at the Copenhagen Royal Theater when it was packed with royals and dignitaries, mostly from Europe, for a special performance to entertain and celebrate the marriage of Princess Margrethe to Count Henri de Laborde de Monpezat of France. That night, Mum and Dad, King Frederick and Queen Ingrid, lent their theater box to their daughter and her fiancé. There was so much security that I had to be cleared six times by six different countries. When the auditorium lights went down and the stage lights came up, all the precious jewelry started to sparkle like stars in the sky. The next day, we were asked to go into the front of the theater to the grand hall where there had been a reception and bring back some standing lights that had been used for extra illumination. Before us were dozens of long tables, enough to seat two hundred or more, and the remains of what looked like a royal feast. I looked at my coworker, and he looked at me. There on the tables were bottles upon bottles of opened wine bottles. Did I mention bottles too many times? We decided that this would be our only chance in this lifetime to taste a vintage of such high quality. Looking around and seeing that the coast was clear, we grabbed three nearly full bottles each and hid them outside the hall. We removed the lights and returned them as quickly as possible, and then we went back to get our stash. Later that evening, we both agreed that the wine was so smooth that it seemed to evaporate in our mouths. It warmed the chest and relaxed the mind. We tested it a few times to reach this conclusion.

On another occasion, I had to go through a security check and had no idea why. I got into place to work the spotlight and saw a brown face in a seat of honor. I had seen pictures of him, and I recognized his features. It was Emperor Haile Selassie I, who was Ethiopia's 225th and last emperor. This man was very special to me. I had followed his life and noble work. His historic line could be traced back to Menelik I, who was credited with being the child of King Solomon and the Queen of Sheba. Seeing him was like seeing someone from thousands of years ago still in the flesh.

Working in the theater taught me to be aware of what is going on around me, but to still be in a relaxed state. I have used this in many situations to avoid danger and in mindfulness in my yoga practice. That was 1968, and the theater is still in my bones and my heart all these years later.

Paintings of Past Years

I was looking at some of my more recent paintings and wondering what happened to the ones I made five decades ago. I started to paint—I mean seriously paint, at twenty-seven years old. I'd been working at the Royal Danish Theater when I had a nervous breakdown. It must have been the accumulation of the effects of being a wartime child, the violence in my home, the racism in the streets, and my sense of isolation as one of the few at the time who broke the glass ceiling for people of color at work and socially in London and Denmark. My marriage had become a disaster and was in collapse. It was so painful that I was afraid to come home. I was devastated by one thing after another until I couldn't take it anymore. One day during a rehearsal, I snapped and left the stage. I started to punch a metal wardrobe until my fist was bleeding. Many of my fellow workers grabbed me and held me back, and I blacked out. I have no memory of the following two days. I became paranoid and delusional. I believed that everyone was looking at me with critical eyes and bad intentions. Familiar places appeared unrecognizable to me, and I was totally disoriented. All the normal treatments that society had to offer did not work. Psychotherapy and meds were of no help. The psychiatrist assigned to me was bonkers. I arrived in his office, which looked like a palace. He asked me if I liked music, and he invited me to play on his full-size grand piano. After I played, he said, "You know you'll never be a professional pianist, right?" Somehow, even in my psychotic state, I realized the psychiatrist needed more help than I did.

My instinct told me that I had only one choice—to fix myself. Some time had gone by, and I was now living on my own. Sitting on a park bench, looking over the several man-made lakes close to the center of Copenhagen, I felt the fresh air and the warmth from the summer sun. In my mind's eye, I saw my very small apartment morph into a hospital room. What would I do to transform it into a healing space?

Within walking distance was an old-fashioned material store with rolls and rolls of all types of cloth for all kinds of needs. So I went in, looked around, and found lightweight bleached cotton curtain stuff in a big roll. Perfect. Hospital curtains. I estimated how much I would need for my two windows. I saw a paint shop and bought two cans of white paint and one small can of red. I arrived back at my apartment, sat down, looked around, and closed my eyes. Before me appeared exactly what needed to be done. I took down the old curtains, moved my bed to the center of the room, and piled all my furniture on top. I stripped off my clothes and started to paint stark naked. Everything white—the walls, the doors, the ceiling. Even the bed frame, table, and chairs. I nearly started on the floor, but the polished two-hundred-year-old lacquered floorboards insisted, "Stop! Enough!" The paint fumes were overpowering, so I opened windows.

That wasn't sufficient, but I didn't know what was missing. I had to go out and find it. I left—by the way, I did dress again—and wandered through cobblestone squares and side streets. This had a soothing effect on me. When I arrived on the main walking street, I was met by a full contingent of tourists and shoppers, so I ducked down the next side street to escape. There in front of me appeared a music shop. In the window were all kinds of instruments. The shop was empty of customers, and it felt safe to go in. Things started to leap out at me. I found myself with a guitar in my arms. It was a perfect fit—a three-quarter-size handmade acoustic Czechoslovakian model, fashioned with a viola-style body. Next, a penny whistle flute chose me. Then an instrument that sounded like a cross between a mouth harp and an accordion. I bought these without hesitation and could not get home quick enough.

That night I painted in large red letters, "Front Door" on the front door, "Kitchen Door" on the kitchen door, followed by the bed, table, and chairs. I fell asleep while hand-sewing the white curtains. I woke early, finished the curtains, and hung them. There was still something missing. I didn't know what it was, but I knew, again, I would have to go out and hunt it down. I stayed clear of the main walking street this time and found the area in Copenhagen with all the small family-run shops. There, as if ordered, my eyes adjusted and settled on an artist's supply store. You could tell it had been around a long time. I walked in, avoiding the other customers. I was now on a mission of completion. I bought canvas, frames, oil paint, brushes, paint thinner, varnish, and a standing easel. Carrying my load, I headed home. I must have looked like a madman struggling with all this through the streets.

I got home, set everything up, arranged the musical instruments and the painting easel, and put out my paints and other supplies on the small table. I made a cup of tea and sat and sat and sat. This was going to be my hospital room for however long it would take to find myself again. Something was guiding me. I was very sick and lost.

I started first by playing the guitar. It was the least challenging, as I had played before. Slowly, very slowly, it came back to me—the three chords of the blues. I played the other musical instruments. After a few weeks of going out only at night to buy food and provisions, I started to paint. I painted nonstop, everyday into the night, and sometimes through the night. As oils take time to dry, I bought a drying medium and painted on three canvases at a time in a series, propping two of them on chairs or the table. When they were dry enough, I took them off the stretcher frames, laid them out to cure, and then rolled them. I taught myself to stretch a new canvas on the old frame. This small apartment became a creative healing factory of color and music.

After three months of music and painting and four walls, an impulse drew me out one day early in the morning. No one else was about, and I started to walk. In a few minutes, I was sitting up against a tree in King's Park. Tired from painting all night, I covered myself with my coat and fell asleep. When I woke, there were people all around me having their lunch break. They were focused on eating. Some were with friends talking or laughing. Mothers were playing with their children. I noticed a man walking his dog on a leash. In that moment, the tide turned, and something changed inside me. It all shifted. All the paranoia. All the disillusionment. All the disorientation. All the pain. Over the next three months, I came out every day and sat under that same tree. Before long, some Bohemian types and students gathered under my tree, and we talked and played music and shared. One day I invited some of them over to my apartment to see my paintings, and the spell was broken. Something spiritual had arisen. Music, painting, and all expressions of creativity had become my new path.

My First Harmonica

I had now been separated from my first wife and children for a while. I can't remember how long, but it was short enough to be sad and to really hurt, and long enough for me to feel the loneliness on a deeper level. At the time, I was smitten with the blues—I mean the wailing and moaning. This male expression of feelings struck a deep chord. It pulled on my heartstrings and created an avenue to express the great loss I was experiencing. I couldn't stop listening to it. I was driven to seek it out.

One day, I went out the door and walked to a store that sold musical instruments. I had stopped by many times and looked through the window at all the instruments, especially the harmonicas. Each time, I had the impulse to go in, but I never did. I just walked away. This time I went in and walked right up to the counter and asked to see the three best mouth harps they had. The manager slid open the door of a glass cabinet, set four on the counter, and ceremoniously opened their cases. Then he laid down a red velvet cloth and stood back. He proclaimed, "You may not place any of them near to your lips or blow into them before purchasing. Once bought and played, you own it. Do you understand?"

I asked which one was the best, and he picked out the fourth one. He took it out of its case and, with great reverence, laid it on the velvet. "This is the Hohner. It is German. The best. The world's best." I hesitated, so he showed me the others. I knew the Hohner was the one. I didn't think of the price. I just paid and walked out. I felt as though I had stolen something and gotten away free.

I later realized I felt this way because the harmonica that I had acquired was a gateway to another world much more valuable than the object. I went home and put it into warm water as the shop owner had instructed. This was to loosen up the reeds. I first placed it to my lips, and it fit perfectly. I started to gently breathe in and out on it, allowing the sounds to resonate. After about five hours in this world of "my sound," I realized it was now dark. I went out and bought a bottle of wine and played through the night until I fell asleep. I woke at around 6:00 a.m. and went out a little drunk and stood on the Stroget, the main walking street in Copenhagen, and started to play.

People began to walk to work, and I continued to play for them and myself. I stopped only when I tasted blood and realized my top lip was swollen and bleeding. The mouth harp, the harmonica, had revealed to me how to play it. I was playing the blues in the same way I had heard it, with the same depth of feeling and emotion. That's over four decades ago, and now I have lived in the United States for many years. Once in a while, not often enough, I still open the case and see the shiny engraved exterior announcing its name, award medals, and pedigree. I still place it in warm water to loosen up the metal reeds, shake it, and wipe it with its dust cloth, rest the black mouthpiece against my lips, breathe in, and gently blow the blues. I am reminded my black sisters and brothers are still struggling. It's a long, long road. I feel the suffering in my bones and my stomach, and then I am transported by the music to a place beyond time and space where healing is possible.

When I Was between Jobs or Carlsberg Brewery

After recovering from my nervous breakdown, I recognized that returning to the theater culture of recreational drinking, smoking, and all that goes with clubbing would be like diving down the same dark hole again. I decided that I was an artist at heart. Learning to play musical instruments and taking out the brushes, dipping them in oil paint and applying them to canvas was the true road for me. My self-induced rehabilitation changed my world, restored balance, and brought light back into my days. Having stepped out of the system of a "bright future" with a handsome government retirement in lighting at the Royal Danish Theater, I was now on my own. It was soon evident I needed some kind of cash flow. Up till then, I had jumped more or less from good job to great job to wonderful and amazing job. So now what?

They were always hiring at Carlsberg Brewery. My job was to check that every crate was full of the staple diet of any respectable and loyal Dane—ale. The smell of hops, yeast, and stale ale—beer to the rest of us—permeated every pore of my skin, hair, and, of course, clothes. After a few days, the aromas even permeated my apartment and hallway, so everyone—I mean everyone, even passersby who lived there—knew where I now worked. Many generations of students in Copenhagen had worked there in the summer months, so even as adults, they recognized the smell and knew. "Oh! You're working at Carlsberg." There was Tuborg, the other large brewery, but the trained nose of the local population immediately deciphered the difference. Now an initiate, I became a member of a tribe of men and women tracing their roots back to the Viking age and beyond.

However, the smell wasn't the only thing. In fact, after a while, it was welcome—like a form of aromatherapy. No, the noise level of the machines, conveyor belts, and the rustling of thousands of bottles for eight hours a day was the overall encompassing impression on my person. It got to the point that I could still hear the sound in my head for a few hours after I clocked off. My dreams began to be all about the factory. I was clocking off, but I couldn't find the exit and was trapped. I was invited to sit on top of one of the many enormous stainless steel brewing vats by a very attractive Danish young woman. Remember, I was young at the time, and resistance was futile, thank you. She disappeared, and I was stranded up there all night, hoping to be rescued by the day shift, but they never arrived. Some of the nightmares were repeaters.

Carlsberg, being a Danish company, and the Danes, being a compassionate people, took pity on us and allowed us to take four beers home each day. You could choose from any of their many brews. One of their ales was Elephant Beer. On the label was a picture of an elephant. What has an elephant to do with beer? Back in the day, early 1800s, they decided to have four full-size granite elephants at the gates of the factory. Elephant Beer was and is their strongest. I mean, just half of one of these babies could provide you with a kick in the front and back of your head, and sides, if you weighed less than 200 pounds. Most Danes were over six feet tall and ate well. Just to get through a Danish winter, you needed some padding. I weighed in at 170 pounds, so it took courage and determination and four or five hours at one of the many parks in Copenhagen to process a five-day working week. Half a bottle became my max—the rest I started to barter. All of us on that work shift would head to the King's Park via a hotdog stand or a smorgasbord, a Danish open sandwich shop, to the same spot under a tree, where we laughed and frolicked.

After a short while, I realized this was taking a backward curve for my cure and hindering me as the Artist. Especially, as my art was beginning to sell. I left Carlsberg, went back to London, signed on to my union, and worked a few productions. One was at the Cambridge Theater, the Tommy Steele show, *Half a Sixpence*, and the other at the Prince of Wales Theater, a revue with lots of feathers and dancers with long legs. I lost attraction for the after-show lifestyle of drinking and staying out all night and started to make friends who had other interests. Eventually, I realized that London was not for me. Why? I don't know. Going back, it is all a mystery why and how I came to decisions. I think it was because I missed my children, and although we were separated and there was difficulty seeing them, there was always hope. So I went back to Denmark.

Vietnam in Copenhagen

I returned to major demonstrations in the streets of Copenhagen in protest of the Vietnam War. Laos and Cambodia were being bombed heavily by U.S. forces to stop the Vietcong (VC) and the North Vietnamese Army from using those countries as a passageway and entrance point for attacks on South Vietnam. Every ten days, 821,000 cluster bombs were being dropped on Laos, killing and injuring countless civilians and decimating the country. It was the heaviest bombing in history in any place on the planet. It was done in secrecy, and when the news got out, people reacted with outrage and an upsurge of antiwar activity. I joined the protest movement.

I was single again, without a partner, and loved hanging out in clubs listening to live music. My passion was jazz. From where I lived, it was no more than five to ten minutes' walk to four or five jazz clubs. My favorite was the legendary jazz club Montmartre. During the 1960s and the1970s, the club served as a European home for American jazz giants like Ben Webster, Dexter Gordon, Stan Getz, Kenny Drew, and many others. The small, intimate club had you within ten feet of the Best of the Best. America had forgotten these greats, having moved on to Motown, rock 'n' roll, the Beatles, and the Stones.

While patronizing these clubs, I started to meet "my Americans." U.S. Soldiers were being flown from the warfront to army bases in Europe for medical attention and/or R & R (rest and recreation) cycles. Some went to Hamburg, Germany, and took leave to come to Copenhagen. These young men, mostly black, shared their stories with me. The North Vietnamese had launched a campaign of surprise attacks, the Tet Offensive, on major cities of South Vietnam, which had placed my Americans in the center of the conflict. U.S. Forces sustained heavy losses.

"We stunk. We were fighting for days in dense tropical jungle. There were poisonous everything, everywhere. Bugs that bore into your feet and lay eggs. If you caught it too late, off came the foot. Snakes, spiders, and millipedes, man! If they got you, twenty minutes at the most. I've seen it. You'd be pronounced killed in action and awarded a medal for bravery. Brothers would die right in front of you, and you couldn't help them."

There were a lot of expletives delivered with passion and remorse. "They told us, never leave a man behind. We did. What could we do? Sometimes, in the confusion, you could even get wiped by friendly fire. You gotta know—there were times we were totally lost. We had no idea where we were, and communication was piss poor in the jungle. That's what the jungle does. Did I mention the heavy rain? We're talking monsoon, brother. For days on end, we were soaking wet. Even the wet got wetter, so you couldn't take your clothes off. They were glued to your body. Then there were booby traps. They could be anywhere. Like a small hole covered with leaves. You'd put your foot down, and bamboo that had been sharpened to a point would stick up and go through your foot. Lots of f——d-up stuff like that. On top of all this, the VC were like an army of ghosts. We never knew where they were until they were on us. They would appear, all hell would break out, and then in a blink, they'd be gone. We lost so many guys."

Then they would go quiet. Some would just sit and stare out of empty eyes and have nothing to say. There were episodes. Something would trigger a memory, someone would go feral, and we'd have to hold them down. Only a buddy could calm them. Some would not go to the toilet unless a buddy was standing outside. Just the loud sound of a toilet flushing could instantly send them back to the hell of war and the nightmare of their mind. To the outside world, they could appear to be normal, but underneath, there was something else, a compounded fear of being killed at any moment. It was nearly as tangible as cigarette smoke in a closed room. I instinctively fell into place, reading the subtle messages of their world, and they picked this up. Somehow my wartime exposure as a baby and a child and years of living with the constant danger of the IRA (Irish Republican Army) bombings in London as a youth tuned me in.

There were lighter times when the sun shone and pushed the horror of the past to a remote place. Then I learned what was cool, what was even cooler, and what was not cool in the USA. Lesson 1: Never drink cheap cherry brandy. The worst hangover ever. Never ask about the Vietnam War. Just listen without question, but don't appear to avoid the subject. Never use the N-word, even though they used it all the time. It was difficult to figure out how to laugh in all the right places. I faked it in the beginning, and they knew it, but it seemed to be OK. I was taught that the N-word had dozens of meanings. That is, even the way it was used, pronounced, or intoned in a sentence changed the meaning of the sentence. These lessons later helped me understand how my own people in India used words that were derogatory toward themselves. Maybe it was a leftover from hundreds of years of British colonial oppression. Women treated my Americans as if they were exotic aliens from another planet. I never saw them flirt back. In fact, they appeared to be oblivious, avoiding any sexual advances toward them. This seemed to press the button and make them even more attractive to the girls-into-women. Eventually, whatever it was that was holding them in their prison, let go, and they started to date. However, the silent ones, hovering in a place of war shock, remained unapproachable, off limits.

One day, after I had decided to call it a night and was home relatively early, 1:00 a.m., there was a knock on my door. It was pitch black in the passage. I asked who it was through the door, and then I heard the voice of my soon-to-be-ex-wife. I got a little apprehensive. It was late—what could bring her here? Was it to do with one of the children? I opened the door and stood back. In the doorway was a six feet three black man in a coat that was much too heavy for this time of year. He was sweating and didn't look well at all. My wife quickly explained that she had met him at a club and that he was sick. Could I let him stay the night with me? He had nowhere to go. With that, she left and left me with him.

He was suffering from a fever. Trying to hold his balance, he toppled a few feet into the room. I didn't have chairs. It was the age of bean bags. He sank into one, and I did what anyone originating from England would do. I put the kettle on for a cup of tea. He told me his name. Robbie. He mumbled that he had been in Copenhagen for a week and he had flown in from Toronto, Canada. He added that he had an infection, that he was lost and didn't have any idea what to do. My wife had told him I would know how to help.

I got him to a hospital clinic, and he got a shot of antibiotics. At the time, health care in Denmark was free to all, even to foreigners. I told him he could stay with me until he felt better. He was twenty-three, from Chicago. His number had been drawn in the lottery for compulsory enrollment in the military. His black friends who had returned from Vietnam said they were put in harm's way more often than other soldiers. Word got back that black soldiers were being put in front units soon after they arrived without adequate on-the-ground orientation. The sheer number of those returning from his neighborhood and the surrounding area in body bags was shocking. Robbie had lost count of how many funerals he had attended, hearts broken, girlfriends, wives, sisters, and mothers weeping. He decided he could be a soldier, but he would not be a wasted target like the boys he grew up with, now lying in early graves. He crossed into Canada, flew to Copenhagen, and had planned to seek protection in neutral Sweden. At the time, if you flew into Sweden, you would be sent back, but they turned a blind eye in Copenhagen and on the ferry to Sweden.

Robbie and I got on so well that he decided to stay in Denmark. He began to bring fellow Americans my way, and my humble home became a halfway house. Over a hundred came through in the two years he lived with me. There was Spoon. He was big—I mean a really big man, six feet six and three hundred pounds. He got his name because he always ate with a spoon. When finished, he would clean it off and push it deep into his afro. Some had come in like Robbie. Others had been in Nam, gone AWOL and were not going back to that "hellhole." Then there was Fast Eddie. He stuttered. Sweet, sweet man and a great cook. Michael, very thoughtful and studious. Mostly silent. You couldn't get more than a few comments from him, but he would spontaneously recite his poetry. Many, many more came to my house to eat from my big pot of Indian stew. At the time, we were all broke, so whatever went into that pot had to be on the cheap side. Pork bones with scraps of meat, pig's feet and knuckles, chicken wings, or beef "a la economique." To this was added bread, wine, or ale and some kind of dessert, set out on a table that had been made from the kitchen door and four beer crates. Life was good. We all sat on the floor, bowl in one hand, spoon in the other, listening to the coolest of cool jazz. Sometimes there were as many as sixteen staying in my one room. I was surprised that the comings and goings of all of these "foreigners" did not get reported by the neighbors.

From my Americans, I gained empathy and an understanding of the truth about war. If war is hell, then those who order their children to fight are devils. Homer's, *The Odyssey*, the story of a war fought over one woman, Helen of Troy, reminds us that the nature of war has not changed across the centuries. I think of Ulysses, leaving his beloved home, Ithaca, his wife and child, in a ship filled with fellow warriors and heroes to fulfill a pledge that resulted in the meaningless slaughter of men, women, and children. It appears to me that all wars, even the Second World War, were never about honor, glory, and the flag, as we were told. They were and are about a few individuals manipulating the power structure for their own benefit, costing hundreds of millions of innocent lives, murdered as collateral damage. Not to mention injuries, physical and mental, that are suffered for generations.

Even now, when I listen to blues or jazz, my Americans, those alive
and those who went back and died in that war, are right here with me.
We are all sitting around the kitchen door that became a table, in that
small room, with the big pot of curry stew and cool jazz as the added
spice. Some are talking, some laughing, some still as the night, staring
into space. All my brothers are still with me, forever.

Christiania, a Freedom State of Mind

On the outskirts of old Copenhagen, there was an abandoned
military complex. Someone found out about a law that went back many
hundreds of years that was still on the books. It stated that if a property
owned by the military was abandoned over a period of time, it was legal
for the civilian population to occupy that property to be used as their
place of residence. So a group of squatters, hippies, and free-thinkers
broke in and started to occupy.

When the news came through the grapevine, I quickly formed
a crew consisting of Robbie, my roomie, and two Danes, one a poet
and singer and the other a groupie, both women. We planned it like a
commando raid. We moved into action on the second day of the squat.
We crawled through a fence opening. People were already staking out
their claim to barracks, office and supply buildings, and houses. I knew
that if we were to find an empty location and avoid conflict, we had
to get a clear picture of the movement of other squatters. As you can
imagine, it was quite chaotic. I climbed onto a roof, then jumped onto
a tree. From here I could see that there was activity around a cluster
of buildings on a main road. So climbing down, I took my team in the
opposite direction. We came across four empty large buildings. A quick
inspection of three showed leaky roofs, broken windows, and other
damage. For a moment, I felt we would have to look elsewhere, but . . .
the fourth? Good roof, windows that could be repaired, and two wood
stoves.

We went in through the kitchen door. The gas stove was usable and
ran on propane. After running, jumping up and down, and screaming
with glee, we put up our homemade flag of occupation. We painted a

sign, "Yoga, Meditation, Dance, and Music Center" and with what was left over, we painted the front door and window frames. This was our spot. It looked like it had housed about thirty soldiers. We put plastic on the windows and stuffed cracks with insulation to keep out the cold. Then we fixed the two wood stoves and fired them up with leftovers from a building site on the other side of the wall. Our new digs came with a line of six toilets in a washroom with showers. Although this occupation was being contested, it was still legal. So we were able to get our water and electricity turned on. There was still much to do. While we were fixing the last of the things that were broken, I painted some colorful murals, and we scavenged for furniture around the city.

Within a week, we opened the only drug-free, drunk-free haven in the new free state we called Christiania. All day, every day in our center, there was live acoustic music and some multimedia art project. I gave free yoga and meditation classes. Community started to form around the center, and people chipped in, so there was always tea or coffee, and we would share food. I made curry and rice and sold it, and local groups came and donated concerts, all of which paid for the utilities and other expenses. We had art exhibitions, ethnic dances, and ran a mini bakery. We had pop-up events before pop-ups were called pop-ups. We held a few weddings there, and I played keyboard and bass in the band. We even made a documentary on Christiania, and I composed the music.

Christiania was a lawless place. The police had no jurisdiction. All the drugs and paraphernalia were being dealt on Main Street. It was really dangerous there, and we were happy that we had chosen a location far from it. The center evolved so much in a period of three years that hundreds of friends and visitors came through our doors from all over the world. To name a few, there was Delaware, a very well-built blonde American. She loved to help me in the kitchen, hiding away from the hounds and wolves she attracted with her voluptuous figure. She was interested in philosophy and metaphysics and opened up and shared her feelings about the bigger picture of everyday life. We had a little Indian guru who just smiled and mumbled mantra for a week. There were East Germans who had escaped Soviet communism and were on their way to find their freedom. A troupe of Mayan musicians, including a shaman, poets, professional dancers, healers, philosophers, a unique

clothes tailor, hip police officers, liberal local politicians, a candlestick
maker, a musical instrument designer, and many, many "dreamers of a
better world," all graced our humble home away from home.

When we moved into Christiania, there was a dimensional change
in my sense of freedom. There were no rules, so we made our own.
There were no landlords, no lawmakers, no restrictions whatsoever.
We, as people, were in a totally free state. I don't remember one fight or
conflict in our center during the time we were there. However, outside
in the rest of Christiania, there was mayhem, chaos, and confusion,
vying for power, drug lord conflicts, and misuse of drugs. Struggling
within this environment, there was an honest, noble group of people
who were trying hard to create a positive structure, but their efforts were
constantly being challenged. Christiania was going through labor pains,
trying to find its footing with how to be a civil society. Eventually, the
darker forces of Christiania spread out, and we were broken into and
vandalized several times. It became impossible to be there, and with
great reluctance, we had to fold up and leave.

That was a long time ago. Presently, Christiania has upscale
restaurants, venues for cinema, concert and theater productions, a radio
station, and a famous Christmas market. People come as tourists from
as far as Japan to witness the unusual phenomenon that was once an
independent free state within a sovereign nation. The Christiania of
today has its own governing rules, its own flag, its own currency, but it
pays taxes and is subject to Danish law. I was there a few Christmases
ago with my son and family. I sensed the invisible presence of the vision
that a rainbow of people had attempted to create all those years ago—
creativity with rules that support safety and fairness, yet maintain the
spirit of freedom.

Chapter 7

Journey Within the Journey, Ramani Rangan

Formentera

Denmark, in the winter back in the early 1970s, was colder than now. Cold would be an understatement. Think Newfoundland, Canada, in a three-month continuous winter storm. I remember walking at an angle of nearly forty-five degrees because of the freezing, biting fangs of Viking sleet. The Oresund strait between Denmark and Sweden would become solid ice, and people would skate across. It became a must to fly south to the relief and welcome of a warmer weather. So I followed a special girlfriend to the village of El Pilar, at the southernmost tip of Formentera, one of Spain's Balearic isles in the Mediterranean. There was, at the time, a noticeable tension among the population toward Generalisimo Franco, the dictator of Spain. The area was part of Catalonia, where the people had a history of being stubbornly independent and rebellious. There was a distinct difference in their dialect. Indeed, they were proud of their language—Catalan. It wasn't recognized as an official language by the rulers of Spain until 1979.

El Pilar was small, just two hundred or so locals, with one general store, which also served as the post office. A swelling of fifty or sixty mixed foreigners, mostly European nationals, came and went for a few days. Others, like myself, rented a house through the winter. We brought color and oddity to this village, which was established back during the Roman Empire. It was only the previous year that a road had been built, as before there was just a donkey trail winding its way up from sea level two hours' walk below.

The house that I rented that winter was three hundred years old and constructed of granite blocks made of walls two and a half feet thick. It had a flat roof with a three-inch slant, directing the rain down a tiled channel to be naturally filtered underground, replenishing the adjacent ancient Roman well. The windows in the house were very small, single pane, didn't open, and had crisscrossed iron bars. Over the front door, there was a freestanding canopy made of wooden branches and a canvas top, most probably set up by a previous occupant to shield from the afternoon sun. As you entered through two heavy double doors, the first thing you would see was the fireplace in a large room nearly the size of the whole house. The interior was bare, with a dirt floor and walls reaching high up to a wood frame roof support. To one side was a built-in cupboard with an old wooden door with peeling blue paint. I was told that the house was built when pirates still roamed the seas and plundered islands for anything they could sell, use, or barter. It was close to the cliff's edge, with a narrow landing below, making it particularly vulnerable to attack. So if the assailants managed to penetrate the front door, the occupants could seek refuge in the bedroom, which was built like a fortress, designed to be a place of last resort.

The landscape was stark, except for the stone walls built by clearing the land and placing the stones at the edge of the intended field. These stone walls served to shield what little would grow here from the punishing winds and rain, to define the property, and to keep the goats and sheep from wandering too far. The house was on an acre of rocky dry land covered with large patches of wild thyme, sage, and bushes of rosemary. There were three brave trees huddled close to the well, two figs, and an old grandmother almond still offering the nutty centers of her fruit. The well was sheltered by a small brick housing, tall enough to enter if you ducked down. I had brought my guitar with me and found that if I sat on a stool and played inside with the doors open, I could get the most wonderful acoustic effect, which would send me into what I can only describe as a timeless zone.

To settle in, I bought a gas stove and rented propane bottles. I paid a local farmer to deliver a cartload of seasoned firewood, enough to build a fire for three months. This was necessary to take the chill off the early morning and bring some warmth to the evening. Being in a place that had so little to do with the outside world sparked my imagination and changed my sense of time and space. There was nothing pushing me to "get on with it," to have to meet someone's or something's goal. Strangely enough, at the time, I was less reflective and began to respond more to a creative impulse. Ideas I had only thought about in the past now seemed to be plausible. I decided to go on a ten-day fast—just juices, herb teas, and broths. I found it surprisingly easy, though I had a few really strange dreams. In one, my bed turned into a layer cake with whipped cream, and I was eating my way through to escape. During the fast, the thought of eating food began to seem abnormal. When it was over, I had to coach myself slowly into eating again. I felt lighter, a weight had lifted off my shoulders, and I was calmer than I had been in all my thirty-four years.

My usual morning ritual on any given day started with roasting whole coffee beans in a dry cast-iron frying pan, one of the few things that came with the house. Then, sitting outside in the light of dawn, I would put them into a grinder, turn the handle, and breathe in the enveloping aroma. There was always water in the bucket I kept in the house overnight, which I would use to fill up an old-fashioned stovetop tin coffee percolator. I would spoon the ground coffee into the top container, place the lid on, and bring it to the boil. Then I would let it simmer. Soon I was sipping my brew along with heated local fresh milk and brown sugar. Wedges of warm bread that I had made in a clay oven from grains milled earlier that week were smothered with butter sourced from the same cows as the milk. These were slathered with honey that had been gathered from bees feeding on the wild herbal fields nearby. Such were my usual companions before facing those of the human kind. Or, on the rare occasions bananas were delivered to the general store, I would whip up a dish of Bananas Flambé. Yes, Bananas Flambé. You know, when you pour brandy over frying bananas and light it. Whoosh! Flash! A worthy addition to the morning ritual.

The days were mostly engaged in painting. I made my frames from local tree branches. These I constructed from four limbs of the same size and tied together near their ends, forming a square. I then took two longer branches that crossed in the middle, attaching each end to the corners. This stabilized the frame. I would ask the baker or general store for sacks, and I would unstitch and re-stitch them to make my canvas. I would then apply a commercial white paint mixed with wood glue as a gesso for the surface. The frames could be reused several times, as I would take the finished painting off when it was dry and tie on a fresh canvas. This was my all-time favorite surface to paint on. It had a rough and organic feel.

The natural light faded early in the winter, so oil lamps and candles lit the evening. It was perfect for gathering around an open fire with other like-minded spirited beings. Wrapping ourselves in blankets, we would sit on colorful rugs, placed over cushions made of potato sacks which had been filled with straw. We would chat and laugh and tell stories, true or imagined while we sipped on honey-sweetened herbal tea or hot wine with clove, cinnamon, and brown sugar.

Later, when my son was born and my special girlfriend (now his mother) and I came down to Formentera, it was just our little family together. I loved to make food, and even though he was so small, my son loved to help me. He was curious about everything and would spend hours staring at ant colonies as the members went about their business. He liked to sit next to me while I played guitar by the well. He would be calm and still, even though we might be there a very long time.

The word got around, and my curries and spicy roasts became famous. The house came with an outside clay oven. It was too expensive to fire it up for just us, so I invited other foreigners over every Monday to bake. Around four or five families would turn up. After the week's bread was done, we would stoke the fire and roast. Those days, I ate red meat. I would order a whole lamb from a farmer. After dressing it with herbs and spices, rubbing it down with olive oil, garlic, and salt inside and out, it would go in the oven. The door was put in place, and then the art of guessing would begin. How long would it take? Chickens or turkeys, and once, a turkey stuffed with a chicken, stuffed with stuffing, were presented on the table, prepared in the same fashion. While waiting, we would sit in a circle and make mayonnaise from scratch and get the vegetables ready to put in the oven twenty minutes before, so everything would finish at the same time. I found a long, thin metal tube and used it to baste, so once in a while, I would check the lamb, goat, turkey, or chicken. If it needed more moisture, I would take a mouthful of olive oil and blow it hard through the tube into the oven and onto the cooking meat. After a few glasses of good farmer's wine and what I call magic, talking and singing and playing guitar, flute, and drum, we would be primed for the fest. I fashioned a table from an old door propped on boxes. To this, a cotton tablecloth was added. Guests would begin to set down their homemade cooked or fresh offerings to complement the meal. When all were seated, I would first bring the roasted vegetables to the table and then return ceremoniously with the main course, which was greeted by cheers. Enjoyment came naturally for these '70s/hippie/ Bohemians. As the evening wore on, children fell asleep and were nestled between the coats on the bed in the bedroom or under the table wrapped in a blanket.

Each year when I got to El Pilar, I fashioned the bed and small chairs and table from timber and the shelves for clothes and kitchenware from discarded wooden fruit crates. Each year, when it was time to leave, all the furnishings I had made were broken down and set alight in a large bonfire, to which I invited the people I had made friends with over the months. I would roll up the canvases from all the paintings I had created in a protective sack cover and take them with me on the several boats and trains through Spain, France, and Germany, which were necessary to get them to their final destination—Denmark. There they would be re-stretched and exhibited in the spring.

These were treasured times.

Step by Step

My two young daughters were in the first month of a three-month visit with me on Formentera. Finding themselves near a small village at the end of a small isolated island with none of the distractions they were used to in Copenhagen, they quickly became bored. "When are we going to do something?" Apparently, gathering wild herbs and helping around the house wasn't exciting enough. The mystique of visiting the general store to pick up provisions and mail had long worn off. There was need for some adventure.

The house I was renting was a short walk to the cliff's edge. There was a rugged path down to a narrow pebble beach, and I thought it would be nice to take them there and treasure hunt. It was a breezy Mediterranean winter's afternoon. Well wrapped in sweaters, coats, hats, gloves, and scarves, we braved the head wind and walked through the several fields of thyme, oregano, and hardy wildflowers struggling through the rocky dry earth. As we approached the cliff's edge, the wind subsided, and we looked down two hundred feet to the beach and started to walk down the path. I kept the pace slow as it was only two persons wide with a sheer drop to one side.

We reached the beach, and the girls were off in a gallop, dispersing like young horses let out of the stable. Their spirit was contagious, and I found myself scavenging with them. There were a few shells, and even fewer gems of weathered sea glass. It had been a clear sky when we left with just an occasional small cloud passing by. They had decided to combine their collection in one pile and sort them out when they got home. I knew that even after we had stuffed our pockets, there were still many that would have to be left. After a few hours, I felt it was time to go back. The light of the day was just beginning to roll over, hinting at the approach of early evening.

I was admiring their catch when out of the corner of my eye, I noticed heavy dark clouds beginning to cover the sky. I looked with horror and saw that the tide had rapidly begun to rise and the waves were getting higher. I immediately alerted the girls that we had to start back home. They went to collect their treasures, and we found that the waves and the rocks were blocking our path, making it impossible to return the same way. As I searched for another way to get up the cliff, the waves got higher and bolder.

I have a mechanism that fires off in times of danger where I become calm and alert at the same time. It stemmed from my childhood. My daughters picked up on the seriousness of our situation and ran to me and froze. They looked at the sea as it boiled and roared at us while I scanned the cliffside. I noted every detail—every stone and every possible avenue of escape before the white-top foaming waves would reach us and sweep us away. It's funny how the mind works. A fleeting thought passed through my mind of how their mother would take the news of the death of her children at the hands of a dangerously deranged ex-husband.

I spied the narrowest of narrow ledges, perfect for mountain goats. In a flash, I pointed and grasped my daughters' hands and raced to the foot of the ledge. I held them close to my side so they could have no doubt that their father was there, present and peaceful. I had to shout over the crescendo of the din of the advancing legions of watery monsters. "Follow me, stay close, don't look down, feel the side of the cliff with your foot as you walk. Slowly. Take one step at a time. Do you trust me?" I repeated, getting close to their faces and looking deep into their eyes, "Do you trust me? Do you trust your father?"

They nodded.

We began the ascent as the waves were lapping at the foot of the ledge. There was no choice. This was it. We had gone halfway up when the ledge narrowed to the width of my foot. I thought I had reached the depth of my calmness, but an even more profound peace came over me, and I signaled them to stop and not look down. They were being so heroic and focused. Without that, we could not have gotten so far. At that point, the ledge became too narrow for us to continue walking as we were. The only option appeared. I would have to take the youngest first and then turn back for her sister. This was an obvious invitation for panic, and I had to avoid it at all costs. I asked for their agreement. It had begun to rain, and their little faces were soaked. With rain in their eyes, they nodded bravely. I addressed the eldest softly to reassure her. "I am walking just a short way away within eyesight with your sister. You will be able to see me at all times. Do you understand?" There was a deep breath that moved my body. "I will come back for you. Stay exactly where you are. It's important that you don't move. Daddy will be right back. Do you understand?" I repeated.

She nodded.

With each step I first cleared the way of small round stones that might cause us to lose our footing. I knew that if she lost her balance, I would not be able to hold her, and I would fall with her. As the rain poured down, creating a veil of opacity, my youngest held onto the corners of my pockets, precisely following my footsteps. In what seemed to be the longest minute in the universe, we reached the spot I had chosen. "I want you to stay here. Don't move. Just lean up against the side." I leaned down and looked into her face and added, "Daddy will be back. I am going to get your sister and bring her here. Do you understand? I am right here with you. Hold on to the side." I think it was as much to give me assurance as it was for her.

I left her, my mind empty, then singularly focused on the movement of my feet and the figure of my little girl a minute away. When I reached her, she was shivering. I guided her in the same way. Holding on, we blindly inched forward and up. The tide had not reached its peak, and waves were still chasing us up the cliff. We all three were united on a ledge with still a very long way to go. Continuing this method and alternating with one girl at a time, inch by inch, step by step, it took an endless painful hour to reach the top. By that time, it was pitch black. As we made our way to the sanctuary of our home, I held on to their little hands tightly as if they were still in mortal danger.

Once there, we dried off and started a fire. I wrapped them both in one blanket together and made hot tea. My tea got cold as I stared at them for a long while, making sure they were truly safe and sound. There was very little said, nothing about the ordeal. They were tired. I tucked them into bed, went into the living room, and felt tears run down my cheeks.

Pig's Tale

When was the last time you saw a pig? I mean a real pig? In the city, we see pictures of pigs on labels, advertising stickers, on posters, wearing little jackets, and maybe a bowtie—never pants. I've even seen them in sailors' suits. It's nearly always a male, with a cute wiggly tail. Pigs even speak and star in movies. There are famous pigs immortalized in ancient fairy tales. In supermarkets, pigs come framed in neatly packaged cuts. Then they stop being pigs and are immaculately transformed into pork, like some religious transfiguration. The general population does not witness this ultimate sacrifice. However, back on Formentera, I witnessed a sight that goes back thousands of years.

Even after wintering there for two years and establishing some rapport with the locals, I was still a stranger. When my two beautiful daughters visited, everything changed, and we were invited to join a village tradition in El Pilar. The tradition was to share a pig. A pig had been selected from a squad of other piglets when it was small by the patriarch of ten families and was set aside. This pig now had status and would be fed the best. Not only would its owners feed it, but acceptable food gifts would be offered by other families. This could be apple cores, corn husks, or the stalks and outer leaves of vegetables. Children were told not to give sweets, but they did. The pig became a member of the community. It could be seen around town being walked on a leash, hind legs fettered with just enough rope so it could walk but not run.

In the morning, the first thing you would hear were the cocks crowing to establish their territory. Then the call of ravens, wrens, a few hawks looking for mice and rats for breakfast, and the cooing and chirping of scruffy pigeons and sparrows outside the bakery. This was followed by dogs, goats, and the braying of a mule as it was taking the harness for the day's labor. Then, with eyes closed, listening between the cacophony of improvised noises, you could hear the grunting and occasional squealing of the pig.

The family who owned the pig didn't give it a name, but out of the collective subconscious of the village, a name emerged. In this case, it was Philippi. Philippi was mostly black, with white patches that were closer to a yellowy gray. The left side of his face was totally black, and the other was the same white that wasn't white. His eyelashes were long enough to make women jealous, except they were bleach white. The way he twitched his snout, surfing the smells in the air, made him resemble his owner.

So Philippi's day had arrived, and it was to be tomorrow. I had an argument with my girlfriend's brother and his wife over whether my two daughters should witness the process that was going to unfold. They had two children and had decided to abstain on moral grounds. I felt that this was part of real life, and it was a once-in-a-lifetime opportunity.

Fat Lady was the title given to the owner of the town's general store and cafe by the foreigners, which she wore with pride. She rarely broke a smile, but when she heard her name, she would drop her mask slightly. She was in her early eighties and spoke only the local dialect. She wore the traditional costume of several layers of plain dark-gray, brown, or black skirts, spanning an inch lower than the top of her shoes, and a plain dark vest over a well-fitted jacket with many buttons stretching up to her chin. Around her waist was a white apron, the only sign of femininity in its hand-stitched flowery edging. The style had not changed in centuries. She had left the island only once with her parents as a child to visit the cathedral in Barcelona. She wasn't impressed by the grandeur of the city, so she married at eighteen and never left the town again. Many children and years later, gravity and life had molded her five-feet-two-inch body into a force of nature. The dark, leathery skin of her face and hands revealed years of exposure to the elements. Long hair had been meticulously groomed each morning into a braid wound with a dark ribbon that hung behind her to her waist. Her large Spanish eyes, with a hint of the Moor, projected calm while at the same time commanding respect. It was this powerful elder of the town who was the unchallenged officiator of the killing of the pig.

Her son Gabriel, in his late forties, a mountain of a man, was her obvious choice for the honor of slaughtering the sacrificial animal. Gabriel had been pacing for a good half an hour in the plaza in front of Fat Lady's General Store, where it would all take place. Families arrived and placed their chairs in order of status, with the grandparents and the special-needs members of the family under an awning in the front row. There was a person with Down's syndrome, someone with MS, several men and women with restricted abilities, and a child in a dilapidated, yet functional wheelchair. The last to show up were the younger generations with their tawny complexion, shiny jet-black hair, and riveting large black eyes. Their youthful energy made a striking contrast against the background of rustic three-hundred-year-old homes. All were dressed in their Sunday best, and the atmosphere was charged with excitement and tension. It was beginning to get hot, and the smell of coffee and baked goods was being replaced by cigar smoke and local wine. Gabriel glanced to his mother, Fat Lady. She gave him a subtle signal to go get the pig, and that is exactly what he did.

A good few minutes passed before Philippi, the now very large pig, was led in. The last few weeks, he had been encouraged to eat as soon as he awoke in the morning till he fell asleep from sheer gorging exhaustion. With Philippi's appearance, everything stopped. Even the children became quiet. It was so shockingly still that even the sound of a feather falling would have been heard. For Philippi, it was just another nice day to go for a walk. He sniffed the air, scrutinizing the ground. All eyes were on him. One child ran forward to pet him, but he was quickly stopped and brought back into the fold. Gabriel tied the rope that was around the pig's neck to a post. He reached into one pocket and pulled out a handful of corn and from the other a small turnip and dropped them on the ground. These offerings were immediately detected by

Philippi. While he was devouring them, Gabriel walked ceremonially
to his mother's store and reappeared with a sack and a bucket. I noticed
a line of empty pails up against the store wall and a chair with a large
piece of plastic draped over it. This was not there before, and it was
obviously connected to the next happening.

Gabriel moved quickly behind Philippi. Philippi was finishing up
the corn and sniffing to see if he had missed any when Gabriel, with the
help of three men, wrestled Philippi to the ground. Suddenly, Philippi
found himself on his side, his legs bound, and a sack over his face. It
took a noticeable few seconds for Philippi to register that he had been
attacked by those he had known as his friends. Philippi let out a squeal
that can only be described as urgent horror. My whole body contracted
as if I was the one in mortal danger. The knife appeared. Its sixteen-
inch dark iron blade had been freshly sharpened and polished. Gabriel
knelt down on his right knee and, grasping the knife by its bone handle,
reached around Philippi's throat, sinking the point in first, then, in
one movement, running the knife three inches deep. Philippi's screams
stopped. A few babies awoke and began to cry. The three men who
had assisted Gabriel stepped back, and two women stepped up, placing
plastic underneath Philippi's dead, but still shaking and vibrating, body.
They then started to collect the blood in the pails. Philippi had gone
to pig heaven with nothing positive to say about his human neighbors.
My daughters, bored with the long wait, had wandered off and didn't
witness this scene. I turned away. I had seen enough.

The celebration was three hours later. The host family had put
up a large tent in front of their door in the garden. I was with my two
daughters. As we entered, we were assaulted by the reek of fresh animal
flesh, and my daughters screamed and ran outside. We gathered wild
thyme and held it to our nose. I told them the family expected us to go
in, and if we didn't, they would be very unhappy. Eventually, I was able
to convince them.

Inside, there were at least sixty of the host family and villagers. As
my eyes adjusted to the light, I saw that they were working in groups,
preparing every part of the remains of Philippi. I had a strong impulse
to run out too. In one corner, there were six people attending a very
large round iron frying pan, stirring the parts that had mostly fat and

skin. In another corner were two grandmothers cleaning the intestines to make sausages. In yet another corner, Philippi's blood was being prepared to make blood sausage with herbs, pepper, and finely chopped pieces of fat. Some were already finished, and strings of them were hanging up. Nearby, his head was being boiled with bay leaves, pepper, and rosemary. I was told that when ready, all would be taken off the skull and put into bread pans, allowed to set, and made into loaves that could be eaten cold.

I was invited with my two girls to join ten others around a large iron frying pan that was on a huge gas ring hooked up to a propane tank. We were to make paella for all sixty people. Each was given a job to do by the chef. There were onions and garlic to dice. Fish, chicken, and Philippi were cleaned and chopped. Tomatoes were boiled, links of chorizo were sliced, large shrimp washed and left in their shells, a rabbit skinned and cut into many pieces. Fresh parsley and thyme, saffron, paprika, lemons, rice, chicken and pork stock, bell and red peppers, flat green beans, and more olive oil than I had ever seen used at one time were all made ready for the chef to do his magic. Songs were sung, and there was much talk and laughter. Slowly, the terrible smell was replaced with amazing cooking smells. My girls lost interest and went out and played with other foreigner children. Homemade Muscatel, a spiced herbal wine, was passed around. Too sweet for my pallet, but watered down, it was so very good. It took an hour to get all the ingredients in the pan and the huge lid on.

While we were waiting for the paella to cook, another circle was formed to make mayonnaise. My girls came back in and helped. We started to take turns, each with our ingredients. Three of us finely chopped a small kilo of garlic and, in a giant mortar-and-pestle, smashed them to a fine paste. Others ground herbs. My girls were part of the group that slowly poured olive oil into an enormous bowl over nearly a hundred egg yolks while others stirred. When it was right, we were all instructed to add our ingredient to the bowl. Fresh bread had been baked that day. More wine was poured, Philippi was toasted, and we took the bread and dipped it in the mayonnaise and ate it with slices of tomato.

All of this, plus the wine, was circulated around the tent, and Philippi was toasted many more times. The air was filled with traditional music played by the locals on violin, accordion, and hand drum. When the chef pronounced the paella ready, all stood up, and a prayer was shared. Glasses were refilled, and my children were given a little to sip. Several toasts were proposed and completed. One of the elderly grandmothers spoke, and signs of the cross were made. The music started again. Everyone sat down in one big circle, and we were served paella as if it were the Eucharist.

We were there till well into the evening, and the girls were getting tired. So we begged our leave, and after reciprocating kisses on both cheeks from men and women alike, we set off under a star-filled sky and sung our way home. Thank you, Philippi. Thank you and all your brethren. Forgive us if we didn't acknowledge at the time how precious you are on this sacred planet called Earth.

Anarchists in My Well

I was back in my favorite winter retreat, Formentera, and had planned to devote this time to fasting, meditation, painting, and playing my guitar. I managed to rent the same rustic house I had for the last three years. It was one of two houses, last on the edge of the peninsula, and wonderfully isolated. One evening, I was picking up my mail at the general store/post office and sitting in the attached cafe when a man across the room caught my eye. He was not one of the locals, and I had not seen him before. His smile revealed a quality of openness.

The next day, in the evening, there was a knock on the door. Except for the farmer who owned the house, it had been weeks since anyone had come calling, especially at night. In those times, the secret service police, the Guardia Civil, could storm down your door. They could search your house, turn everything over, take your passport, and even haul you off with no reason. It was not unusual for people to disappear, never to be heard from again. This was not the pounding of an official, so I went to the door and, from behind its protection, asked who it was. I recognized the neighbor's voice and opened the door. In he walked with his wife and three male Spaniards in their mid-twenties. They spoke English and conveyed to me that they were from Barcelona on the mainland. I trusted my neighbor, and therefore trusted anyone he would bring to my home.

I offered them tea and homemade biscuits and then put more wood on the fire. My neighbor had been a top DJ for a national radio station in Denmark. He introduced Bob Dylan and the Doors to Denmark, so I assumed his friends were somehow connected to the music scene. They stayed for just an hour, and we chatted about all things and nothing.

The next day, the man I had seen smiling in the general store was on the path leading to my house and looked lost. I greeted him, and he said that he was looking for my neighbor's house. I was standing by the Roman well with my guitar. He said he played too, so I struck a few chords to demonstrate the amazing acoustics created by the well. He was quiet and shut his eyes. After playing for a few minutes, I pointed him in the right direction, and he departed.

As a reminder—Spain was under the dictatorship of Generalisimo Franco. Catalonia, the part of Spain I was in, was notorious for rebellion. Over the next few days, it was revealed that the man with the smile and the other three men who had visited me that night with my neighbor were anarchists, active in the movement to overthrow Franco. They had come to hide out for a while and create and record songs of insurrection to be played on a ghost radio station that was always on the move. It turned out that my neighbor had brought them to meet me in order to give them confidence that I could be trusted if I were to see them around. I was told it was imperative that I not reveal their political leanings to anyone, even my closest friends. They wanted to use the well for sound effects. I loved the idea. It was perfect. They warned me that I would be in grave danger. I said I understood.

So over the next week, they set up a car battery and wired their primitive equipment to it. One microphone recorded the singer and the guitar, and the other microphone went down the well. The two were mixed to enhance the sound. For that week, I was told to keep my usual routines, going into the village, getting my mail, drinking my coffee, chatting with people. It was nerve-wracking every time I saw an official or a policeman. I unconsciously felt that people knew and I would be found out. How does one "try" to seem normal? In the end, I was glad I had stood up for something I believed in and had taken a small part in fighting the good fight for freedom.

Chapter 8

I Am, You Are..., Ramani Rangan

Target Practice

I was in Canada working in an art store a few miles outside Vancouver. I got the job through a friend of a friend of someone I met. The pay was very good and gave me time to do my own painting. The store was on a highway. The first week, there was not one customer. When I went to pick up my wages, I mentioned this. The boss said, "Don't worry about it. Just keep your hours. Everything's fine."

In the second week, again, no customers . . . till Friday afternoon. I had my easel up and was painting. Then suddenly, three heavily armed special police force officers crashed through the skylight on ropes. Four more burst through the front and back doors and pinned me to the floor within seconds of their arrival. Needless to say, I was in shock and felt as though I was suddenly in an alternate reality. One of the longest minutes of my life passed before a plainclothes detective, obviously in charge, entered the room. They did a body search and, finding nothing, invited me to sit down. The detective turned out to be an immigrant from Scotland. Hearing my British accent, he determined that I was not his everyday bad man. He started to question me to find out how deeply I was involved. Realizing that I happened to be in the wrong place at the wrong time, he began to relate his story.

The story went like this. They were after some very nasty members of a gang. This gang had the habit of kidnapping runners for a drug syndicate, putting masks over their heads, driving them up into the mountains, taking the drug money the runners were transporting, and then letting them go unharmed. Something went wrong for our bad guys. The runner in question was kidnapped, given sleeping pills, and put in the boot of the car so he would not be able to identify the abductees and see where he was being taken. To their surprise, when they opened the boot, he was dead. He had died of asphyxiation. They took his body, put it in a large bag, weighed it down with rocks, brought it out to sea, and dumped it, thinking no one would find it there. However! The body bag got tangled up in a fisherman's net and was brought up from its watery grave and handed over to the police. The drug syndicate, tipped off by someone in the police department, put a bounty on the head of whoever had done this to their man. The police traced the whereabouts of the gang members who had been stealing from the syndicate and arrested most of them in several sting operations. The gang members were being kept in hiding so the drug syndicate couldn't find them and they could live long enough to be brought to justice.

There were a few loose ends, and I was one of them. The store was a front for the gang members. The police had been watching me coming and going for the last few days, in the hope that one of the top gang members who was still loose would turn up. The detective told me he had information through one of his contacts in the prison system that the drug syndicate had a mark on me and I was on their sub list to be snuffed out. He told me that he could not protect me but advised me to lie low, hide, and leave Canada within twenty-four hours. He said he would pass the message down the line that I was just an idiot looking after a store. He hoped they would weigh the need to kill me against the need to keep their profile low and not bother to follow me.

Well, being the cool customer that I am, I immediately tried to fly into the USA, but a telephone enquiry to the American embassy informed me that the border between Canada and the United States was closed. Someone had threatened President Gerald Ford's life. So I had to go somewhere, and I was determined not to go back to Denmark. What if they followed me there and it led to my family? An acquaintance reluctantly let me hide out in his garage overnight. On the wall was a map of the Americas. I found some darts and decided to close my eyes and throw one at the map. It landed in Jamaica, and so did I.

Jamaica in the 1970s

Arriving in the Kingston airport in Jamaica, I was passing through customs when a very stern-faced policeman stopped me and, in a monotone, commanded, "Come with me." He gestured me to follow him to a small office. My mind whispered, *Oh dear.* He asked me where I was going, and I said to a hotel. "Which one?" he asked.

I said, "I don't know." Then I added, "I was going to ask the taxi driver."

He pointed for me to sit and picked up the phone and spoke to someone. "Come with me."

I followed him, struggling with my two bags, to the taxi stand. The policeman told me to listen very carefully as he spoke to a taxi driver. He told him he had noted his cab license number and his taxi driving permit. Then he proceeded to scan his driving license. He instructed him to take me to a specific hotel. He said he had telephoned ahead, and they were expecting me. He emphasized that it would take twenty-three minutes to drive there at this time of day. He was going to call the hotel when we left, and they were going to call him when I arrived so he knew I was safe. Something in the back of my mind alerted me to pay close attention and to fight the fatigue of waking up early, getting to the airport in Vancouver, a long flight, going through customs, and a thirty-degree rise in temperature. The policeman then looked at me and asked me to repeat what I had heard him say to the driver. I did. He looked straight into my eyes, searching to see if I had grasped the situation, and said, "Jamaica is not a paradise." He paused. "Things are very dangerous here. Be very, very careful." He stood up to his full size, stepped back, and gave the driver a final piercing look. Then he turned and walked away.

Afterward, I speculated that guardian angels come in many forms.

The driver, responding as though this were a usual occurrence, checked his watch, and we drove off. Within a few minutes, we were passing by a sixteen-foot chain wall fence topped with heavy barbed wire that went on for a good three miles. I asked him what was behind the fence. He told me that Kingston was more or less under siege and what we were passing was a holding prison for gangs of up to three hundred who were terrorizing, killing, and robbing the people. He said it was widespread and described what I could only understand to be a civil unrest, bordering on a civil war.

Sure enough, we arrived at the hotel twenty-three minutes later. It looked like a barricaded compound and was surrounded by two twelve-foot fences, one outer, one inner, with a ten-foot distance between them. The gates, when opened, acted as an enclosed passageway between the two fences. Centered between the fences were high metal rails. Attached to the rails were chains, each attached, on the other end, to the collars of

Rhodesian Ridgeback hounds. I counted eight, but later was told there were twelve, in four sections, each with three hounds. Thus the whole hotel was protected by these ninety-pound all-muscle and kill doggies. Rhodesian Ridgeback hounds were traditionally bred to hunt lions. By the way, did I mention there were several heavily armed guards as well? I checked in and was shown to my room. As well as heavy bars on my windows, there were also thinner bars to stop vampire bats, known to carry rabies, from coming in through the windows and sucking blood from the guests. A finer netting blocked mosquitoes from transmitting malaria and other nasty diseases. I was seriously wondering what I'd gotten myself into.

I must have been well entrenched in a narcissistic dream world, because the next day, I ventured out with my mobile artist's painting easel, got lost, found a large building with grounds and a guard, and asked where I was. Either he didn't understand my accent, or he had never been confronted with this situation. He picked up a phone, spoke to someone, and a woman came to the gate. I told her I was from London to make it easier to relate, and that I was an artist and was lost. She looked me up and down, then ushered me in and said they were holding the first annual international convention for women—something like that—and "please come in and meet them." We entered a large room occupied by roughly one hundred women from all parts of the globe. I was asked my name, where I was from, and how I came to be there. They greeted me with smiles and a round of applause. I thanked them and was led to a room and given iced orange juice. I went outside and set up my easel and painted an abstract image of what I was feeling.

I left it to dry, went out the gate, and started to walk, thinking that I would find a shop or a like building and could then get directions for how to get back. But as I walked, the buildings grew more and more run-down. I thought that if I kept on going, a main road would magically appear and I could find a phone and call the hotel to send a taxi. Instead, the signs of poverty increased. I knew I was having a serious problem when I passed a chain gang repairing the road. Each of them had dirty rags around their ankles to protect them somewhat from the wounds caused by the heavy iron manacles they wore. I felt I was in enemy territory and was steadily getting more and more panicky.

Eventually, locals began to look at me as if I were planning suicide just by being there, and I wanted their help to complete the deed.

Hopelessly lost and now in the darkest, scariest neighborhood my imagination could conjure up, I suddenly saw way off in the distance what I thought was a large "M" sign. It had to be a mirage, because for all practical purposes, this was a desert. I walked toward the "M," and it got bigger and bigger, and then there it was—a MacDonald's. It was real. The "M" sign could just as well have been a cross on top of a Catholic church. I headed straight for it, looking for sanctuary. Entering the premises, a sense of safety flooded over me, along with the air conditioning. After sitting down for a well-needed few minutes and then looking at the menu board, I noticed the daily special to the side. It was goat curry and rice. Goat curry and rice? Hey! If that's what the locals want, well, that's supply and demand. It tasted doubly good to this Indian. The woman behind the counter was so nice when I explained my situation. She looked at me as if I had come from another world— and I had! I asked her if she would please do me a special favor and call the hotel. She did, and the hotel sent a taxi. I gave her a tip, and she gave me a smile that signaled, *Come back sometime.*

I started to breathe, and so did my taxi driver when we turned onto a main road. I arrived. The gates were opened and shut for the taxi. I went to my room and showered for half an hour, not only to get clean and cool off, but to try to wash the fear away. By the third rum and coke at the bar, I decided I had to get out of Kingston soon—very soon. I resolved to leave my portable artist's easel at the women's convention and chalk it up as fair trade for getting back to the hotel in one piece. I was told Montego Bay at the other end of the island was better for tourists, so I took a taxi to the bus station. The bus was ancient and rickety, leaving me still with a feeling of being unprotected and unsafe. As we drove through the jungle interior and passed through beautiful landscapes, I finally began to relax.

It was immediately obvious that the police had an iron grip on the whole town of Montego Bay, so visitors would feel safe to come and spend their Yankee dollars. Flying in over Jamaica, I had seen mountain after mountain covered with tropical forest so thick that it looked like broccoli—a tight, dark-green canopy. I was told that these forests made the perfect hiding place for ruthless gangs. Jamaica had been known as Hispaniola, a popular spot for pirates in its day, and the tradition was still alive. Instead of travelers on the open sea, the target for gathering booty was now banks and businesses and the rich and famous. Some small shops were owned by East Indians, but at this time, 90 percent of business, smaller hotels, and private homes were owned by the Chinese. Apparently, these business owners treated the locals with disdain. Their prices were inflated on necessary items, which meant that Native Jamaicans ran up debt so high they could never pay it off. There was a cycle of poverty which became extreme enough that the people had snapped. The year before I arrived, there had been a national uprising and a massacre of thousands of Chinese and East Indian businessmen and their families. The perpetrators hid out in the interior and formed cult gangs, with many practices including ritual sacrifice. Among these and other groups, there was support for an ongoing violent rebellion. None of this was reported in the international press to protect the tourist industry. There were still pockets of animosity toward the surviving Indians, and many had left. At the time, I didn't grasp the seriousness of the situation.

I heard that Negril, a small beach town south of Montego, was a good place to visit. There, white non-Jamaicans mixed with the new Rastafarians who believed that Haile Selassie, the king of Ethiopia, was the Lion of Judah, and therefore the true representative of God, a.k.a. Jah. With the mix of reggae and ganja (marijuana), there was a new identification that helped some on the island to have a sense of pride and an identity independent of the old colonial rulers. The swimming in Negril was good, and the food even better. I stayed in the White Bird, an all-bamboo hotel. After a few days, I was asleep in my room when I awoke in pitch black to a man holding a six-inch ceramic cone full of hashish, called a chillum. He had blown a few mouthfuls of smoke in my face. By the time I realized what was happening, the ganja was working, and I didn't really care. He then disappeared, leaving in the same way he came. The next day, I mentioned it at the hotel desk. They told me no one knew his real name, but he was referred to as King George. He had been doing this for a few years, and they could not catch him no matter how they tried. Only his name written on scraps of paper showed he had been there.

This was a strange and interesting place. For some reason, I felt safe for the first time since I arrived in Jamaica. For lunch, I ate at an open-air restaurant patronized by locals. I was befriended by a few of them, as well as by a few visiting Americans. There was one local male in his mid-twenties I had spoken with, and we became friendly. He asked me if I wanted to experience real Jamaica. I answered, "Yes, very much." We made arrangements for him to take me into the interior to meet his family in a few days.

The next day in the restaurant, he brought up the subject of Indian businessmen in Jamaica. I said that I hated the mentality of Indians or people of any nationality who went to other countries, opened businesses, manipulated the population, cheated them, and treated them with contempt. I mentioned that I had grown up in poverty and had experienced this form of racism myself.

The next day, he asked me to meet him at the restaurant to go with him to visit his family in the mountains. He came on time and sat quietly, asking me to do the same. He then confessed that he and his friends had planned to torture and kill me once we were in the mountains. Because of what I had said the day before about Indian businessmen, identifying myself with him and the Jamaican people and their plight, he had decided that I was one of them and would not kill me. He told me he was ashamed of seeing me only as an Indian and not as a person, and that it was a lesson he had needed to learn. We parted, and the full implication of what had nearly happened sank in. I knew I needed to get off this island as soon as possible.

Kidnapped

The next day, I was recovering and processing my narrow escape from being tortured and murdered. Lying in the shade, gathering my nerves and soaking up some tranquility, I started planning my next move. I was joined by an American couple who were on vacation from their work on the Alaska pipeline, Mary and Bill. We started to chat and got on really well. They asked if I wanted to rent a car with them and see more of Jamaica's coast. The warmth of their invitation tempered my fear. We asked at the desk, and they arranged for us to take a taxi to a car rental office about ten miles away. They required a deposit of two hundred dollars, which we paid by credit card. With snorkels, masks, and flippers, we sought out the beaches and coves that were best for seeing the greatest variety of fish.

Upon our return, the assistant told us that the computer was down, so he could not refund the deposit onto the card, but he could give us the two hundred dollars in cash. We agreed. He said he would call for a taxi to get us back to the hotel. The taxi arrived, we were greeted with a smile, and we piled in.

The taxi followed the coast road back to the hotel, but then it took a turn away from the coast. It continued onto a side street, which was paved and then changed to gravel. I leaned forward to ask the driver if we were taking a shortcut. It was then I heard the click of doors locking. The panic was immediate.

In disbelief, I tried them all. They wouldn't open, and the windows wouldn't roll down. My companions had not registered what had just happened, so they were startled by my response. I informed them that we were being kidnapped. I took command of the situation and instructed them to sit back and breathe as there wasn't anything we could do. The small window between the driver and the passenger's side was thick and reinforced with iron bars, so there was no way to get to the driver.

The road became steeper by the minute and turned into a muddy mountain path only wide enough for one vehicle at a time. My heart was pounding, but I was trying to maintain an appearance of calm and control for my companions. I tried to speak, but nothing came out, so I sat back in my seat and waited while my companions struggled with the doors and pounded on the divider panel. Meanwhile, we wound up the mountainside driving over large rocks that jolted us up off our seats. I signaled to them to sit down and repeated that there was nothing we could do till the taxi stopped. It was logical, but not convincing enough.

It must have been twenty minutes from the time the taxi turned off the main road till it came to a clearing and stopped. Mary became hysterical and started to shout that we were going to get killed. She was banging the door, and I grabbed hold of her arms to stop her from injuring herself. Bill was in shock and was motionless. A whole very long minute went by as the taxi driver got out and one man finally came out of the bushes and approached the taxi. I could only hear the mumble of the two men talking because of the sound of my heart pumping blood into my head.

Finally, the door locks were released, and the door was opened. In front of me was a tall, strong-looking Jamaican holding an old rusty ten-inch blade. With that hand, he waved us to exit the taxi. I came out first. My whole body was now dripping with sweat and soaking my clothes, so that it felt as though I had been caught in the downpour of a thunderstorm. Mary followed me. I went back for Bill and walked him out. The shock had totally closed down his normal motor responses. It seemed that I was going to be the one to navigate our kidnapping.

The driver stood back, and the man with the knife stepped forward and quickly pressed the point of the blade into my throat deep enough that I could feel the pressure on my Adam's apple, but not deep enough to break the skin. His face was within a few inches of mine. He shouted something I didn't understand, as I too was in shock. It sounded like a completely different language. My shoulders must have been up, because they dropped, and I felt my body become cold, and my breathing slow down. The words "What do you want?" came out of my mouth, but seemed to be projected by another force.

His eyes widened, and the hand that was holding the knife started to tremble. I knew this was not good. He was nervous, and this meant he might do something he was not planning to do and kill me.

"You is the police?" he blared out, repeating it several times. He stepped back a few paces, drawing the knife away from my throat.

The mind is a strange thing. Here I was, in the most dangerous situation, my life threatened, and I was looking at the knife and thinking that if he stabbed me, I could get lockjaw and die from the rust on the knife. It was then I saw a flash of something metal reflecting in the bushes. I calculated that it was a man with a gun.

"You *is* the police!" he said, eyes darting around as if I were part of a police sting.

"No," I replied so calmly that not only was he confused, but I was too, about how calmly the statement had proceeded from my mouth.

All this time, Bill was motionless, and Mary began to bait him to do something. She looked at me and began to scream, "They're just black men. Do something. You can beat them easily." I was horrified. Her statement felt like it included me. I was outraged at her words. What had been calm turned within seconds to anger—anger toward her. I slapped her on the face and grabbed the handbag she was carrying, swearing, "Who the . . . do you think you are?" I opened it and emptied all its contents on the ground, rummaged for the two-hundred-dollar deposit in cash and any other money, grabbed her hand, and pried a ring off one of her fingers and threw it onto the heap of her belongings.

The man with the knife was obviously flustered as I apologized for the insult she had directed at him and the driver and whoever was hiding in the bushes. He grabbed the money, the ring, and a few other things. Looking up in the air, all around, and finally at me with a look of bewilderment, he signaled the driver to get in. Then everything happened so fast that I can only remember all three getting into the taxi and driving off.

Bill was still paralyzed, and Mary had sunk to the ground weeping. I ignored her sobbing and her petty muttering over all her losses and went over to Bill. I held his hand and whispered, "It's over. We're OK now." I told Mary she had to get up and pull it together. I was still angry with her, but I knew it would not help, because we had to get off this mountain and down to the road in one piece.

It took two hours. Every time we passed a village or small clusters of houses, people would come out and point at us and laugh. They knew the routine, and we had fallen for it. Once we reached the road, we had to walk two more hours in the baking sun. No one stopped when we hailed them. We must have looked a mess when we finally got into town and found the police station.

We asked to see the inspector and were shown seats in the corridor to sit on. There was a cacophony of sound outside—people singing and shouting and a parade with live bands passing by. We were there for an hour before we were ushered into an office.

"What do you want?" the officer asked, not looking up. I started to tell him and partway through, he stopped me. "Are you hurt? Injured?"

I answered, "No."

"You are lucky to be alive."

I protested with a few "buts."

He continued, "Can you hear what is happening outside?"

"Yes," I replied. Bill and Mary were silent all this time, as if I were their legal counsel.

"You are wasting my time. I have hundreds of people on the street drinkin' and being stupid, celebratin' a local festival. You still alive? Get out." He looked down again at the papers on his desk and waved at a figure behind us. We were escorted to the street into the alternative reality of a jubilant mayhem of extremely happy people having fun.

Caribbean Island Hopping

I found out that there was a ship—that is to say, it was registered as a ship, but I would have no hesitation describing it as an oversized rusty tin can—that ferried the poorest of Caribbean people with their bundles, bags, goats, and chickens, etc., from island to island as deck passengers. The price was $185 to sail from Kingston, Jamaica, to Port of Spain, Trinidad, stopping at fifteen islands on the way on an eighteen-day trip. The trip included meals consisting of a variety of Caribbean root vegetables with rice, beans, and a chili hot sauce, which made it palatable. There were enough deck passengers to cover the deck and other non-paying passengers in the living form of thousands of beetles, millions of ants, and tribes of rats. They came out at night and headed for the kitchen.

After a very uncomfortable night, I worked out a nocturnal strategy. I made a place for myself to sleep by tying a plank between the ship and a lifeboat, then strapping myself to the plank with only the waves below. During the day, my plank transformed into the perfect observation point for spying the occasional sea mammal, pod, or other animated aquatic creatures of the deep. This gave me a visceral feeling of being part of an immense mystical watery world.

We sailed for two days. Our first port of call was Saint Kitts. It was about seven in the morning with a clear, beautiful sky when we tied up at the dock. Most of the deck passengers were local, so some were coming back home carrying things that were cheaper or available only in Jamaica, others perhaps visiting family and friends. These were open and smiling people willing to share a greeting, a story, and a sip of their homemade rum. We disembarked and I waved goodbye to those I had made friends with.

The scene depicted before me was like an 1880's movie set. There were no cars or visible signs of modern times. The people on the dock were dressed in simple clothes, practical for work and the hot climate. There were no T-shirts printed with free advertising, images, or slogans to be seen. I was traveling light with just a small case stowed aboard under lock and key. I also had a backpack which I carried with me everywhere. I kept a flat wallet strapped around my waist, which felt sufficiently hidden under my shirt. Ready to leave the safety of the boat, I walked the gangplank down to a cobblestone terra firma.

The dock was filled with activity, boats being loaded and unloaded. Children were in school uniforms, much like one would see back in England. Small stands lining the opening to the street looked inviting. Especially after two days of vegetables and rice. I was in pursuit of mangoes, bananas, a cake, and coffee and whatever treat would evoke a salivation response. The mood of the people was so warm and bright that I felt free and safe.

I was starting to take my first few steps toward the stands when a breathtakingly beautiful young woman, as black as raven wings, stepped up and blocked my path. She smiled so her perfect glistening white teeth flashed in front of me and stopped me in my tracks. "You is lovely," she announced with such confidence that I was stunned and had no reply. "Give me your shirt," she requested, as if she had known me her whole life. "I love it," she proclaimed. It was then I remembered I was wearing a T-shirt with an image of Stevie Wonder on it. "You can have mine." She lowered her head and looked up at me through her top eyelashes like a child working the emotions of an adult to buy them an ice cream. Grasping the bottom of her loosely hanging blouse, she started to take it off. I signaled for her to stop. She was now very close to me, within a few feet of my face and getting closer. I panicked and mumbled something, simultaneously turning around and walking quickly back to the ferry with her now following, teasing me with compliments and continuing her soft demand of the object I was wearing. I was still walking fast on the gangplank till I got back on the ferry. She had stopped. I glanced out of the corner of my eye as she turned away and saw a smile that I interpreted as a sense of cheeky triumph. This encounter was being observed by some of the crew, who were laughing hysterically. I eventually got over my embarrassment, ventured out bravely to a vendor, and purchased breakfast while scouting the terrain for any other surprises that Saint Kitts might have up its sleeve.

It took us less than an hour to cast off, sail, and reach our next destination, Nevis. Nevis is even smaller than Saint Kitts. The two together make a country. We had three hours ashore. Being a deck passenger was rigorous, and I needed to relax. I decided that I was going to leave the road, walk to a beach, sit in the shade, and look at the clearest water I've ever seen. Before long, I came to a beach that was totally black with lava pebbles and sand. It was the first time I had ever seen this, and it shocked me. I had to take my shoes off and walk on it to make sure it was real. There was plenty of shade, so it was easy to find my perfect spot among many perfect spots and just sit. My body sank into itself, and I let go in a way I hadn't for a long time. My awareness was enhanced, and the gentle waves seemed to have as much to say as the windswept coasters. I was totally alone in this retreat of mine, with a sense that my tranquility would not be disturbed. When I moved my feet, the pebbles and sand made a tonal ring, one small frequency from a perfect musical note. Ripples spread out in the shallows, catching a sparkle of sunlight and passing it on. As my eyes lifted to see further, the color changed to a blue that held a promise of peace in the world.

We all have moments that are presented to us. If we are lucky, we stop and open and allow them to take over our senses, like when we were babies. An hour must have gone by. I found that I had stripped naked. Floating in the warmth of the primal waters, I completely surrendered, allowing the sun to regenerate my body and spirit. It was time to go back. I couldn't resist stopping several times and turning to see if it was still there—my black beach that spoke to me of myself, and the sense of feeling different my whole life. Now there would always be a beach in the world, reminding me that everything was possible—I was possible. Not the limitation that I had grasped from what the world had presented to me, but the possibility that difference could be magical.

The experience was so profound that I was not aware of my surroundings until I found myself back at the port. I was early, so I bought three coconuts from a fierce looking, yet sweet, grandmother lady. I sat down and drank each one and then returned for her son to split them open, so I could eat the delicate soft white meat on the inside. That night, as we sailed to our next destination, I didn't need supper. I was full.

I had heard about Antigua and a little about its history of slavery. At the time, it was very beautiful, with a mix of colonial and modern architecture. People were friendly, relaxed, and peaceful. Yet thoughts crowded my mind—images of people worked to death, tortured, and enduring unimaginable abuses. I looked for some presence or sign of those times, but if it was there, I didn't find it. We were allowed half a day on the island. I quickly tired of being a town tourist and ended up at a jackpot beach. I estimated it was half a mile long and about sixty feet wide. It was covered with millions and millions of shells, in colors, shapes, and patterns of unlimited variation. I had brought my backpack with me and started to scavenge for the "special" ones. The challenge was overwhelming, like waking up in Ali Baba's cave full of treasure and having to choose from the enormity of the find. Time was alive on another planet, but here the beach had become a sorcerer. I was bewitched and hungry for more of the smiling shells that seemed to come alive and say, "Take me! I'm right here! I'm better than that one!" Or, "Don't put me down!"

The heat was getting to me. I was getting signals to rest. I found a shady spot and smoothed out a space to lie down. I closed my eyes for what I thought was just a moment. Next thing I knew, I was woken by the direct rays of the sun. I looked at my watch and saw time had flown by. I had less than a few swallows of water from my canteen and one hour to get back to the ferry.

On my first try to lift my backpack, it wouldn't budge. I tried again, putting more force into it and succeeded to get it up to waist height, only to set it down again. Quickly, my built-in bio-computer ran the numbers for the distance to the ferry, the time of day, the temperature, and the condition of the surface of the route. It became clear that the only answer was to empty some of the shells. "There must be another equation," my mind searched. Nothing. The clock was ticking. I emptied, first, a quarter. Still too heavy. Then a half. I put on my backpack and started to walk a few steps. No good. Still way too heavy. In less than a minute, I was down to a few handfuls, a little heavier of heart with each lessening of load. On the edge of the beach, I stopped, turned, and heard a vague whisper to let them all go. I laid the two handfuls down, back with their family members. There were three or four hiding in the creases of the pack. I retrieved them and, one by one, placed them down on the others. Like they were an offering that I couldn't give, because I had taken them—but somehow, nevertheless, a gift of thanks for sharing for a while. I made sure all had been returned, turned away, and escaped the clutches of my desire for riches beyond imagination.

As we approached Saint Vincent, I was on my sleeping plank. Looking down, I saw a pod of dolphins racing the ferry. As they disappeared below the surface and then appeared again, weaving in and out, they could easily pace us. This was the first time I had come so close to our aquatic mammal cousins. We were separated by only ten feet. I felt the connectedness of life and hoped they could sense my fellowship with them. By now, all of the foreigners had disembarked on previous islands, and I was the only non-local.

The ferry was going to leave us on Saint Vincent while they delivered and picked up goods from one of the Grenadines islands. On land, there were forested hills and narrow roads visible from the dock. Knowing I had eight hours ashore, I decided I was going to walk into the hills and meet some locals. As I was leaving town, I saw a group of about ten men and women walking toward me who looked to be of European descent. I presumed they were visiting tourists, but as they got closer, I could hear they were speaking English with the local accent. I was surprised. Not only by the experience, but also by how my mind could be limited and narrow in its perception of the world. On later research, I found that the island in the past, besides African slaves, also had English, French, other European and East Indian indentured laborers.

We had docked at dawn, and the morning bustle was just getting off to a start. I stopped to buy some fruit, butter, and rolls and walked till I reached the edge of town. Now it was just me and rich tropical trees on both sides of the road. The undergrowth was so dense that I could see only a foot in, as all the plants intermixed with each other to form a lush solid wall of ever-changing greens in an endless variety of size and shape. It was about 8:00 a.m. when I came to a break in the jungle's fortification, revealing a path. Here, I stopped, sat down, and rested. It was getting hot, and being a "sweater," I was already soaked enough that I had to continuously wipe my forehead so as not to flood the sandwich I was munching on.

I walked another two hours, passing open spaces where the jungle had been cleared and palms had been planted in rows that stretched off into the distant foothills of a mountain. A few trucks had passed by in both directions, but no one on foot. I was thinking I better flag one down and ask how far the next town was when I came upon a clearing with several houses and storage buildings. I could see parts of other humble dwellings in the background. I ventured into the center of the clearing and was about to announce myself when I heard a voice coming from my left and high enough it could have come from one of the trees.

I turned to see a large three-story building that was made from the surrounding natural materials and blended in with the background. The voice came from the top floor. It sounded like a male in his mid-thirties. I could not see him. He asked me who I was. I told him my name, where I was from, and about my journey. On hearing this, several faces came forward and showed themselves. The ground floor was about twenty feet high and looked like a business of some sort. As more people from the top appeared, I noticed that the ground floor was barricaded up with planks, old advertising billboards, and iron bars. There were now about twenty-five adults looking down on me. The person behind the voice told me to wait. "Don't move." He disappeared, and other eyes searched beyond me in all directions, as if they were guarding themselves from someone or something that meant them harm.

It was less than a minute when the man appeared on the ground from a corner of the building, signaling me to follow him. I made a split decision, which is very typical of me, and followed him around the back of the building. We crawled into a hidden space that was quickly secured behind us. We continued in pitch black to the head of an opening, and I followed him up steep homemade steps. I emerged into the brightness of day and the gleaming faces of many welcoming hearts. After more words of my adventure and their enquiry about what was happening in the big world, they started to tell me their story.

The building was a school, and those surrounding me were teachers and people supporting them. They told me they were on strike because the bare essential and necessary school supplies were not being issued. They could not teach their children, and so the children could not take the test to go to the next grade. They were asking for better working conditions and a reasonable livelihood, the minimum requirements to fulfill their duties and live a decent life. It was impossible to get the word out because the press was not covering the story at the time. They had been up there, barricaded in for two weeks, part of a mass strike with other schools participating. They feared they would be arrested or punished for striking.

I felt a profound intimacy and would have wanted to hear more and be of comfort, but they said it was dangerous for me to be there. Then they conveyed a sober request. "Please don't forget us! Please go out and tell the world what is happening here on Saint Vincent." I gave them the food I had and other things I felt they could use from my backpack. I made a point not to carry too much money with me, so what little I had, I left with them.

It was hard for me to leave. Even though I had spent only an hour with them, I felt that I was leaving my tribe—a tribe that was honorable and loving. I turned several times to wave, and each time, I had a sense that I was abandoning them. I had been commissioned to be their courier and now I had a mission to complete. I headed back to the ship even though it was early. Upon reaching the main street of the port, I sat in a restaurant puzzling over the scant menu but ended just ordering drinks. I didn't know who to contact or how.

The next stop was the end of the trip—Trinidad. I found a hotel and showered several times, as the ship's two galleys were disgusting, visited by everyone on board. I needed to wash off not only the dirt and grime but also the heaviness that I had taken on from the last port of call.

The journey aboard the ferry was a time of major life lessons. Most important was getting to talk and share with the Caribbean islanders. I saw a marked difference between people from each island. I must say I began to identify with them. They had shown me an alternative way to be in the world. Their pace was slowed down, not rushed, yet everything got done. In them, I experienced a gracefulness, calmness, and cheerfulness in the face of adversity. The journey I had taken outside was now inviting me on a journey inside, and I discovered a place within me that I could fill with more love.

As I was low on money, I asked for a transfer of funds from my bank, but was denied. I had a plane ticket to return to England from Canada and was able to change it and return from Trinidad. When I got to my bank in London, I found that the manager had been my assistant in a London theater. When I asked him why I had sufficient funds but my transfer was denied, he said with a smirk, "It was time for you to come home."

The Nordkaperen and the Storm

Back in Denmark, I was invited to join friends on a small island called La Gomera in the Canary Islands off the coast of Africa. There was some awkwardness between us, and I needed to take a break, so I rented a small house up in the mountains at the cloud line. I would wake and open all the doors in the house. Sitting up in my bed, I would watch the clouds start to roll into the room. Within a few minutes, the clouds would burn off, and small birds would test their safety, flying partway into the kitchen, then flying out again. When they were sure the coast was clear, they would fly all the way into the kitchen and begin to hunt mosquitoes and other insects for their breakfast. While I was still in bed, they would then clean out the bedroom, devour the last morsel, and leave by the bedroom door. It was now safe for me to arise and prepare my own meal. Their brave circle, coming in through the kitchen and then out through the bedroom, was a blessing to my morning and started my daily routine.

Every few days, I would have to walk one hour down to town to buy provisions, as I was limited by how much I could carry up the mountain at a time. I had finished shopping, and it was now too hot to climb back up, so I decided that I would wait a few hours in town till it was cooler. I went to a small restaurant overlooking the pier, where I loved to watch the fishing boats tie up to unload their catch. The pier was built of granite, about three hundred feet out from the shoreline, tall enough to service the boats at high and low tides, with a single lamppost at the end acting as a beacon. It was a treat to eat out once in a while and take a break from my own cooking.

Under a shaded table, looking out over a beautiful calm sea and a clear sky, I overheard Danish being spoken. I was fluent, having lived there for many years. Smiling to myself, I walked over and introduced myself in Danish, creating a startled response. We all chuckled, and they motioned me to join them. They were the captain and crew of the yacht *Nordkaperen*, which was circumnavigating the earth. Before they were to cast off, I was invited to visit and come on board.

The next day, excited with the unique opportunity, I descended from my perch above the clouds and, as agreed, met one of the crew members, who rowed me to where the *Nordkaperen* was anchored. I had brought some cheese, fresh bread, olives, and a bottle of wine. They added some sausages and fresh fruit, and we gently rocked on a calm sea, ate, and exchanged stories.

After an hour or so, we noticed our bright sunny day darkening. The yacht began to pitch and sway, so that I began to feel sick to my stomach. The captain went up top and returned with a puzzled expression on his face. The weather forecast had predicted a possibility of a light shower, but this looked like something more. He checked the onboard radio and immediately ordered everyone to leave the cabin and go on top. Within minutes, it was so overcast it was nearly as dark as night. He began to cross the deck, shouting out orders.

By now, I was feeling so sick that I had to lie down. The crew sprang to full attention, and it was clear that something scary was happening. The yacht was swaying so violently that the whole vessel was being lifted up and slammed down. I began to feel physically as if I were dying. It was then the captain came to me shouting over the volume of the wind that a rare, freak, mega storm had developed suddenly. They had to drop anchor and sail away from the harbor out to sea immediately. It was too dangerous to stay there as they would lose their moorings and be dashed against the rocks. He gave me the alternatives. I would either have to stay and sail with them to South America or get off the yacht straightaway. I was in such a dire state that there was no choice. I couldn't take it anymore. I had to get off. I told him I wouldn't stay. He instructed one of his crew to provide me with a boat to row ashore and left.

The boat was very small, about eight feet long and well used. It was lowered into the sea, which was now like a gigantic pot of water boiling over. The anchors were raised, the sails were down, the engine was engaged with full power, and we were already moving away. Flashes of lightning outlined glimpses of human forms, animated and drenched, as they did what mariners have done for thousands of years, struggling on the edge of life and death.

The crewman held the boat steady and I climbed down. It was floating around like a leaf in the wind, slamming up against the side of the yacht. Adrenaline rushed through my system and totally wiped out the sensation of the worst seasickness I had ever experienced. I was thrown into a state of hyperawareness. I managed to time the rising and falling of the waves and sit down without injuring myself, release the rope that was tied to the yacht, and grab the oars. I saw the yacht disappear in waves that were much higher than its masts. I pointed my boat in the exact opposite direction and began to row.

My sense of time was now determined by the movement of the waves. On the peak, I looked down three stories high. From the trough, there was just a hint of sky. The roar and the vibration of the tempest around me shook my whole body and pushed my mind inward. It seemed there was no path to safety—safety was gone. I expected a wave to crash into the boat and turn it over, flood it, and sweep me away.

Wrestling with the sea was sucking the energy from my arms. It seemed like an hour had passed and I had made no progress. I was flooded with the futility and fragility of my life. I realized I had to stop fighting and try to synchronize and align myself with this storm, let go, be in the moment, and respond intuitively. At some point the boat and I became one, my little boat against a sky of billowing blackness, lit by lightning, echoed by thunder. This assembled collection of wooden planks held together with nails and glue and oars that at any moment could be wrenched from my grasp...This was my life. With endless repetition, wave upon wave, there was a split second of no movement as we balanced on a crest and then fell weightlessly, sucked down into a bottomless pit to sure death, only to be resurrected and rise again.

At some point, my mind returned to the surface for observation and presented me with a conclusion. There was no other choice, but to continue. Typical for a rowboat, my back was to the direction I was heading. So I couldn't see where I was going. I just had to do my best to keep the boat in what I thought was the direction of land, with watery monsters chasing me from behind. I saw no end, no finish line—it seemed to go on forever.

I was rowing, glancing around, when I felt a change in the movement of the waves. I turned, and there looming behind me appeared the granite pier wall. I was shocked. How, in this immensity, could I have found it? But I was too dangerously close. As the waves receded, the water level fell twenty feet, exposing the foundation of the pier and the beach. As they rose, they leaped over the top of the lamppost and continued over the length of the pier landing. I could feel the waves beginning to pull me in. I had to put more distance between me and the pier, so I had to row back out.

As I struggled to turn around, I realized that I had to time it so I wouldn't be capsized by a wave catching me sideways. I hadn't gotten my momentum yet, so the next wave continued to push me closer to the rocky landing. I was totally spent, but the sight of the little light on the top of the lamppost moved something deep inside of me, and my body surged with new energy. The body that had just battled with an invincible foe was now refreshed and ready for the next battle. I heard the whisper of a voice within me. Not the mind voice as it speaks inside the head but a feeling voice, a knowing that started to guide me. I turned and faced the landing. I knew the only way I was going to save my life was to get onto the pier. On both sides of the pier were rocks that would smash the boat to splinters. The waves were pushing me off, and I had to continually adjust to hold my position.

Then I noticed that the waves had a pattern. There would be several relatively smaller waves, a larger wave, and then a massive wave that would rise up over the landing, the lamppost and sail to the end onto land. I began to study the rhythm of the waves. I knew that I would have to turn myself around in the boat so I could see where I was going. I pulled the oars in, went onto my knees and crawled into my new position, put the oars back in and struggled to regain control. I knew I had only one attempt. There wasn't a second chance. So I counted the waves, studying the changing pattern, looking for the massive wave. The one I needed.

After five minutes of eternity, I knew the rhythm. There was no doubt or hesitation. I counted three sets of the smaller waves, the big one, and then waited for the massive wave. I saw it begin to swell, and I rowed with all my might to catch the front of the crest just right, like a surfer. I was now within fifteen feet of the landing, and the wave was still a few feet below the surface of the pier. Then the wave ascended, picking the boat up like an afterthought, higher and higher. It was like flying and floating. The wave topped the lamppost with me in the boat. I continued sailing on ten feet of water, then nine, eight, seven and six, five, four, three. Then the wave receded, dropping the boat like a bird making yet another perfect landing. I was now fifty feet beyond the pier. I took a deep breath, stood up, and began to run, to make sure the next wave didn't catch me.

Facing the pier was the restaurant where I had met the Danes. Soaked from head to foot, I rushed in. Everyone stared at me, wondering how and from where I had manifested. I ordered a fresh tuna steak caught that morning and a bottle of wine. When I looked out the window, my boat was gone.

Chapter 9

Out by Moonlight, Ramani Rangan

The American with Dark Eyes

It was 1976, and I was in between theater productions in London when I decided to visit a close friend in Copenhagen. He was an American expat who had settled there, was now married to a Dane, and had two preteen daughters. As long as I can remember, he had always left important details out when communicating, and I was met with one when I reached his address and knocked on the door.

My friend was in his late thirties, but I was met by a man of seventy, an obvious non-Dane. Looking me up and down, he suggested that I use the back stairs to deliver. It was at that moment I saw a little bit of my friend in this man's face and heard him, from somewhere deep in the apartment, ask who was at the door. I shouted out my name, and he came and saved me. What he had failed to tell me was that his father and his sister were visiting at the same time. We both had a good laugh about how his father had seen my dark Indian face and thought I was obviously delivering pizza.

While we were catching up, he told me that his sister had gone out. He lived on one of the main streets downtown in a huge Victorian-style apartment. It had high ceilings with decorative moldings, and in the living room, a rosette in the center featured a chandelier. From there, double French doors led to the dining room. Beyond that were enough bedrooms for all of us. His father had only been in Denmark a week and was not impressed. Where was McDonald's? It had not yet invaded. His sister was tired of being trapped in the apartment and wanted to see the sights. He was relieved to have his old friend appear to save the day.

It was now late evening, and I was getting tired. I had started out early and had been traveling for twenty-four hours by train, ferry, and then train again. I was hungry, so I thought I would eat and crash when in walked his sister, Leah. All of a sudden, I wasn't tired anymore. We chatted a bit. The next day, I planned to visit all my favorite spots, and I asked Leah if she wanted to join me. She liked the idea.

It was wonderful to show her my Copenhagen. We seemed to hit it off. I even think she started to like me. They were from South Philadelphia. It took a while for me to understand her expressions, gestures, and attitudes, which I found baffling and interesting at the same time. In the last week she was visiting, we got closer, and we arranged to stay in touch. They left. I stayed a few weeks longer, really enjoying hanging out with my friend and his family and our common friends, and then returned to London.

Leah and I wrote to each other many times over that winter. She expressed to me that she was not happy with her life in the States. I was going to have some free time in late spring and invited her to come over and visit a few countries in Europe. She agreed, and we met up in London. After a few days here and a few days there, we ended up on Samos, a Greek island. Our relationship deepened, and we eventually got used to each other's ways. Having the freedom to rent a nice house, eat simple and great food, and not worry about work or responsibilities helped a lot.

We returned to London and stayed at our family home with my mother, who was not too happy with the arrangement. We were now into a new year. Leah's British visa was running out, and she couldn't get an extension. After much discussion, we decided that we didn't want to be separated. Next thing I knew, we were running late and driving down the wrong side of the road against oncoming traffic on the way to Camden Town Hall for our wedding ceremony. Our idea of a wonderful way to spend the rest of the day was to visit the London Zoo and walk in Regent's Park as the sun went down.

Living with my mother wasn't working, and London was very expensive and getting congested, so we decided to go back to Copenhagen. My friend Leah's brother was moving to a smaller apartment, and we were ecstatic to inherit his Victorian. It was extraordinarily inexpensive. We were there for a few years, and in that time, I started training at a yoga school. I connected with one of the first all-organic/biodynamic collectives called Urtakrammer, a small store in a cellar in the middle of downtown. I helped them to cater large events as a specialty cook doing mainly Indian vegetarian meals. One of these events was the annual Roskilde Music Festival, where we fed thousands of hungry mouths.

One day Leah was looking at a small diary and was considering throwing it out. It looked interesting, and I asked her what it was. She replied that she had been a baker and that this was her book of personal recipes. I asked her to bake something. She did, and it was amazing. I had never tasted anything like it. England was not famous for its cooking, and Denmark was very traditional, seldom varying from recipes that had been passed on for generations. So here was something deliciously different. Leah's flavors were revolutionary.

I had an idea. I asked Leah to choose a few recipes. One was banana gingerbread, another was almond cinnamon bread, and a third was date and walnut bread. We cut the loaves in squares and took them to Urtakrammer and gave them a taste. It was a resounding hit! That is how we started a pirate bakery in our large old-fashioned kitchen. The business grew so much that I had to secretly haul an extra gas stove up three flights of narrow back stairs and illegally hook it up. At its peak, we were delivering three times a week, over two hundred pieces. The sign of a great baker is consistency. Leah broke all records in that period.

Simultaneously, I finished going to yoga school and had small groups come over to practice. This developed into many friendships, people from all walks of life. Musicians, ballet dancers, singers, artists, writers, and lots of other interesting personalities stopped by. I would cook, and we would all share our talents. Our house hosted gurus from India and other dignitaries, some who were members of the Theosophical Society. We also had students stay with us from around the world, studying alternative therapies. People from the Swedenborg Institute came and gave presentations. Amazing children accompanied their parents. This was a very special period in my life.

Despite all this and what wonderful, wonderful Copenhagen had to offer, Leah was still not happy and wanted to go home. I had never been to the United States and, quite frankly, had not thought of it. I asked if we could give Denmark another year, and if she still didn't want to stay, I would promise to try the States. I was sure she would get used to being there, but after the agreed time, she was still pining to go back. There were still complications which made it impossible to see my children. It was heartbreaking and there was no resolution in sight. I did not want to leave the children or the possibility that things could change. I loved Denmark and knew it would always be a home for me, but I had made a contract with Leah and reluctantly, I kept my promise.

I was asked if I was ever a member of a certain political party or knew anyone who was a member and answered, "No." I was then required to swear to defend something that was read up, and I agreed. I was given a green card, and we walked out of the American embassy. Shortly, I found myself in an airport in the United States, in a new country and a new life. As we left the secure area, I saw my first policeman with a gun, and I got a real shock.

We lived in Philadelphia for a year. It wasn't working. We used a twenty-one-day airline ticket to visit many cities across the country, but none of them seemed right. With friends, I expressed my despair at not finding a place I could call home in America. "Don't give up yet. Go visit New Mexico," one of them encouraged me. We went there, and it was perfect. We settled in and loved the Land of Enchantment.

Within several years, our relationship became strained, and I moved in with friends. After a period of time, we officially separated, and later divorced. For a few years after, we were there for each other during times of need. Now, though we rarely see each other, I still feel love and respect for her.

The Land of Enchantment and the Rez

I was now living in Albuquerque, the central engine for New Mexico's commerce and home to the university, the state fair and the world's largest hot air balloon festival. I loved the expanse of the surrounding landscape, diversity of peoples and the food. I'm talking real huevos rancheros with world-famous Hatch green chile salsa that could bring tears to an elephant's eyes at fifty yards.

One of the jobs I had was making Southwestern style belt buckles as a wax mold maker and finisher for Rusty, an ex hippy, also husband and father of three young girls. At the same time I was teaching yoga and meditation at the Freedom University, which meant you got paid what the students could afford. Most people had at least two jobs to make a "scrape by" lifestyle work, with the exception of rich ranch owners, white collar and government employees...and preachers. I suspect about 80 percent of all monetary endeavors were under-the-table, and the table was very long and wide.

In this environment of Native Pueblo Tribal Peoples, the old New Mexican Hispanic community, the Euro-Americans, and a smattering of every other ethnic group you could think of, one would meet all kinds of fellow travelers. We had mad and genius scientists from the Sandia Labs, cowboys and cowgirls who really did wrangle cattle, prospectors scratching for "the big one" in closed-down mines, teachers and students from UNM. In the mix were Lowriders, generally from the Hispanic community.

For those who do not know, a Lowrider is religiously in love with the automobile. Not any automobile—the automobile in his or her possession. Usually, this was an older, highly desired make and model that they had worked on for thousands of hours, cleaning, gleaming, and custom machining. Each was an expression of personal creativity, detailed, some with intricate designs. Most could raise the whole body up several feet from the wheels with hydraulics, and some had independent suspension for each wheel. The chassis was usually set very low to the ground. The back was often entirely refitted with a sophisticated sound system that shook your whole body as it passed you by. On any given summer Saturday, thirty to forty impeccably fashioned vehicles could be seen parading on Central, the main street.

Native peoples could be seen around town, dressed in traditional clothing, going about their business. Their influence was evident in the general population, creating a unique New Mexican identity. This was a fusion of Native, Hispanic, and cowboy culture. Professionals, including those in the highest level of government, complimented their suits with a bolo tie, a cluster of turquoise nuggets, or other gems, surrounded with ornately fashioned solid silver. This would hang on a braided leather cord, terminating in silver points to be worn around the neck. Long hair was tied back in an immaculately neat ponytail hanging a good foot and a half down the back. Patterned leather cowboy boots were favored over polished shoes. This is a mere glimpse of the painting that is New Mexico, but enough to set the scene for my story.

Getting together with family, friends, and guests in adobe-style homes with a background of big sky, mesas, desert gardens, and flowering cactus to eat good food and drink some wine or beer was a weekly event. The aroma of tacos, enchiladas, chiles rellenos, tamales, empanadas, beans, pozole, and corn tortillas saturated the air and made our mouths water in anticipation. At one such party I met a teacher, Alvita, a Black Caribbean who taught on an Indian Reservation, referred to as the Rez by the locals. We got on well, and she invited me to meet her family.

Hearing that I was a painter, she asked me if I would give an art class at her school in the Four Corners area where Arizona, Colorado, Utah, and New Mexico meet. Yes! It was way, way out there. You may know by now that I have moments where I act before I think, and this was one of those occasions. So we started off early and drove for what turned out to be eight hours due to the unpaved—should I call them— roads? We finally arrived at dusk to find a small settlement which looked, to my untrained eye, like an abandoned 1920s mining camp. After I was shown to my bedroom, I collapsed into a welcome sleep.

I was woken at 6:00 a.m. the next day to shower and have breakfast. Alvita led me to a prefabricated two-story oblong building and ushered me into the classroom. Did I mention that I had shaved my head? In front of me were eighteen dark faces, as dark and darker than mine, hair the color of a moonless midnight, but shining like the wings of a raven with a purple hue. I was speechless with their beauty.

As soon as they saw me, they looked down, eyes staying open, but facing the top of their desks. Alvita introduced me, and there was not one eye that looked up. I nervously cleared my throat after each sentence. Eventually, I managed to ask them what was the most important and favorite thing they liked to do. Exercising my peripheral vision, I noticed them look at me when they thought I was out of eye contact. Whatever I said fell flat, and there was no response. For me, the reception was cold, cold, and more cold. After lunch, in desperation, I looked around the classroom, trying to get a clue of what I could do, but there was nothing. I managed to get them to draw and then paint with watercolors, but they were totally in charge and instructed and helped each other as if I was not there. Alvita came in and took over, as arranged.

It was 2:00 p.m., and I was exhausted. I went out for a walk, but not too far because everything around me looked the same. I knew that if I went over one hill, I would be lost forever, and all they would eventually find would be my bones with a little morsel left for some creatures to fight over. It was baking hot, so I soon went back to my room and, laying my head down to rest, I fell into a coma-like sleep.

That evening, I was invited over to eat at Alvita's place with some of her fellow teachers. I described what I had experienced and announced that I had failed and could not go back in the morning. Alvita looked at me, her eyes shining brightly, and said, "They loved you." I was shocked. Alvita continued, saying that they could not stop asking about me over and over. They wanted to know every little detail. So when she took over, the class was focused on what and who I was. "But . . . but. . ." A lot of buts sprang forth from my mouth. She told me that they loved me because I was like them but not like them at the same time. They were curious, but they didn't know how to behave with me, and they were shy. Making minimal eye contact was normal in the culture. "Where did all his hair go?" they had asked. She said they were excited to come to school the next day.

Entering the classroom the next morning, I was greeted with a collective scream and a group hug. Time stopped. Now, with all eyes on me, I said that we were going to work together to make a painting the size of the wall, which was twenty feet by ten feet. They looked at the wall, puzzled. "How are we going to do that?" I asked them to think of a subject that they had all experienced, and that was easy to imagine. Within a minute, they chose a project, the annual rodeo. I asked them to close their eyes and tell me what it would look like, then open their eyes and direct me in doing a color pencil sketch-up. They gathered around as I listened to suggestions. There were so many of them, yet they agreed very easily, as if they tapped into a collective space they all shared, and now I was part of that space. The result was a master watercolor and pastel. I divided it into as many squares as there were children, numbering each one. Each child was given a square and set out to sketch and paint it on a larger sheet of paper. The room was focused and still. We then taped them all together in order and reinforced the back. There was an atmosphere of excitement and wonder. We moved some tables together and, standing on them, stuck the completed mural on the classroom wall facing the front door. It was colorful, full of movement, with a rodeo rider on a bucking mustang, men dressed in clown suits standing by to protect the rider and Navajo people of all ages on the outside of the ring, with just one black face and one baldheaded brown face present. It was bigger than life and expressed so much of who they were.

Alvita and I left early the next day before school started, and all the children were there to see us off. I had a mixed feeling of love and a sense of abandoning them. I saw Alvita a week later, and she told me they had asked if there were other brown people out there off the Rez. She said to them, "The world is full of brown people, like you."

I saw Alvita a few times on a family visit, and then she was gone. Sometimes I wonder if people come into one's life for a reason, and when that reason is fulfilled, they go on to fulfill another need on the path of life, and that is simply what all this is about.

The Hot Springs

I heard of natural hot springs scattered all over the state, most of them off the beaten track. I understood that over the millennium, Native peoples would use them to purify in preparation for traditional tribal or medicine ceremonies. They were also used for healing, simple rejuvenation, and to harmonize with the natural order. Living near the campus of the University of New Mexico, I had lots of students as my friends. So it came to pass that one of the students mentioned she was going to a hot spring near Battleship Rock in the Jemez Mountains. Hearing that I didn't have a car and had never been there, she invited me to come along.

It was early on a Saturday morning in May when we headed out. The driving time would have been about three and three quarter hours, but we stopped and gathered herbs and took pictures on the way. We saw a few rattlers, jackrabbits, falcons, and lots of lizards. It all took much longer than we had thought. It was now 11:00 a.m., and it was beginning to get hot, but we figured we had a window of an hour before having to seek sufficient shade. We walked for five minutes until we reached rocks with steam rising from behind. As we got closer, we saw the surfaces were shiny wet and glimmering in the sunlight. So much steam was rising from the pool, it looked like the water was boiling.

I was apprehensive, but my friend, without blinking, threw off all her clothes, sat down at the edge, slowly moved forward, and touched the water with her toes. That she went into the spring naked seemed so natural, I didn't even register it at the time. I was more focused on a vicarious experience of imagined pain, but she looked over to me and laughed, half at my facial expression and half at her own relief. Before long, she was submerged, with just her head and her shoulders above water. I sheepishly followed suit, and with a few painful digs to my bare feet from the rocks, I too entered into the water.

It felt scalding hot, but my body adjusted. I was drawn into a timeless zone. The steam made everything outside the circle of rocks invisible, as if there was nothing beyond the pool. I looked up and saw the bluest of skies. The water was so very hot that I could only stay under a short while before I would have to stand up to cool off, but then I could not resist, and this ancient spring would pull me down again. We had talked a lot on the way up, but words seemed meaningless now. The gentle popping of bubbles and the calls of a circling eagle were the only sounds. We were just being.

We must have been in and out three or four times before we decided with just the subtlest of signals and without verbal agreement that it was time. She got out, and I followed her to a pool of mud. She began to roll in it until there was not a part of her that wasn't covered, including her hair. As a good apprentice, I asked myself, *Should I follow?* I did. Then we frolicked in the mud and talked about what we had just experienced. We got out and lay in the sun until the mud dried and caked. Then we danced around, shaking as much off as we could and washed the rest at a cooler spring nearby.

Dressed, we drove to a visitors' center and broke our fast with fruit. She wanted to walk around a little, but I needed to lie down, so I found a place outside in the shade, fell asleep, and dreamed. In my dream, I was an eagle, soaring high in a different sky, looking down on the earth many hundreds of years ago.

In reflection, sex never crossed my mind. Maybe I was lucky that the electrical and chemical impulses in my brain didn't make their millions of synaptic jumps and take advantage of my male hormone delivery system. Several times in my life, I have had, and continue to have, the very precious gift of profound friendship and organic transcendent spiritual experience with women. For this I am truly grateful.

Dragon Tooth

A close friend had invited me and a small group over for dinner. It was a bright, late summer day, and the sun was shining on buildings and adobe walls with an incandescent orange redness. Albuquerque was cooling down from its summer heat attack, and families were outside enjoying the relief that comes at dusk. My friend, the hostess, was a fellow yoga instructor. She had prepared steamed corn on the cob to be rolled in butter with a sprinkle of red or green pepper powder. This was New Mexico. Chile was a necessary staple.

We were talking and having fun. While I was chewing on the corn on the cob, something snapped in my mouth. I wore a partial denture and thought I had broken it. This embarrassing situation had happened before in public several times, and I had learned to deal with it. I thought I could excuse myself like I had done before, buy a kit from the pharmacy, and fix it. So I sought the refuge of the bathroom, where I intended to plan my untimely exit. Examining my dentures, I found nothing. They were intact. On reinserting them, I touched a front tooth and nearly fell to the floor from the pain. I had cracked a tooth. My mouth was slowly registering the presence of blood.

I went into my usual survival mode—calm and clear. Returning to my friends, I announced that I had cracked a tooth but didn't reveal the level of pain I was in or the seriousness of the injury. Somehow I got home. On examining my tooth, I found that it had cracked in half, running vertical, so it went up into my skull. Explicit language came to mind and was expressed. It was now 7:00 p.m., and all dental services were closed except for real emergencies. I figured that if I went to the ER, they would just refer me to a dentist in the morning. I considered taking a double shot of tequila, tying the offending tooth to the knob of a door, and slamming it shut. I couldn't do that. So my strategy plan was to call up three dentists and leave a message for the morning. I would make an appointment with the one who returned my call first.

That done and the scramble for painkillers over, I revisited the tooth in question. When I was thirteen, a boy standing on a wall in the playground jumped down on top of me. I was knocked to the ground face first. The impact pushed my upper front tooth deep into its cavity, fracturing my skull. Despite my obvious distress and the blood all over my face and shirt, the teacher told me to sit down and be quiet. For two hours, I sat through class, and it was only when school was out that I was allowed to run home. My mother rushed me in a taxi to the University College London Eastman Dental Institute, and they put me under and worked on me for four hours. When I returned to a conscious state, the dental surgeon told me he tried to save the tooth but had to remove it because too much time had elapsed to be able to reconstruct it successfully. If I had come in straightaway, he would have been able to save it. That lesson sprang to mind. Now I was in a similarly grave predicament with the other upper front tooth. After looking in the mirror and studying my poor tooth, I visualized what I needed to do to try to save it. I would construct a splint. Yes! I would look around for a piece of wood or fashion one and tie it around the tooth with dental floss. A toothpick was too round, and a cocktail stirrer too wide, but a matchstick...Yes! It was perfect. I broke off the strike end and, after a few attempts, achieved the right length. I was hoping that if I united the two halves, they would still be exchanging their life force, and in the morning, the dentist would simply cement them together. I would leave with instructions to not eat solid food for a week, and that would be that.

A new confidence flushed through my body and mind. I had to close my mouth for a bit as I was aching from holding it wide open. I touched the tooth with my tongue. The shooting pain reminded me that it was not all a bad dream. I took a shot of whiskey and took another with me into the bathroom. I turned on the bath, waited till it was at the right level, and turned it off. I lined up the soap, set out some candles, found my favorite beach towel, and placed the dental floss and the tailored matchstick on a glass shelf. To position myself, I had to stand on a stool. I would have to visually compensate because I was relying on my reflection through a mirror. I made a loop of floss, like a small lasso, and carefully drew it up to the widest part of the tooth so it would not slip. Then I tightened it slowly. The gap between the two halves started to close, and the throbbing seemed to ease. Next I placed the matchstick splint vertically behind the tooth and started to wrap the floss around the tooth and the splint. I did this four times till it felt just right. Then I made a loop knot and tied it, pulling the loose end so it was now holding everything snug. I cut the floss with scissors, and there it was—complete.

With the help of the whiskey and the adrenaline that had flushed my whole body and now subsided, I experienced a state of relaxation. I removed what clothing was separating me from sinking into the warmth of the awaiting bath, lit three candles, turned on Stevie Wonder, and retreated into my cocoon. I slept reasonably well, considering. When I woke, I started calling dentists. On the second try, I got an appointment for that morning and had to walk a jarring and painful couple miles to get there, as I didn't drive at the time.

I filled out the annoying paperwork, was ushered into the room, and sat down in the Frankenstein chair with the glaring interrogation lamp. I explained my dilemma. Examining my mouth, the dentist saw the tooth with its first aid attachments. As he slowly unraveled my tooth's support, he commented on what I had done. "It is ingeniously constructed. For a non-professional, quite amazing." He further commended me on my efforts in the field. It sounded like it might have worked. A sense of optimism washed over me. He studied my x-rays and then said he was sorry to tell me that the tooth in question had snapped to the root and couldn't be saved. He would have to take it out. I was despondent. That was not all. I had extensive deterioration. My bone line was receding, there was infection, and my health was in danger. He recommended taking out the top teeth. Eventually, he said, they would all have to be extracted. The split tooth had to come out—that was all I could manage. I paid my eighty dollars and went home with a gap in my mouth that my tongue could not stop feeling. Now I was devastated.

I love morning glories, the way they weave themselves around fences, open and point their colorful skirts toward the sun as they slow-dance across the sky and close again in the evening. Normally, they greet me. This time, they didn't whisper a word. Or if they did, I didn't hear them as I entered my house and firmly closed the door behind me. Leaning on the door, I knew everything had changed. While I hid away for a few days, I came to realize there had been certain events in my life that were cornerstones, like the stations of the cross that Jesus passed through on his way to be crucified. This was one of my stations. The ones of the past loomed over me. I was only forty-four years old, and I was facing a preview of my mortality. Dramatic, yes! But there it was. This was a "no turning back" station. It was final. There would be more like this all the way to the last station.

I called the dentist back and the price he quoted was way over my head. I was lost. What was I going to do? I heard that people could get dental work in Mexico for a much better price. So I decided to take a Peter Pan bus to El Paso, Texas, and cross the bridge to the border town of Juarez. This was before Juarez was riddled with drug cartel wars and became known as the murder capital of the world. After a few hours of searching, I left the main street and found an old, rusty sign with a peeling image of a three-foot molar and climbed a set of stairs in similar condition. Entering the waiting area, which was in the corridor, I saw the dentist in street clothes, not even wearing an apron. Human teeth were scattered densely on the floor, interrupted only by a pathway to the chair. I went back to the main street and kept on looking until I found a dentist trained in the United States.

To my relief, the clinic was modern, and the receptionist and the dentist were bilingual. So I felt safe opening my mouth to be stretched, probed, prodded, and x-rayed. He came to the same conclusion as the New Mexico dentist. The uppers had to come out. He could save the lowers for now. His quote was a fifth of the U.S. price. He planned to perform the extractions in two stages, half the following day and half the day after that.

That night, my mind rolled through extreme scenarios. One impulse was to go back to Albuquerque, like somehow it was all going to magically get better overnight. I felt as though someone I had loved deeply for most of my life was about to die. A sense of total desolation overcame me. I crossed back to El Paso, where I was staying with a friend of a friend and her daughter. I attempted to convey my situation while at the same time protect them from my feelings. They didn't get the gravity, and it was awkward.

That night, I had a lucid dream. An adult male lion with a full mane appeared. He roared, and I saw he had no teeth. It was clear his teeth made him potent as a male, and without them, he was completely vulnerable. He lay down under a tree, waiting to die. I woke with a pain in the pit of my stomach.

On the third day, I went into the clinic so the dentist could inspect his handiwork. Notice, no mention of the two days of extraction. My poor face was swollen, painful, and aching, even with the meds. He must have told me before, but I had spaced it out. I would have to wait for six weeks to be fitted with dentures. Six weeks, no teeth in my upper mouth.

It turned out that the friend of the friend I was staying with had misinterpreted my intentions and thought I had come down to El Paso to have a relationship with her. Needless to say, my presence was not desired when it became apparent this was not the case. I was asked to leave. Her toilet didn't work properly, so I went out and got the parts and fixed it. Somehow I imagined this might be some compensation for the loss of her projected aspiration. This lion needed to face the world, so I left. But where was I going to go?

The Crystal Warrior

I crossed back over to Juarez and checked into a hotel. I wandered around the streets, lost for a few days. I needed to talk to someone. So I decided that I would take a chance and call an ex-girlfriend. We had not parted under favorable circumstances. Sue was an independent, edgy, creative, cut-through-the-crap, strange kind of maverick, survivalist personality. I described the state I was in. She took a breath. I waited in the silence. I apologized. She kept the silence, making me sweat a little as a payback. Then she melted a bit, and we started to talk. I told her I was feeling desperately alone and depressed and asked if she would come down. I would pay all the expenses. Another breath. We could meet on the El Paso side, cross together, go down to a coastal town in Southern Mexico where it was warm and wait for my gums to heal. She thought it over out loud. She was in California. It was not a simple request. I don't know if it was "all expenses paid" or the sound of hanging out on a beach that clinched it, but she agreed.

Three days later, we were on a train to Mexico City, where we had to change for our final destination, Oaxaca City. We stepped out on the platform to the welcoming aroma of subtropical plants and balmy, warm air. The pace was noticeably slower in comparison to Juarez and Mexico City. The majority of people were closer to my color, of native origin, and with no hint of European features.

We booked into a hotel and had been there for a few days when Sue suddenly became very ill. Within an hour, she was burning up with a fever, and her eyes began to roll up in their sockets. I knew I had to get her to an emergency room immediately. They told me she had contracted a virus. She had rapid dehydration, was in shock, and her kidney functions were in danger of shutting down. They would have to keep her in on IV and medication. Her situation was critical. If her fever broke within thirty-six hours, she might have a chance of survival. They said I was not allowed to stay, there was nothing I could do, and I should return during visiting hours the next day.

Reluctantly, I left my hotel name and phone number with them and went back to the hotel. I put out the "Do Not Disturb" sign and then lay down. I was very tired and must have slept for a few hours. When I awoke, I felt as though I had been pinned to the bed. I tried to open my eyes, but they seemed to be stuck. They were burning with a sensation I can only describe as a wet fire. I had lost all definition of my physical form, but whatever it was, it was slowly being cooked. I panicked and tried to use my willpower to move. There was no response. As I was starting to slip into unconsciousness, the thought passed through my mind without any emotion, "I have the same thing Sue has."

While in this deep fever, I experienced a state of altered wakefulness. One part of me was detached and observed that the body I was in was sweating profusely and was so hot it seemed volcanic. I slipped in and out of sleep and consciousness several times, unable to move and finally going under. Next morning, I woke up horrified with the recognition that I was in crisis. This was really it—I was going to die. I had a passing thought of my mother learning of my death. She would be devastated. I sank back again into a deeper state of fever. The spirit of the fever became a personage, with total power over me. It was an unwanted lover, sucking my life and consuming me like a ripe fruit, as it found new places to occupy in my body and mind. This sinister creature had possessed me, fully.

Right then, at that very moment, my consciousness ruptured, and all past history drained away. My ego became a drop that melted into every other thing. Lines within lines began to form, crisscrossing. First in chaos. Then lines connected to lines, and they formed a matrix. This morphed into triangles and squares, and then pyramids and cubes and other geometric shapes. A thin, clear film defined the surface of each plane. All this took place against a white pearl background of infinite space. I seemed to be in the presence of an intelligence, not directing but allowing an event to take its natural course. These shapes stopped multiplying and began to seek each other out, and eventually, a hint of a unified structure began to appear. The whole network clicked together, in what can only be described as a painfully perfect, faceted, crystalline version of a human form. At its center was a star tetrahedron.

I began to shrink, so I was small enough to fly around its perimeter. Then it changed so I could easily glide in and out of its crystal structure, as if I were defying the integrity of its surface and could at will pass through without any hindrance. It took on many hues, like the rainbow colors on a bubble. At moments, I came to consciousness, and the form was still in front of me, unmoving. Whether my eyes were open or closed, it was still there. It even penetrated my dreams, never changing its quality. It was familiar and unfamiliar at the same time. I had an experience of complete freedom as I had never known before, and in that moment, I understood its true nature—that it was a warrior. The Crystal Warrior. The Crystal Warrior was an all-powerful sentinel, guarding something very important. What it was guarding, I did not know, just that its intent was to hold something in safety.

While my body was on lockdown and fighting desperately for its life, my companion stood fast, never leaving my side. I had no control over the functions of my body, so all movements were spontaneous. Eyes opening, eyes closing, sounds coming from the lungs laboring for breath, noises, mumblings and words all registered, but totally impersonal. My, for a better word, ego seemed to change moment by moment, feeling the fever in my body, being disconnected from the fever in my body, the sense of not even being in my body at all. There all the time in this timelessness was the Crystal Warrior.

I had always experienced my mind as fluctuating. Thoughts jumped from one place to another, ever changing. This movement created my reality. Now here was a permanency, previously unimagined. I had a vague sense that the Crystal Warrior was not just there to hold space for me, but was a benevolent universal presence, holding space for all vestiges of life. For humans, plants, animals, and the mineral world. Then I lost all consciousness and sank into full fevered oblivion.

Altogether, it was a total of thirty-six hours later, when Sue showed up and got the hotel to open the door. There I was, still lying on the bed. They had to wake me by shaking me vigorously. The fever must have broken a little earlier, for at that point, I was just asleep. I was very, very weak and couldn't move by myself. It was obvious that Sue had gone through a great deal. In the short time, she had lost a lot of weight, and her face was drawn, with dark circles under her eyes. She came over to help me stand. I couldn't and staggered over to sit down on one of the chairs. She was mad at me for not coming to the hospital to see her or pick her up, but that all changed when she saw the condition I was in. I too had lost a great deal of weight. The accumulated sweat from the fever had become a stinking glue that stuck my clothes to my body. The mattress I had slept on was damaged from the poisons and toxins excreted. The hotel had no other option but to take it outside and set it on fire. It took quite a few days for me to get my strength back so I could stand up and get to the hospital to get checked out. When they saw me, they were shocked that I had survived. They gave me an IV and then let me go.

I continued to have recurring bouts of the fever over the next couple of years, and always, the Crystal Warrior would appear. At one point, I was in Philly and had a particularly heavy incident. I fell asleep, and next thing I remember, I was standing in the middle of the airport in Atlanta with a ticket in my hand for Albuquerque. No idea how I got there.

Without the fever, I would not have had the vision and the transformational message that the Crystal Warrior holds. I believe the Crystal Warrior saved my life. I had experienced altered states from childhood. The Crystal Warrior gave me confirmation that these things were not imaginary and actually did exist. It encouraged me in the future to be open to the potential of extrasensory phenomenon. The star tetrahedron at the center of the Crystal Warrior turns out to be known as the Merkaba, which literally means "light-spirit-body," divine energy in form.

Trust Your Gut

After my episode with the killer fever, Sue and I decided to take a bus west to the Pacific coastal town of Port Angel. A few things happened while I was there, enough for five, six other stories, but I will stay focused.

One day, I was sitting outside of a restaurant, and I started a conversation with an American who was sitting at the next table. He was dusty and unshaven. His clothes looked as though he had been living out in the jungle or a desert for a good long while. It turned out it was the latter. He said he was practicing a form of meditation that involved a thirty-day fast on water and wild cactus juice. He had just come off his spiritual journey and was having his first smoothie. As the conversation progressed, he told me he made rings from silver or gold-filled wire, a material that was better than plated gold. He sold them in New York at Italian street festivals in the summer and on college campuses in the fall. He obviously was very weak from his fast. While getting his bill, he asked me if I would help him sell in New York. It was November, and he wanted me to join him in April next year. He could use someone to keep watch for stealing, give change, fetch things, and hold down the fort when he needed to answer the call of nature. I immediately concluded that he was out of it, if you know what I mean. Thirty days in the desert on water and cactus juice? I agreed to exchange telephone numbers. He left, I ordered another drink, and all was forgotten.

I had now been six weeks in Mexico without upper teeth. The money was quickly running out, and Sue ran out quickly too. Life is full of lessons, isn't it? I went back to the dentist in Juarez and got my new mouth. Boy, did that feel strange. For all that time, I'd been gumming my food. I had my first solid meal in a small cantina. Roasted garlic bulbs cut in half sideways in olive oil, herbs with sweet and hot chilies, and fresh bread were placed on the table within half a minute of entering the premises. I ordered deep-fried fish tortillas, frijoles, rice, and plantains. I was in heaven.

I love Mexico and would have loved to stay, but it was time to return to Albuquerque. December, Christmas and New Year, January, February, March passed. Now, April and still cold, the telephone rang. A voice asked me, "Where are you?" I was more than puzzled, and waited for information to come through. After a total sweep of my memory banks, I realized it was the man from Port Angel who had been wandering in the desert on a mission to find himself. He asked me if I could come up that weekend, as he needed to start making more jewelry to get ready for the shows. I said I really didn't want to. *This man is mad. Definitely living in an alternate reality*, I thought. He asked me what I was doing to make money. I told him. He said his jewelry gave him a profit of ten times his investment. He would train me and show me how to fashion fifty different styles of rings. This included buying material, shaping it, soldering it, tumbling and finishing it, as well as how to use all the necessary tools and equipment safely, and how to set up a display. I would make two hundred to three hundred dollars per day. While working with him, he would cover all my expenses, lodging, food, and extras. After the festival season was over in August, we would sit down and make a display that would cost three hundred dollars and would have a street value of over three thousand dollars, which would all be mine. I told him I didn't have very much money. He said I only needed about two hundred dollars, and he would look after the rest.

Would you believe it? I was on a Greyhound bus the next day, traveling from Albuquerque, New Mexico, to New York City with two hundred dollars in my pocket. He met me at the bus station and greeted me as if I were an old friend. We immediately drove to the Jewelry District and he asked me if I had the two hundred dollars. I said, "Yes." He gave me a list of materials to buy, with the name of the supplier and directions, and said he would drive around the block as it was impossible to park.

That is how the pulling of a tooth led me to a successful business selling jewelry around the country in many venues for the next eight years. Back home, I acquired a vending license to sell my handmade costume jewelry outside the Student Union at the University of New Mexico. So I would lug my foldout table, boxed merchandise, display and tool box on a two-wheel trolley held by bungee cords for three blocks and set up under my favorite tree. I had a wall around the tree to sit on, and there I would make new earrings. Or I would size silver and gold rings. Jewelry that I had not sold at arts and craft shows was offered to students at a really good price. I still made enough to cover expenses and a little more to buy new materials. This gave me the opportunity to meet wonderful young people. Some would stay and sit with me on my wall, and we would discuss all manner of subjects—philosophy, politics, sociology. Or they might confide in me about the ups and downs of their life and ask for guidance.

When President Reagan came into office and the trickle down didn't trickle down to my customer base anymore, I had to find other means of gainful employment. As a jeweler, I had been independent, creative, and was totally in charge of whether I wanted to work or take time off. Through years of conversing from behind the safety of my table in my role as vendor, I gained a great deal of confidence and became much more comfortable around people. I had been guided by my instinct to follow an illogical, possibly even dangerous, proposition, and it turned out to be perfect for me for all those years. Coincidence or magic?

Cars

Growing up in London, we got around on buses and the Tube, the underground train. Greater London had such an efficient transport system that the thought of needing a car never entered my mind. In my neighborhood, it was rare to see a parked car that wasn't a wedding limo, an ambulance, or a hearse. My first experience of a motorized vehicle was a taxi, which at the time was a totally mind-altering experience. In Copenhagen, they had trams with overhead electric cables, as well as buses and trains, but 30 percent of the population chose to pedal. There were bike lanes everywhere, and bikes had the right of way. You could even catch the prime minister of the country on a cold winter morning on his vintage black bicycle on the way to the government buildings. In Philadelphia I used public transport, as most working people did. Albuquerque was a different story. The bus service was limited. Where I lived near the campus of the University of New Mexico, shops, restaurants, coffee houses, bookstores, and most everything I needed were within walking distance. When I sold my handmade jewelry around the country, I had a partner who did all the driving, and I was discouraged from learning to drive. I was now about forty-five and had never driven a car even once.

Then I met Gloria when I was selling my jewelry at a fair and she was doing psychic readings. We started a relationship. We had an engagement at a winter show in Lubbock, Texas, where I was going to sell and she was going to read. She drove us in her van. Just as we got to the state border and saw the "Welcome to the Lone Star State" sign, the temperature dropped forty degrees, from sunshine to black ice on the highway. It was getting late in the afternoon, and I asked if we should turn back.

Gloria was a strong-headed woman and said we were going to drive on. When we began to see semi trucks flipped on their side on the shoulder of the road, abandoned vehicles, and remnants of collisions, I mentioned as calmly as possible that we were not going to make it. We were now driving at ten miles an hour in the center of the road with poor visibility. We reached a compromise to drive twenty miles to the next filling station and then decide if we would continue.

Arriving there three hours later, with an overcast sky so dark it looked like nighttime, we found that the station was closed and deserted. We knew we were in dire straits. So we huddled for fifteen minutes, figuring out our strategy. If we stayed, we could freeze to death. If we went on, it would be into the unknown. Checking that we had enough gas, we decided we would turn around and go back. It was going to be a grueling four to five hours to the border.

After one hour, Gloria said that she was sick and needed to lie down. She stopped the van in the middle of the road in the pitch black, leaving me up front in the passenger seat. I said, "We can't stop here!"

She had covered herself with a blanket and was curled up in a fetal position. Her muffled reply was, "You have to drive." I reminded her that I had never driven before...ever! She replied in a matter-of-fact tone, "The van is an automatic. One pedal is for the brake, one for the gas. Keep both hands on the steering wheel."

"I can't do it," I said.

"Then we'll have to stay here in the middle of the road until the storm clears or someone stops to help," she answered.

I continued to plead with her, but she wouldn't respond. I had no other option, so I took the wheel for the first time in my life. As soon as I put my foot on the gas, I lost control. I stopped panicking and managed to get back to the center of the road. After many hair-raising experiments, I learned that if I went exactly eighteen miles per hour, we would stay on the road. A little faster, and we would begin to go into a spin. A little slower, and we would begin to slide to the side into the shoulder. I drove us all the way back to the "Welcome to New Mexico, Land of Enchantment" sign.

As I crossed over, the clouds and the black ice completely disappeared. I could see the sun setting in front of me. Looking back, there was a clear line of dark, forbidding clouds stretching from horizon to horizon along the borderline on the Texas side. I pulled over. Gloria woke up and said she was feeling better and could drive the rest of the way.

When I tried to let go of the steering wheel, my arms and my hands were locked in position. I was holding on for dear life for so many hours, that they had set. My shoulders ached for a few days after. That's how I learned to drive. It would be a year before I plucked up enough courage to learn to drive officially and get my license. Out of the blue one day, Gloria mentioned in passing, "I wasn't sick that day on the way back from Lubbock. I was just scared stiff."

Mammoth Memories

Albuquerque attracted all kinds of amazing characters. Like Paul, a friend of a friend. He was a dealer in fossilized ivory artifacts. He would acquire all the legal paperwork necessary and go on an annual expedition to excavate them himself, way up in Alaska near the Arctic Circle. A large man, slow-talking with a calm disposition, he was so relaxed that when he sat back in his favorite armchair, he seemed ready to fall asleep at any moment. He was a hippie in the sixties, and now in the eighties, he still wore his hair long, was rarely seen without a large-brimmed hat, wore loose clothes and chunky bracelets and necklaces made of the fossils he had collected. He told me that his dig sites were over ten thousand years old, created by the ancient tribes when they cast aside broken hunting, fishing, or skinning tools and ceremonial or personal adornments. He showed me pieces that were made from walrus and mammoth tusks, whale bones, and teeth from animals now extinct. I was entranced, and in the few days that he was visiting, I invited myself over with the offer of making Indian food so I could see some of his objects and hear their stories.

The next few days were packed with adventure as he related a story for each object. He made a point of bringing out only a few at a time from a large black metal traveling trunk that had its own two locks built in, reinforced by flat iron bars that wrapped around it and were secured by a padlock the size of my fist. As he placed a piece down, he would stop and look at it as if he, like me, was seeing it for that first time.

The first object was a tooth. It was nearly four inches long. He handed it to me, and I took it as if it were alive and just sleeping. "This came from a saber-toothed tiger. If you look on one side, you will see that it is worn down," he said, sitting back and closing his eyes. "It was probably used as a scraper for hides and for flattening strips of sinew." I looked at it in wonder. My eyes widened even more as he produced a fishhook made out of a mammoth's tusk. With each object, my imagination transported me back to those times. I could see worn hands with deep lines and fingernails that had been split and broken but now healed. I saw children dressed in animal skins, their faces dark brown with big cheeks and eyes squinting from the glare of the sun, reflecting off of ice that stretched as far as the eye could see.

The next objects were three cylindrical beads made of fossilized walrus tusk. They had a hole through the middle and were carved with a wavy pattern and small dots between each wave. I envisioned a room made of animal skins stretched over a frame, constructed of roughly worked branches the diameter of a child's arm. In the center of the room was a fire with smoke rising and escaping from a hole out the top. I was sitting cross-legged in a circle with my tribe. Traders were with us from the South, a place unlike ours, where the forest had no beginning and no end and there was no lapse between the call of birds. Beside me to my right was a kinsman, still dressed in heavy outside clothes. His skin was wrinkled and looked as tough as the leather clothes he was wearing. His hair was like the black of night, with a few graying strands at his temples. He was drilling a hole into a piece of bone held between his feet using a sharpened stone attached to a stick, which he steadied loosely with one hand. With the other hand, he pulled a bow back and forth horizontally. The bow was made of a large creature's rib and sinew and functioned to rotate the stick. In this imaginary world, I was doing the same.

Over the course of the days I was with Paul, he showed me more than two hundred objects and conveyed to me his deep relationship with each—how he imagined it was acquired, crafted, and used. I felt that I had been drawn into the lives of real living, breathing people who struggled on the edge of a harsh and dangerous frozen world. It seemed to me that their values were no different than ours. The important things in life were family and friends. Protecting oneself and each other from the elements and danger. Finding food and wanting respect. Love. Children who grow up to be healthy, and their children's children, who grow up to be healthy too. As the last hours of my day with Paul were drawing to a close and he was ready to take the road, we both realized we had shared something special. He told me that he was going to Tucson, Arizona, to the largest gem and mineral show in the world. He went each year and had a permanently reserved suite at a hotel in the middle of the fair. I was welcome to come down for a few days. I jumped at the offer.

The show was beyond my expectations. Imagine coming into the outskirts of a large city, usual lines of businesses, junk food franchises spaced between strip malls, and a web of cables blocking the sight of a full sky. Then bang, motel after motel, with people taking things in and out of parked vans, trucks, and trailers, in boxes, trays, and large packages. I traveled a mile, and it didn't stop—in fact, it got crazier, with cars triple parked, loading and unloading their merchandise. Foldout tables appeared on street corners and in storefronts. From my point of view, I was seeing the wildest and longest block party ever, and I wasn't even there yet. A sign pointed to the center of the city, "2 miles," where the show was officially located. Then I saw ahead of me the traffic jam of all traffic jams. I realized that if I continued, I would be blocked in, so I took the first side street, pulled over, and called Paul.

I was lucky to get him the first time. He said it would be impossible to get within a mile of his setup, which was in a prime location downtown. So, he directed me to a place half a mile's walk from him next to an arroyo—a large, deep channel that directs floodwaters away from the city. I found it as did others, and while waiting for a space to park my van, I spoke to a vendor who was about to move his trailer to his spot in town. He agreed to give me a lift in. Being a regular for the last twenty years, he knew the ins and outs of the route to take. When he left me off, I called again, and Paul guided me the last ten minutes to his camping trailer.

Even in the winter, it was hot for me, so I was happy to "come on in." The chair Paul was sitting on was facing the same direction in the same corner of the trailer as back at our friend's home. In fact, it was the same chair. His smile was the equivalent of a hug and so I sat down and took a breath. I felt as though we were continuing our conversation from the last time. I could tell he was glad to see me. After driving overnight from Albuquerque to Tucson, four hundred and fifty miles, I was beyond exhaustion, but his greeting washed the tiredness away.

For fifteen years, he had been going to Alaska, "working the hill," and then bringing his merchandise down and setting up in the same place. In this time, he established relationships with returning dealers who traded with him each year. Some were jewelers and fashion scouts on the hunt for the next season's new look, and a smaller few were curators in search of a special piece for their museum collection. Over the next three days, I was introduced to a steady stream of fascinating individuals who knocked on the door of the trailer and greeted Paul as if he were a family member. A whiskey or vodka was chased with sodas, wine, or beer and snacks of chips, crackers with cheese and salsa, countless pizza, and Chinese deliveries.

Paul seemed to instinctively tune in to the interests of each person who came through the door. After chatting with them, he would stop and get quiet, focusing inward. Then he knew where to look in the menagerie of his enormous stockpile. He would open a chest or a drawer and ceremoniously bring forth an object and lay it on one of several small tables as if it were the Holy Grail. He would stand there, feasting his eyes, as though it was the first time. All this was real. There was no acting here. Paul was in awe of what passed through his hands.

They came from all corners of the globe and between the corners, some with English accents so thick I could not understand them—but Paul could. Others came with interpreters or just pointed, frowned, smiled, or nodded their heads. Paul seemed to know if the person recognized the value or quality of the item. If he became impatient with a potential customer, he would excuse himself and leave the trailer and go for a walk. Eventually, the customer, realizing they were never going to be a customer, left. Paul was respectful, straight, sincere, but had no time for people who were not honest, did not know what they were doing and pretended that they did.

Of course, I didn't stay in the trailer all the time, and he, knowing that I made my own costume jewelry, suggested that I check out Quartzite, a small town about three and a half hours away. In fact, the Tucson fair hadn't officially started yet. Feeling that I wouldn't be missing anything, I set off. After driving nearly four hours on a dusty road, I came across one structure with a foundation, a telephone kiosk, and a McDonald's. This couldn't possibly be it, so I continued another five minutes. Looming up on the side of the road were thirty canopies in disarray, with old campers and RVs and people who looked like prospectors. I pulled over, found the nearest shade, and asked, "How far is Quartzite?"

"It just so happens, this is Quartzite. We sell here for three months of the year to the snowbirds. Otherwise, it's just lizards and scorpions." They were a collection of wholesalers and low-end rock, mineral, and rough stone vendors.

I rummaged around for a half hour and noticed a box of milky quartz. They were the size of a fist, shaped like a pyramid with spectacular cathedral-like formations graduating to a point. I was immediately attracted to them. I asked how much. They were five dollars a pound. We negotiated and settled on a box of forty good ones for fifty dollars. When I showed them to Paul, he offered me a table outside his trailer. I was setting out my cathedrals when a couple stopped, picked one up, and asked, "How much?" Out of my mouth came, "Fifty dollars." They handed over the money and said they were from California, where this would normally go for two hundred dollars. That day, I sold ten pieces at fifty dollars each and saw Paul crack a smile. I sold the rest in the next few days.

The show started, attended by 1,200 vendors. It was overwhelming. I saw a full-size adult mammoth skeleton for sale at one million dollars. I saw crystal balls four feet in diameter. There were pink, blue, and blood-red diamonds, and pearls of all shapes and sizes. There was an amethyst cave from Brazil I could walk into, twice my size and fifteen feet wide. The interior was covered with thousands of perfect crystals. All the wonders of the gem and mineral world were represented here in profusion. I saw four Japanese men who looked totally out of place, dressed in smart business suits, carrying black leather briefcases, entering a prestigious hotel. Two black limos magically appeared, precisely as they exited, to whisk them away. Paul explained that they come every year to buy diamonds for something between a hundred and a hundred and fifty million dollars.

In contrast, an unkempt man in dusty, torn clothing went into an office that assesses the value of a gem or mineral. He came out running, screaming, and shouting that he had found a totally new unclassified mineral. We all crowded around him. "I've got to call my grandmother," he said. We followed him to a telephone booth (no cell phones then). I was right there as he cried and asked his grandmother what he should name the new find. She obviously couldn't think of anything. "I'm going to name it after you!" He rushed back into the office and returned waving a certificate of authenticity, declaring, "I discovered a new rock, I discovered a new rock!" as he ran out of sight.

I took my leave of Paul, and before returning to New Mexico, I drove out into the desert away from the glare of the city. I made my bed on the roof of my van under the starry sky of a billion points of twinkling lights. They felt so close. Just as I had done when I was a child, I reached up to touch them before falling asleep.

I Met Jenny, My Wife-to-Be

I had lived in New Mexico for six years when I met Jenny, my wife-to-be. She had grown up in Tierra Amarilla, a small predominantly Spanish-speaking Northern New Mexican town. I met her on the campus of the University of New Mexico where she was studying for her bachelor's degree in fine arts. We had known each other as friends for years before our spark began to ignite into a flame. At the time, she had become a massage therapist and was living in Santa Fe. I had only been out of my last relationship for a few months. After that one, I was seriously thinking of becoming a monk. So I felt the need to detox before even considering starting another relationship. I went on a forty-day cleanse of fresh juices, herbal teas, and broths. I had fasted many times before, but this was one of the longest. There is a discipline in the process of fasting which can create clarity. My feelings for Jenny were deep, and I was ready to take on the challenge of love. For me, Jenny was a mystery woman. She seemed to know about being close to the earth.

One evening, Jenny told me that it was the time of year to harvest wild sage. Local Native Americans had used sage for time immemorial in their sacred ceremonies and rites. It was tied into bundles and lit, the flame extinguished, and the smoke used for cleansing and healing. She asked me to come with her to gather it in the far north of the state. I felt I was being included in something very special and said I would really like that.

The next day, before the sun rose, we set off in the direction of Taos. The New Mexico landscape at dawn was breathtaking, with its red/

ochre earth and tribes of evergreen piñon trees huddled together to share a common source of precious water. We passed mountains, mesas, ancient lava beds, and canyons. Colors and ever-changing shadows painted magic on the unlimited canvases of our minds. Beyond Taos, Jenny turned off the highway onto a paved road that soon turned to dust and gravel, then bumpy with rocks. We drove at a snail's pace until it was impossible to go farther without damage to the car. We stepped out, I looked around, and there we were—nowhere and yet everywhere.

She had been here a few times before and began to stride as though she were on her way to an important meeting. The uneven ground sloped uphill, and prickly plants did not alter the rhythm of her pace. I followed much more slowly, choosing my footsteps carefully. We were both carrying backpacks and bottles of water, which gave me the feeling of being on a safari. I could have been on the plains of an African expanse soon to meet up with exotic animals or in the foothills of the Himalayas on the way to an ancient temple. Only when Jenny stopped and declared that we had arrived did I get my monkey mind to rest.

Where we were standing appeared to me to be no different than any of the other spots. I looked around and could see the horizon in three directions. Jenny guided us to what she called the grandmother bush. It was about the size of six people crouching, each thin stem bearing light, minty green, silvery, fuzzy leaves, stretched out from the density of its interior. Jenny silently prayed, and I closed my eyes. For the first time, I heard the silence. When she finished praying, she explained that she had just asked for and received permission to pick and told me that one should never take from the grandmother.

She started to gently break off stems from nearby bushes and put them in her backpack, indicating that I do the same, all the while maintaining silence. I followed her lead. The aroma of the sage encompassed me, and I was in the most holy place a person could hope to be. When it was time to leave, I had the distinct feeling that I was being called to stay.

Who really knows how the decision is made to bond with another person for life. Could it have been this still, quiet, and peaceful sharing, and the invitation to venture out into the embrace of nature to pick wild sage with a wild woman on a sunny day in the Land of Enchantment?

Encounters of the Mystical Kind

I am an incurable believer in synchronicity. My whole life has been permeated with unexplained experiences—things that have no logical, rational explanation. Some may call them coincidence, a trick of the mind. Maybe so, but I'd like to invite your opinion on a case in point.

Still in the beginning of our relationship, Jenny invited me to visit her in Santa Fe. I had arrived early. She was at work doing massage at 10,000 Waves, a wonderful Japanese spa in the foothills ten minutes outside of town. So I waited for her in the large, empty, unpaved parking area outside the place where she was house-sitting. It was a historic area of town with restored adobe houses painted in all shades of ochre in the hues of the surrounding mesas. All edges were sculpted round, and walls were decorated with inset Mexican tiles. The roofs were supported with *vigas*, horizontal seasoned tree trunks that extended a foot out from the exterior. As the sun arched across the sky, their shadows traced a pattern, marking the passing of time. I found a low wall to sit on, shaded by a struggling almond tree. It was one of those days when the sky was so perfectly blue you couldn't imagine where it started or ended.

Suddenly a rickety, rusty old bus was heading toward me, kicking up dust. It screeched to a stop. The bus was hand-painted orange, and all the windows had drawn, mismatched curtains. As the dust settled, the driver and the person in the front passenger seat stepped out and looked around as if I wasn't there. It was obvious they were lost. Both men were dark enough to be from South America. My mind couldn't grasp this dramatic shift of reality, so I froze, stayed where I was, and watched the scene unfold.

Seeing me, the driver smiled. He stretched and came over and introduced himself and his assistant. We shook hands, and I exhaled. In the next few minutes, he explained that he was driving very important people from the southernmost tip of Argentina to the Arctic Circle in Canada, stopping on the way at special places. The assistant went back to the bus, opened the door, and addressed the people inside. He spoke in a language that I had never ever heard before. He lowered a step in front of the door and out of the darkness appeared the beautiful weathered face of an aged woman. She was followed by seven more women of her generation.

They were all wearing multilayered hand-woven, hand-dyed cotton dresses, one on top of the other. Each outfit was unique and embroidered with brilliant colors. Their blouses were plain and earth-toned, decorated with many mother-of-pearl buttons, topped by waistcoats depicting animal figures, some familiar and some not. Over this they wore a plain shawl that shifted with every movement, revealing bangles, bracelets, and rings of silver glinting in the light.

The driver rolled out a wide canvas shade from above the door while the assistant brought out small child-sized stools for all the women to sit on. Aged goat cheese, pickled cactus, small tomatoes, onion and garlic, crusty bread, herbs, and beer were set out on a table. I was signaled by the driver to come and sit down. Apparently, the women had invited me. I slipped down from the wall and walked over to obey the request. One of the women gestured for me to eat. I marveled that just a moment ago, I was sitting on a wall, minding my own business, and now I was sitting down with eight very old Native women, and I was surprisingly comfortable. Even though I was a total stranger to them, and they to me, it was as though we knew each other.

The driver, serving also as their interpreter, told me that these women were revered shaman healers known as the Grandmothers. They were stopping at all the power points along the spine of the American continent. At each point, they asked for forgiveness, guidance, and healing for the imbalance that humans had created. Their borders and directions were energetic, not geographic, I was told. Somehow they had managed to be immune to passport, visas, and border controls of any sort. They had decided to rest here, take some nourishment, and then head out to do their cleansing ceremony somewhere north.

I had a treasured bottle of water from the runoff of a glacier given to me by my friend Paul, who I mentioned before and who traded in fossilized ivory. He perceived that water had a spirit, and as it had been frozen for millions of years, it was the purest of pure water with a purest of pure spirit. For some reason, I had felt it necessary to put it in my backpack that morning. Just as the water had "spoken" to me to take it along, it "spoke" to me again. I had studied and practiced an

ancient ceremony and mantra from my Indian culture, and I explained
that I would like to perform this ceremony for them. As I related the
story of the water and my intention to the driver, he translated for
the Grandmothers. The Grandmothers' eyes lit up. I could see from
their expressions that they were moved, but not surprised. The driver
followed my instructions to bring a washing bowl. I took out the spirit
water and poured it in the bowl and asked the Grandmothers if they
would take off their sandals. I started to chant the healing mantra, and
one by one, I had each of the Grandmothers put their feet in the water so
I could wash them. At this point, all of time seemed to stand still. After
I finished washing their feet, I took the water and watered the roots of
the tree I had been sitting under before they came.

They must have received what was necessary, as if this was one of
the spots on their healing journey. They started to stand up, and I placed
my hands together over my heart, bowed my head, and said "Namaste"
to each one, the driver, and his assistant. I felt their blessing given, and
they drove off. As their bus, bumping and bouncing, disappeared from
view, dust still in the air, my lovely new friend, Jenny, immediately
appeared. "How are you? Sorry to keep you waiting!"

Chapter 10

Shree Ganesha the Gatekeeper, Ramani Rangan

Traveling in Magical India

Traveling in India for me is always a mind-altering experience. How could it not be? For instance, if one were to go overland, it would not be unusual to pass through at least three different regions within three hours, all with their own unique language and culture.

Jenny and I had planned a spiritual pilgrimage to seek out my ancestry and visit temples and ashrams along the way. Jenny had been more than supportive and had convinced me that this trip to the land of my parents was important and necessary, as my mother had just died and my father had passed away many years before. So it was that at fifty-five years old, I was facing my very first trip into this magical, yet scary, subcontinent of over a billion people who looked like me.

We were in Mumbai, hosted by a wonderful couple who were medical doctors and practitioners of alternative medicine. We were about to board a rickshaw on our way to Victoria Station to embark on an eighteen-hour train ride south. It was so hot that I could, at any given moment, take my finger and run it from one side of my forehead to the other and sweat would shower down as I leaned forward to execute this maneuver. For the locals, it was winter, so they wore sweaters and jackets. We were wearing light, gauzy traditional Indian cotton pants and tunics called *punjabis* that felt as though we were walking around in pajamas in public. The word *pajama*, by the way, evolved through the British colonial mispronunciation of the word *Punjabi*.

As we stepped into the street, immediately, the thousands of people going about their business crowded into our personal space. It was like a dream that gets out of hand and starts to behave like a nightmare. The exhaust from the cars and trucks added to the sense of invasion. Bicycles were everywhere, riders ranging from businessmen in suits, schoolchildren in uniform, and porters carrying loads twenty baskets high. Scooters with as many as two adults, plus their offspring, wove through the traffic mayhem. All braved the stampede, the whole while trying to avoid the wandering sacred cows. For them, it was the natural order of things. For me it was the height of chaos.

People pay good money to go on scary rides at a carnival, but that is nothing compared to riding in peak traffic in an Indian city. While in our rickshaw, other rickshaws were driving so close we could smell the perfume and aftershave of their passengers. Within a blink, that car would have gone and another taken its place, producing a different intimate look into the life of a complete stranger. As all rickshaw cabs are open, we too were also on display. Sometimes we would smile and receive a smile back, or even get waves from children. Meanwhile, our driver was careening through this pandemonium with full confidence that we would get to our destination safely. Did I mention that rickshaw taxis have only three wheels and are light enough for one person to tip over?

The Victoria train station loomed in sight, heralded by a hundred other rickshaw taxis waiting for a fare. The usual complement of holy cows grazed from a small pile of rubbish. It pained me to see plastic ingested by these companions of humanity, who, for thousands of years had been revered as a symbol of the divine bounty of nature. The Europeans and Americans had quizzed me on the illogical reason to let cows roam freely if so many people in India were starving. Why not slaughter them and eat them? I had meditated on this and independently came to the conclusion that there were very practical reasons for protecting the cows and incorporating them into the religion. A living cow produces fresh milk, which can be cultured into yoghurt, ghee, (clarified butter), and cheese. Plus, dried cow patties are an unlimited source of free fuel to cook with and keep warm, saving millions of trees. By now, most of India would have become a desert.

Avoiding the cows, our driver dropped us off at the main entrance to Mumbai's train station. I softly fought off a dozen porters trying to grab the bags out of my hands. My highly developed international hand signal for "Back off" worked, and they scurried away, using their 360 degree vision to identify the next target.

We entered a main hall that was about the size of three football fields, packed with what seemed like thousands of fellow travelers milling about. There were tens of lines, hundreds long, extending from counters with antique signs, originating from the time of Queen Victoria. Near the supporting pillars were extended families sharing a meal on a rug they had spread out. There was even a family with a goat. I began to notice the vast diversity of Indian social, religious, and ethnic groups. So many complexions, features, and physical characteristics were present. Regions could be identified by the way women wrapped their saris, wore their hair, or by the size and shade of their bindis, the red spots applied daily at the center of their forehead. Another indication of region was the way men's turbans were wrapped around their heads. Worn high, for example, they could be from Rajasthan. Some men wore Western clothing. Others wore different traditional styles, one being a long white cotton cloth wrapped around their lower body and a loose thin cotton or embroidered silk shirt, topped with a Western-style jacket. In this hub of humanity was a sampling of India's twenty-two officially recognized languages, more than a hundred distinct dialects and just as many, if not more, cultural differences, practiced for thousands of years. I may have been foreign to the land, but India was my Mother and these were my people.

It became very quickly apparent that we had no idea which line to stand in to get our tickets. Scanning the hordes, I saw a man in a uniform, and we made a beeline toward him. He spoke English and, without hesitation, took us under his wing and signaled us to follow him. He escorted us past the longest of waiting lines to the front window, addressed the clerk with authority, and secured our tickets. We thanked our savior. He responded with a gesture of, *it was nothing*. I saluted him as if he were in the army, and then we parted.

He had told us to go to platform 47 in a 113-platform station. Really, we are talking about a small city of its own. Trains were divided into three classes or more, plus a separate ladies' compartment. Also, the train would be shedding some carriages and taking on others, depending on the destination. It was not going to be straightforward. Looking for platform 47, we carried our bags up and down several flights of stairs high enough to clear the trains and walked along platforms to be met with yet more flights of stairs. We passed beggars of all ages and genders. A religious spiritual leader was followed by his disciples. They were all dressed in white robes and moved through the masses with an air of weightlessness, as if they were dancing in slow motion. The aromatic smell of spices, mixed with the heated oil from the train's mechanical parts, filled the air. So many people, so close, and yet the smell of body odor one would imagine in the heat and situation was strangely absent.

We had taken a wrong turn and were obviously lost. We were at a platform with a higher number. We set down our bags, exhausted, and took a breath. My clothes were totally soaked with perspiration. We had deliberately left early, so there was enough time, but now it was getting close, and we were getting stressed. It was then I let go. My mind stopped, and I noticed a stray dog crossing the tracks. My wife smiled at me, the kind of smile that conveys, *I am here . . . We are here.*

It was then a man dressed in a business suit, tie, shiny shoes, and a briefcase, approached us and asked very politely, "Where, please, is your destination going?"

Sensing it was safe, we showed him our tickets. After studying them, he reached out his hand and grabbed mine, signaling with the other to pick up our bags and follow him. He proceeded to lead us from the platform, up and down more stairways, along more platforms. After ten minutes, we were finally, at last, on platform 47.

He said we needed to position ourselves on the platform so when the train arrived, we would be standing in front of the door of the right carriage. We thanked him and expected him to leave, but he just stayed there. I said thank you again and that he had been so helpful, but we didn't want to keep him any longer. He waved away my statement and asked if we had water for the ride. When I answered "No," he pointed to a vendor who sold bottled water and some food stuffs, and I went to get them while he stood by relaxed, centered, and calm. About ten minutes passed while he read his paper, until we heard the first chug of the train in the background grow louder. It slowed and finally jerked to a screeching stop.

Sure enough, we were right in front of a train door. He had put away his newspaper and was already guiding us to the front so the crowds would not push in front of us. "This is the one, dear sir," he said. He addressed the guard who was blocking the door to the train. The guard looked at our tickets and, with a brief smile, ushered us up the steps and pointed out the direction for us to take once inside. "Your reservations are good. There will be no problem," said our angel in disguise. Just as he had appeared half an hour ago out of thin air, he was gone, lost, as I turned around to look for him in the crowd. At long last, we were in the train finding our compartment, only through the kindness and incredible generosity of strangers who treated us as family.

The Onion Cutter of Mahabalipuram

The train we had boarded in Mumbai took us only part of the way. We had two more trains to negotiate before we arrived in Puttaparthi to visit the ashram of Sai Baba, a guru with millions of followers. My Jenny witnessed him produce what appeared to be a manifestation of *Vibhuti*, sacred ash. He showered it on a woman next to her who asked him for a private audience. I was more impressed with the scores of free hospitals, hundreds of free medical clinics, and many free schools, kitchens, and housing for the poor that his followers had created in his name. While at his ashram, I got sick to my stomach and was grateful for the free treatment I received. The highlight for me occurred while Jenny and I were sitting in the garden. I heard a woman singing a prayer of lament that was so deep it brought me to my knees. In her song, I heard all the losses and sacrifices that women had endured over the ages. She continued for a long while, and only when she finished could I move. This was the first stop of our journey south, and we were excited for what was to come. Yet the paramount lesson I was to learn was not what I had thought India had in store for me.

We took a flight directly from Sai Baba's airport to Madras, now called Chennai, the capital of Tamil Nadu. My father was Tamil, and here we would begin the search for his family roots. His family line had always been a mystery. With several generations born in South Africa, tracing him would be like finding my way through a thick fog. The family in South Africa had no leads. Primarily, to break with the caste system, the ruling bodies of Tamil Nadu in the 1940s had decided to forbid, de facto, the passing on of surnames to the next generation. So following a complicated protocol, children could take their surname from the first name of either parent, the name of the family temple, or the name of the town they were from. Sometimes they might use the whole name, sometimes just an initial. Since this transpired after their departure, my father's family retained their surname, *Rangan*, and passed it on to successive generations. Meanwhile, those relatives who had remained were likely to have changed their name several times. How could we ever find them? I discovered through my research that the name *Rangan* was directly connected to Ranganathaswamy, an aspect of the deity Vishnu. There are many temples devoted to Ranganathaswamy. Jenny and I mapped a plan to go to the one in Srirangam, in Tiruchirappalli, stopping at other temples and sacred sites along the way.

We heard of a famous large bas-relief called Arjuna's Penance that was carved out of rock. It was in Mahabalipuram, just an hour's ride by bus from Chennai following the coast. En route, we could see beaches, empty except for fishing boats returning with their catch, released from the waters of the Bay of Bengal. We checked into a small older hotel. We soon discovered that small items were disappearing. One day we walked into the room just in time to see a cheeky monkey clambering out the window with our fruit and other trinkets in arms.

Day and night, there was a continual staccato of hammering. It was the sound of hundreds of carvers, chip, chip, chipping away on sacred statues, some fifteen feet high. The whole town was engaged in the process of sculpting stone and had been doing this for thousands of years. We spent days marveling at the temples and ancient sculptures of Nandi the bull, full-sized elephants, lions, and mythological creatures. We were just as awed as we witnessed present-time sacred sculptures, created before our very eyes.

Then one morning, while walking a dusty street leading down to the beach, passing a gauntlet of beggars with hands extended for a few coins, something extraordinary happened. There are moments in one's life when the mind blinks, and in that split second, reality presents itself, stepping away from the illusion of what we know as normal. This was such an instant. I smelled the pungent aroma of South Indian curry. It was coming from a dilapidated, weathered building. I felt a pull to go inside. The seating was arranged in long wooden tables and benches. Working men only, of all ages and shades of Indian, were packed shoulder to shoulder, talking and laughing. The large room was dark and an obvious drop in temperature made it inviting. The smiles, flashing teeth framed by dark-skinned faces, eased my sense of being where I might not belong. I waited for a signal to sit, but where?

Set in front of each person was a large banana leaf acting as a plate. A man stripped to the waist, barefoot, and wearing only a loincloth passed between the tables with a pot of cooked lentils and spooned-out portions. Small hills of dry potato pea curry, mixed vegetables, chickpea masala, white rice, two kinds of spicy pickles, and soft yogurt were already in the process of being consumed. Whole wheat chapatis were torn into pieces and served as a scoop. The only other utensils in evidence were the fingers of the right hand, used to make the delivery to the mouth.

I had seated myself when, for no apparent reason, I had an urge to turn toward the door. There I saw a few inches of the back of a man sitting just outside on a flattened cushion. I had not noticed him as I walked in. My banana leaf was being filled, and anticipation brought me back to my taste buds. I paid about one dollar fifty cents for all that I could eat, and with the hum of the heat from the hot chilies in my mouth, I walked outside.

The man was still sitting there, and I felt a magnetic impulse to look closely. Not wanting to stand over him, I walked across the street under a shade tree. I started to watch him, his actions hypnotizing me. He was using his right hand out of my line of sight in a repetitive rhythm, and I could see the movement register in his body. I then saw a boy come from what must have been the kitchen, carrying a large empty stainless steel bowl. He passed the bowl to the man, and the man exchanged it for a full one. It was precisely then I caught a glimpse of what he was holding in his left hand. It was an onion. I realized the bowl was full of onions, all sliced like petals plucked from a great flower.

I had to return the next day. When I arrived, the man was not there. This time the server signaled to me in a matter-of-fact way to go to a water tap and wash my hands and pointed to a place for me to sit. I complied as if he was an officer in the army and I was an ordinary enlisted soldier. The banana leaf was placed before me, and a cart was pushed by with pots filled with the simple, fragrant, tasty fare of the day. I looked around to see what everyone was doing, to follow their lead, and remembered to use only my right hand. Even though I looked like an

Indian, everyone knew I was a foreigner. Yet before long, I was just one of the crew of a ship that never sails. A man next to me demonstrated that by folding the banana leaf, I was signaling that I was finished.

As I went to pay, I saw that the man who was cutting the onions had returned. I walked out into the thirty-degree rise in temperature and immediately began to sweat profusely. I sought shade on the other side of the street as before, sitting on a rock. I was facing the onion man. I wondered how he could be in the direct sun all day. He was very dark, so much so that just the slightest movement of his face reflected back a deep blue of his near-black complexion. His hair was speckled with gray yet was as thick as a young man's. His back was against the wall, and his knees were bent apart, with his soles touching, allowing him to hold a one-inch-thick by four-inch-wide wooden board between the joints of his big toes at one end and against his chest at the other. The one-inch side faced forward and served as the cutting surface. The onion man reached down with his left hand, flowing into the basket by his side, and magically manifested a symbol of the universe, disguised as an onion. Then he sliced, peeled, and freed it from its outer skin. Chop, chop, the well-worn knife moved up and down, creating a percussion sound like a professional drummer. Sharp as a razor, it danced again and again as he reached, sliced, chopped, his body one with his instrument.

I refocused my mind's eye and imagined that his hand was moving without holding the knife and saw a temple dancer's gesture of a sacred mudra, where each position of the fingers and the wrist denoted a desire for enlightenment. This onion was not only being sliced to fill stomachs, but somehow to sustain the spirit, heal the wounds, and fill the gaps of whatever unspoken suffering was present in the room. The onion man looked up just for a second, and I saw a contented man, a balanced man, a complete man, a man who had no question or longing for answers. I felt an impact as if I had eyes inside my head, and they were forced for the first time to open to the blinding of daylight.

Over many years, I had visited gurus, yogis, healers, and wise men and women. Those who have proclaimed that they know and we should buy their book and in the reading and practice of their book, we might know too. At that very moment, he was it, all that they profess. There wasn't anything I could ask him, and I knew this, and it was good. I became silent inside. He appeared before me in the mask costume of a "simple" onion cutter in the sea of India's humanity, yet really, he was the Onion Cutter. If there were such a thing as reincarnation, could it be possible that in his last life he was a great holy man or woman who walked the earth as a healer of souls? Now in his last life, in this worldly soup, could he, at any time, leave and ascend to merge with the infinite? Yet here he was, with just the power of his presence, flooding me with nothing tangible but the awareness that *We are all onion cutters of some sort.*

It seems we are either being peeled by life or we are peeling life. The question for me has become, in my lifetime, will I ever be as fine an onion cutter as the Onion Cutter of Mahabalipuram?

Shiva's Procession

Leaving Mahabalipuram, we took a local bus to a main terminal. We were greeted by the smell of noxious diesel fumes and hundreds of buses. The destination names for each bus were written in Hindi, plus a translation in Tamil and other South Indian languages. None of them were written with English characters, and thus we had no clue where they were going. So Jenny went around to each bus, shouting over the cacophony of people and engines, "Chidambaram? Chidambaram? Chidambaram?" We were directed from one bus to another until after many tries, we finally found the right one. It turned out that the bus we were on was not direct. We actually had to change buses again to an even slower one, which stopped at every village and made many detours. This bus was close to antique with suspension repaired way past its normal life span. Standing room only, with bump on top of bump and much shake, rattle, and roll, we took the slow, scenic route to arrive at our final destination—a temple dedicated to Shiva.

We had our first glimpse of the temple from the balcony of our hotel room. The next day, as we stood before it, we were overwhelmed. It was magnificent. The main entry was through a four-sided tower at least seven stories tall, richly decorated with hundreds of brightly painted, colorful figures derived from Hindu religion and mythology. We found ourselves in a stone courtyard of many acres. A group of young men dressed in white were sitting in the shade. They waved us over and warmly invited us to join them. A few spoke a little English and asked the usual questions, who we were, where we were from, and why we were in India. Within a few minutes, some of the young men said that I should stay, meaning that I should live there permanently. One even put his head in my lap, closed his eyes, and rested. Only in India! The spell was broken by a voice calling. They all stood up as one and ran toward the temple building. Suddenly we were on our own to investigate yet another unrecognized wonder of the world.

There was so much to see and not enough eyes to behold it all. Within the outer courtyard was the temple building, which was itself enormous. Multiple colonnades led in different directions. Their granite pillars were intricately carved. We came to another shaded courtyard where devotees could rest and gather themselves before or after making their devotions. Beyond this was a large enclosed area where our eyes had to adjust to the darkness. There were priests making puja, (prayers), classes of children studying, and a mass of the faithful seeking an answer from the invisible. Despite all this activity, there was an atmosphere of reverence, calm, and perfect sanctuary. Everything became sacred. Here was a spiritual anarchy. People made offerings and performed rituals without external direction. The priest appeared to be more like a facilitator or advisor, providing ceremony or blessings on request, but each person allowed themselves direct communication with the divine.

We hung out for a bit, soaking up the vibrant peace, and we were about to leave when one of the young men we had met in the beginning came running up to us. He explained that this was a very important day where the statue of the Lord Shiva had to be wheeled around the temple in his chariot, and that he could not find enough priests to help him. He asked us to help, and we agreed.

We were led to an enclosure where the chariot was being stored behind a large wooden gate. It was huge and appeared to be many hundreds of years old. The wheels alone were about our height. The platform reached our chest. On top of this, the deity was enshrined and adorned with flowers on a massive, intricately carved wooden throne. All in all, the total height was about four times our size. Other priests joined us so we numbered about ten.

It was extremely hot as Jenny and I found a place and began to push. We were in our bare feet, as it was required that we remove our sandals when entering the temple grounds. We expected we were to circle the interior of the temple around the courtyard, but the chariot did not turn. I asked why, and the priest replied, "We push it around the outer temple walls...three times." I quickly did the math and figured it was about one mile around the whole of the exterior, about three miles all together.

When we left the temple walls, thousands of people were gathered to watch the procession. Our feet met the burning heat of midday sun on concrete, relieved only for split seconds as each foot took its turn off the ground. We pushed for about three hours. At one point, I asked if anyone who was not a priest ever pushed the Chariot. He said, "I doubt it."

I looked at Jenny and asked, "What about women?"

"No! No, definitely not!" He smiled. "First time, first time."

"How old is this tradition of pushing the deity around the temple?" I asked.

"Hundreds of years. Possibly thousands."

When we returned to the temple, it was quiet inside. No one was around. The chariot was returned to the keep, and we took leave of the priests. We then heard the distant sound of people and traced it to a doorway that opened to a huge reservoir of water called a ghat. There we found thousands of people, some in the water and some standing on terraced steps. A group of priests carried a bundle to the edge of the water. They lifted a veil, and there was the statue of the deity we had just wheeled around the temple. We witnessed as it was lowered into the water for purification. The crowd lifted their voice in celebration. We had started the day as tourists and ended the day as part of a sacred ceremony.

Temple Stories

Some say that trees were the precursors of temples. In ancient times, people would seek the shade of a tree. This tree would bear flowers, fruit, and nuts. It nourished and sustained them. So they honored it and tended it, that it might thrive and continue to give its gifts. They considered that the tree must have a beneficent spirit and began to worship it as a deity. Then slowly, over the millennium, altars were created. Some of these evolved into small structures, gradually increasing in size to eventually become the elaborate temples of today.

Jenny and I had visited the Ranganathaswamy Temple in Srirangam, Tiruchirappalli, the Meenakshi Temple in Madurai, and others along the way. We noticed that there was always a revered tree within the temple courtyard. We also noticed a pattern. The entrance tower gate to each temple was impressive and gloriously decorated. Each successive gate was less ornate. As we passed through the courtyard and into the main temple building, the structures also became progressively plain. Until the inner sanctum was just bare walls and pillars, with perhaps a stone carved Yoni and/or Lingam (representative of the feminine and masculine), the resident deity, or just empty space.

On our way to one of the temples, we passed through a marketplace exploding with colorful objects for devotional practices. There were mini-deity statues, fresh fruits, and incense, and my favorite—thousands of garland necklaces, threaded together from freshly cut marigold heads. Leaving the market, we passed through the entrance gates and rested by a tree. The tree was in its own raised bed. At its base were many lit candles and bowls formed from banana leaves containing flowers, fruit, folded prayers, and other offerings. Some women were on their knees praying.

We walked into the coolness of the temple complex. The floor was polished marble with geometric patterns that extended many hundreds of feet. The ceiling was festooned with bright inlay and supported by multitudes of matching carved columns. Gentle breezes, created by the design of the halls and walkways, eased our path. Reaching the next open space, we were met with crowds of devotees and priests doing mantra and puja over fires burning in small copper upturned pyramid-shaped vessels with flat bottoms. The smell of burning incense and ghee filled the air. At the end of the hall, to my amazement, stood the largest elephant I had ever seen. It was wearing a garland, and it bore the mark of Shiva between its eyes—three horizontal lines painted in white. People were standing in a queue. I was told this was "very special, very special," so I joined in. When it was my turn, I found myself looking straight up to this giant of a creature. It lifted its trunk and placed it on my forehead. I received the most humongous wet kiss ever. A blessing!

As we approached the inner sanctum, a priest stopped us and very respectfully informed us that only Hindu men could go in and that I had to strip to the waist. I looked at Jenny, and she nodded and acknowledged that only I could enter. I took off my shirt and handed it to her. She smiled, and I walked through the darkened passageway.

I could see light coming from an opening ahead and walked toward it. I came out into a space about five paces wide that was open to the sky and surrounded a central sanctum. On each side of the entrance to the sanctum were identical figures of a goddess carved in stone. On seeing them, I felt a sharp, piercing, yet soft pain in my heart. Tears surged from my eyes. I was holding myself up, stopping myself from falling to the ground. I could not move. Then I was flooded with streams of images and impressions of belonging to a long, long line of ancestral connection to India. It was as if I had always been of this bloodline. Faces and figures flashed by in seconds, clear and sharp. Whole lifetimes passed by like waves splashing up on the shore. As quickly as it had come, it disappeared, along with the uncontrollable flow of tears. I could move again, despite the ache in my stomach.

Now I could walk through the entrance and found myself in a passageway that got narrower and narrower, spiraling toward the center. At one point, it was so narrow I had to angle my body toward the wall to continue. I was in pitch black, arms tucked into my sides, with my hands feeling the wall. I let go of fear and continued. I then began to recognize the faint, sweet smell of burning ghee. I stepped foot length to foot length. A flicker of light in front of me patterned the rough side of one of the walls, and I heard a male voice chanting.

I emerged into a small round room. In the center was a large, human-sized, carved stone lingam. It was plain and dome-shaped on top, tapering out at its base into a shallow trough. There a priest was repeating a mantra. As he finished each round, he would chant *Svaha*, (So Be It), and pour a little of the ghee on the lingam. He did not look up at me, just kept chanting and making the offering. I looked around the room and saw that the whole of the inner temple I was standing in had been carved from one rock. As the fire played its game of changing shadows, I realized that I recognized the mantra, and it was one of the few I knew by heart. It had been taught to me many years ago in Denmark, by a visiting devotee of *Agnihotra*, the ancient fire ceremony. I joined the priest for a few minutes in chanting, not knowing if it was appropriate, but it seemed natural.

When I felt it was time to go, I retraced my steps and emerged with a sense that a door that had been closed was now open. To what I didn't know. I was pleased to see Jenny. From her expression, I looked different. She noticed I was wearing a single red thread hanging from my left shoulder and crossing over to the right side at my hip. I had no idea how it got there. I put on my shirt, and we continued our earthly journey.

At the Tip of India

We had arrived in Kanyakumari at the southern tip of India where the Arabian Sea, the Bay of Bengal, and the Indian Ocean meet. How could there be an end to India? Yet there it was. Looking out on the confluence of these three bodies of water stood a quiet memorial to Mahatma Gandhi, painted in soft pastel colors. There we paid homage to the humble man who motivated millions to free India from tyranny. His brave trust in the power of nonviolence has inspired and will continue to motivate generations to come.

We saw many things in Kanyakumari, but the most puzzling and surprising, yet so India, was a temple we visited that was dedicated to Lord Hanuman, the monkey god. The temple was magnificent. We had seen a figure of Lord Ganesh, the elephant god, at the entrance to every temple and Hindu home we had entered, but on the main gate of this temple, he was nowhere to be found.

It was dark inside with many chambers. In the main chamber was an eighteen-foot statue of Hanuman. He was painted all blue, but that was not the thing that stopped me in my tracks. It was the fact that his long tail was coming out of the center of his forehead, stemming from what is known in the West as the pineal gland. In yogic tradition, it is called the third eye, with the ability, when awakened, to see beyond what we perceive as material reality. What could this mean?

Then I started to notice more and more unusual things in this temple—too many to mention. We left through a designated exit, which had an unusually insignificant appearance. I had an intuitive impulse to look back. There on the exit arch, above the door, was the statue of Lord Ganesh. Not at the entrance, but at the exit.

The whole place seemed to be back to front. Like a puzzle, a riddle made especially for us to ask a question. But what question? What were so many funny things doing in a sacred temple at the southernmost end of the mainland of India? My mind loves things that are baffling, but for the meanwhile, I let it rest. Later, it came to me that perhaps, because it is the last temple on the subcontinent of India and the farthest from the sacred Himalayas, it would be perceived as the end of a journey. However, the end is also the beginning. Perhaps the implication is that the journey is un-ending until we transcend the five-sense mind construct to a higher level of perception.

We had arrived at our hotel very early in the morning, and there was a twenty-four-hour stay. We would have to leave our hotel at the same time or pay for another day. So the next morning, we left while it was still dark and there was a couple hours before our train would depart. We decided to go to the beach and watch the sunrise.

We thought we would be the only ones there, but as we passed the last row of houses, in front of us were gathered hundreds of people. It was so quiet. Not a word or movement broke the silence. It was as if we, unknowingly, had walked into the most sacred temple on earth. There were many families with small children, couples, and singles, women with flowers in their hair, men wearing garlands. All standing and facing east, looking beyond the waves to the place where the ocean meets the sky.

The reverence projected from this multitude of pilgrims entered my whole being. We slowly found the perfect spot and waited. In front of us was a small rock island with a memorial dedicated to one of India's most revered saints—Vivekananda. The first hue of light gently rose on the horizon. Not a sound, not a murmur from the hundreds. Open palms were brought together, thumbs touching the center of chests. Children, seeing this, did the same. The muted sound of waves breaking on the rocks below held the space for nature to sing her song. Then the first piercing sliver of the sun reached out to us and bathed our faces in gold. I felt as though we were all transfixed. From this burden of a world of time and space, we entered together an eternal moment of transfiguration—a place that is our true home, a sanctuary of pure love.

When the sun was fully free from its horizon, then and only then did people begin to whisper to each other quietly, as one would early in the morning. Children and elders were tended to as many started to depart, having received the blessings bestowed. Others, like us, stayed a little longer, to adjust, hold the space, and witness the start of the passage of the solar arc across the heavens. The richness of the experience lingered long after Jenny and I left to continue on our pilgrimage.

The Elephant Rampage, Thirty Elephants, Sir!

We were in Varkala, a coastal town in Kerala, resting from travel for a few weeks. We had been told that there was going to be a big festival with a procession and thirty elephants. Usually, thirty meant three, so we were skeptical.

It was early evening, and the sun had gone down. We arrived at the outskirts of the celebration and were met with rows and rows of colored electric lights, strung from everywhere possible. Thousands of joyful devotees carried lit torches or offerings of small arrangements of flowers, fruit, coins, and ghee candles. We watched as men and women, ten across, holding banners and flags with sacred motifs, paraded before us. We felt the heat of the torches, and the air was permeated with an earthy smell of incense and a distinct tone of animal.

It was then I saw the biggest elephant I had ever seen, even larger than the one who blessed me in the temple. It wore an elaborate face mask and a crown of gold. Its ears were adorned with colorful symbols, and it was draped with a royal red fabric, fringed with golden tassels. Its tusks were shortened and capped with ornate silver. Riding on top was a man dressed in traditional costume with a lavishly decorated turban wound tall. He was wearing a long coat, fit for the wealthiest raja, completed with sequined shoes with toes that dramatically turned up to a point. If that weren't enough, this lumbering giant was followed by another, equally enormous, equally adorned, but uniquely decorated. Their immense presence made me feel fragile and small. Then came a float bearing a statue of Shiva. There was also a float for Hanuman. Children followed, boys dressed as Shiva or Krishna and girls as Parvati or Radha. Interspersed between the floats were elephant after elephant. In this case, there actually were thirty elephants, possibly more!

The head of the procession had passed and was now turning on to another road. One of the elephants refused to make the turn, started to protest and trumpet. Other elephants picked up the call and began to panic, and mahouts (riders) lost control. Within seconds, masses of people were running, shoving, and pushing in our direction, with an elephant stampeding close behind. The earth shook. There was a mayhem of sound with frantic screaming and the terrifying trumpeting of elephants responding to each other. The people around us were looking for a place to hide. Some ran into what they thought was the safety of their homes, and our eyes met as they looked out from their windows. It occurred to me that the houses were so flimsy that if an elephant charged in their direction, they could be crushed like a paper bag.

It was happening so fast that I did not see where to run. By now, the first elephant was close, and I could literally see the whites of its eyes. Its trunk was raised, head was lowered, and ears pinned back. It was clear we were in mortal danger. We were standing under arches with supporting columns as wide as a person. I grabbed hold of Jenny, and we hid behind the columns. Terror was all around. Dust billowed up, and the columns reverberated as this formidable entity had its taste of freedom and stormed by. Soon we saw the coast was clear and, as one unit, made our getaway. I hoped the elephants had some peace, stillness, and quiet before they were recaptured.

The Rangans of Mysore

From the time of my childhood, if my father thought I was showing any sign of weakness, he would say, "You are a Rangan. Never forget, you are a Rangan. What are you?"

The answer would have to be "Rangan." Being a stranger in a strange land with no Indians around, I had no clue what that meant, but I had the impression it entailed certain responsibilities others didn't have.

Much later on, when I was trying to make sense of my life, an Indian man in a business suit sat in line to get an intuitive consultation from me. When it was his turn, he opened his briefcase and told me he had studied my name, and it meant, "Light and Sound." Taking just one minute of my time, he packed up and left and I never saw him again. This prompted my research into the name, "Rangan." I found out that the name was incorporated into many Sanskrit titles in Hinduism. This is how I discovered the Ranganathaswamy temples in India.

When we were at the temple in Srirangam, Tiruchirappalli, I saw the image of Vishnu as Ranganatha. In the Hindu cosmology, Vishnu is one of the three primary deities. He sustains and preserves the order and harmony of the universe. Brahma creates, and Shiva destroys. In Vishnu's aspect as Ranganatha, he is reclining in a state of perfect stillness on the coiled body of the snake god Adisesha, with its seven serpent heads hovering over him like a canopy.

I had studied *Yoga Nidra*, "the Sleep of the Yogi." At the moment before sleep, everything falls away—time and space and the sum of one's history and memory. At that instant, a corridor opens up that leads to the core of beingness. This is also true at the moment of death. *Yoga Nidra* is the practice of expanding this moment and creating a direct link, consciously, with your true nature. I sensed that Vishnu as Ranganatha was in a perpetual state of *Yoga Nidra*. Perhaps we are being invited through this manifestation of Vishnu to join him in a pure state of awareness, where moksha, liberation from karma and rebirth, is found.

It turns out that there are many Ranganathaswamy temples. Leaving Varkala in Kerala, we took a trip on a simple boat through the backwaters, where we harvested spices and stopped at Amma's ashram, a guru referred to as the Hugging Mother. We saw the Jewish synagogue and the Chinese fishing nets in Kochi. Now we were in Mysore, in Karnataka.

If Mahabalipuram is the place to find stone carving, Mysore is the place to find everything carved in wood. It is a royal city with many palaces. The Maharaja and family still reside there, though their ruling days are long gone. Come to find there is also a Ranganathaswamy temple nearby.

We arrived on a bright day and checked into a hotel that overlooked a central square, also home to hundreds of parrots who rose and circled in the sky like a cloud of vibrating perfect green. Next day, we got up early, and with our trusty map and the help of a rickshaw driver, we ventured out to find the Ranganathaswamy temple.

It was built on the first island upstream on the Kaveri River, which could be reached by crossing a bridge from the mainland. Inside the temple was a man standing by himself, bare chested, dressed in a dhoti, a simple length of cotton sheet wrapped and tied at the waist covering the lower body. Jenny and I told him my name, and that I had come to India on a quest to find my roots. He said that his name was Rangan too, and we studied each other for a few seconds. He added that he would like to introduce us to his family, but he was in the middle of his duties and asked if we could come back in a while.

When we returned, he took us to his home on the temple grounds, where we were met by his wife, several grown offspring, his sister, and her family. One of his daughters had a good command of English. She was shy but very welcoming. She introduced us all and translated for me as I told my story. They listened to me with attention and interest. We were offered tea, fruit, and cake. The question of my surname and theirs being the same was pondered, and we came to the consensus that there was a possibility we were related.

Of course, we had our picture taken, and we took theirs. The daughter who spoke English spent time talking with Jenny, fascinated by this woman from another world. I listened in as she shared personal details of her life.

When it was time to go, we took our leave with warmth and gratitude. Crossing back over the bridge to the mainland, I reflected that my father had never been to India. This journey was for both of us.

Dorothy and the Fig Tree

"Dorothy, Dorothy."

"Coming, Grandma."

This is how my mother would start the story she had related to me hundreds of times. My mother loved to tell the stories of her childhood, especially about when she went to stay with her grandmother in the country. Within a few moments of starting her story, she would be transported there. Her face and body would express and animate every word as if it were all happening for the first time. With eyes looking to a place outside the four walls of the room, she would continue. I was never tired of listening to her. It was our world, and I didn't have to share it with anyone.

"Have you been a naughty girl?"

"No, Grandma!"

"I told you not to climb the fig tree."

"I didn't." My mother would frown, mimicking her grandma's expression.

"You know your grandfather has no teeth, and those figs are the only fruit he can eat."

"Yes, Grandma!"

"I was a very, very bad girl. Wicked," she confessed. "I would wait till no one was watching and look for the ripest fig and climb the tree and steal it. Even more wicked, when my grandma saw that the fig was gone, she would ask me, 'Did you take it, Dorothy?' And I would say, 'No, Grandma!' And blame it on the servant boy. He would get a few slaps as he was denying he knew anything about it. I was really very bad," she would add.

The image of her stealing a fig from the tree was imprinted on my mind. Now here I was, in India, planning to find the place she talked about so many times. All I had to go on was that her grandfather was a Presbyterian pastor of the diocese of Malegaon in Maharashtra in the early 1900s. They lived in a house on the grounds of the church, and her grandmother was the only midwife for the area. That was it.

Jenny and I found Malegaon on the map. The first leg of our journey took us to a hotel where we stayed overnight and continued by bus the next day.

My mother had described Malegaon as a collection of houses around the church, surrounded by many small villages. As we passed the sign announcing we were close, I saw hundreds of houses and shops. Then there were factories and the haze of pollution and more houses. The bus entered a well-used terminal station and stopped. Surely, this wasn't Malegaon.

We got out and looked around, bewildered. My hopes were crushed. I said to Jenny, "It's not here. I think we won't find it."

She faced me, looked into my eyes, and said, "Don't give up. We will find it."

In front of us were many motorized rickshaw taxis and their drivers standing in a group talking. I approached them and managed to speak to one and explain my mission. He said there were no churches in Malegaon. He translated for his fellow drivers, and they all agreed. We went inside the station and looked for the station master with the intention of finding out when we could take the next bus for our return.

The station master was in his office with five other men. He spoke very good English. This prompted me to tell him my story and mention my grandfather and the church. "A church in Malegaon... no church... mosque, yes!" He translated for the other men, and they were all engaged in a buzz of enquiry, seeking in their minds for a clue. A few seconds went by, and one of the men exclaimed something, which was related to us by the station master. "Yes, there is a church! A Christian family has been living there for many, many years." Their faces were lit up and showed a genuine excitement at being able to help me in my quest.

The station master walked with us out to the rickshaws and instructed a driver where to take us. He told him to wait while we were inside and return us to the station. He negotiated a price and told us how much we should pay and then bid us a warm farewell. We expressed our immense gratitude.

With little time to settle into our seats, we were off at a challenging speed. Weaving in and out of traffic toward the outskirts of town on a dirt road, we came to a twelve-foot-tall chain-link fence gate with a cement frame and walls on both sides extending the length of the block. Our driver jumped out and called for someone to come. A man appeared with other members of his family behind him of all ages and both genders. They looked at us, puzzled. The driver began to explain. The man addressed us in clear, gentle, broken English. He said, "I don't know, but you have come a long way. Please, please come in." He opened the gate and gestured for us to enter.

We were escorted past the church and into their house, where we were invited to sit down and the family was introduced to us. Tea and biscuits were offered as I told my mother's history and the details she had given me about the church and her grandparents. He and his wife seemed to be the only English speakers. They said there had been a large Christian community in the area, but slowly, over a long period of time, they had left. "We are the last Christians here," he stated with a soft smile. They said they had no recollection of my grandfather or of the name *Parke*. It would have been at least sixty years ago, and their records did not go that far back.

My mother's story flashed in my mind, and suddenly, I remembered. "My mother always talked about a fig tree and how she would steal from it."

"There are no fig trees here," the gentleman said. Then his daughter whispered in his ear. He said, "She says there is a tree in the courtyard." The whole family accompanied us as we were led outside to a dusty open space. The daughter pointed to the saddest, weakest tree. Its trunk was thinner than my wrist, with a few living branches that had some lonely leaves. Jenny and I at the same time thought to look at the shape of the leaves. "They are fig leaves," I declared. Jenny agreed. "This is a fig tree." It was not flourishing as my mother had described, but here it was. "What are the chances that there is another Christian church with another fig tree in Malegaon?" I asked the couple.

They were amazed and said, "None!"

I asked Jenny to take a picture of me with the tree and a few with the family, just to prove it was real. I was overcome by a flood of feelings too difficult to describe. They asked us if we would like to stay the night. It was sincerely offered, but I declined. I was overwhelmed and needed some time to adjust to what had just happened.

We left, feeling connected to this wonderful family. I can imagine that every time they went out in the backyard, they would think of us. Finally arriving back at our hotel and thanking Jenny for all her encouragement, I lay down and thought just before falling asleep, *My mum would be proud of her son.*

Fanuswalla Buildings

We had been in India for three months, and it was time for us to return home. So much had happened—amazing things, challenging things, and heartfelt moments. There was one more thing I needed to complete, and that was to find Fanuswalla Buildings. This was where my mother grew up with her father, her mother, and her siblings in the 1930s. It was in a poor area of Mumbai, a few steps up from a slum. She left in 1937, at a time when the population of the city was 1.5 million. It was now 1997 and had grown to 10 million. This was going to be like looking for a particular needle in a hill of needles in a giant stack of hay. The name of the building was never spelled out, so I had only a phonetic rendering. My mother had mentioned that the name meant "umbrella maker," but when I looked it up in Hindi, it didn't mean that. We decided to try anyway and set our minds on finding it.

We spoke with a rickshaw driver, giving him just the name of the building complex. After much back-and-forth, he agreed to start off and drove us to an area where he suspected it might be. He stopped to ask people, shop owners, and other taxi drivers on the way. Like a good detective, he sorted out the improbable from the maybes, using his intuition. People are very helpful in India and would often rather say, "It's over there," than "I don't know."

After much zigzagging in the heat of the day, we were starting to lose hope when the driver asked a man who happened to be walking by. Yes, the name had been changed, he said, and that was why we couldn't find it. He gave us directions, and after a few minutes, the driver stopped outside of a run-down community complex. Lettering on a stone pillar declared, "Chatriwalla Buildings," the new name.

Jenny and I stepped out of the rickshaw and stood for a few moments to gather ourselves. We walked through double iron gates, like the ones my mother had described. Over the decades, the humidity, hot weather, and the annual monsoon had refashioned the two-story, mostly wooden structures, so they looked as though they had fallen into partial ruin. We saw that there were a few children playing in the courtyard. I approached the eldest and told him my family, the Parkes, had lived there many years ago. He must have sent one of the younger children to fetch someone, because within less than a minute, a woman came running, calling out my cousin's name. She looked at my fifty-six-year-old face and, with hope in her eyes, repeated his name. I told her I wasn't him—I was his cousin. She showed a fleeting moment of disappointment, then smiled and welcomed us.

My mother and her middle sister, my Auntie Irene, were the first to leave India. Then in 1954, her two brothers immigrated and came to stay with us in England. Her father retired and arrived a few years after. The last to come was my cousin, who was thirteen at the time.

I told the woman, "My mother was Dorothy." Her eyes watered, and she told me she had been a child when my mother left, but she remembered her. She had heard many stories from her father about my family. She pointed out the apartment they lived in. It was the building in front of us on the second floor. She shared some stories of my cousin, of my grandfather, and the death of his wife, Tara, my grandmother. She became quiet and then showed us where my mother's youngest sister had jumped to her death from the wooden railings. She conveyed how sorry she was.

Then her expression changed, and her body softened. She told us that before and during the Second World War, there was a scarcity of food, and all the families in the complex were hungry. When my mother and her sister were working in Europe, they sent money back to my grandfather. My grandfather, in turn, bought sacks of rice, lentils, beans, and other provisions, not only for our family, but for all the families in all the buildings for many years. She seemed proud to tell me of my grandfather and the goodness of his heart. He had saved so many people's lives. The people of Fanuswalla Buildings were sad when he immigrated.

I was not prepared for this story. The grandfather I knew who came to live with us never mentioned this, but here was a witness to his generosity. This put me in mind of my mother's generosity. When we had so very little ourselves, she opened our house to poverty-stricken families in our Irish neighborhood. Their children would come several times a week to have their only solid meal at our table. At one point, there was a boy who stayed with us for a whole year. Also, my father told me, his family would take whatever was left over from their harvest on their farm in South Africa and leave it outside the front door for travelers to feed themselves. I felt an appreciation for the values I had inherited from both my mother and my father's family line.

I was so moved and grateful that we had found this solid, verifiable link to my mother's past. We shared our good-byes with this wonderful neighbor of our family, she went back in her house, and we turned to leave, but not before taking a picture of the sign that would remind us we had found Fanuswalla Buildings.

Chapter 11

Sacred Vision Inside, Ramani Rangan

India Calls Again

It was November 2007, my second trip to India. This time, I needed to be by myself. The first time I went to find my ancestral roots, this time I was here to find my spiritual connection with India, something that had been missing for the sixty-six years I'd been on planet Earth. I had heard of Rishikesh, a sacred city famous for its temples, hundreds of ashrams, and yoga and Vedic schools.

I arrived in New Delhi to find overwhelming pollution from the burning fires of a recent festival, Diwali. The air cleared the next morning, and I got a deal to tour the Golden Triangle—a three-day trip exploring sites in Delhi, the Taj Mahal in Agra, and a huge fortress in Rajasthan, with a final destination of Rishikesh. I was at breakfast at my hotel in Rishikesh, and I asked the waiter if he could recommend an ashram. He pointed to another waiter and said, "Speak to him." I repeated my request, and he suggested his guru. I agreed. He said he would call ahead and tell him I would be arriving the next day. He gave me a piece of paper with the name of the ashram and the name of the town, Uttarkashi.

The next morning, I took a bus into the foothills of the Himalayas on a single-lane road with drops on one side descending hundreds of meters into the valley. Periodically, an extra width was carved out of the mountainside for traffic from the opposite direction to pass. When I dared to look, I saw a few rusty old buses below that had not survived the turns, and at one point, a more recent victim of misjudgment. Who knows what happened to the passengers.

The eight-hour journey was hair-raising, to say the least, and I arrived in the dark. I showed my piece of paper, and no one could read it because it was written in English and not in the local language. Finally, I found a rickshaw driver who recognized the name of the ashram. Totally exhausted and with no other options, I knew I had to trust. He drove for half an hour and we arrived.

Along one of the walls in the front room were young men sitting drinking tea. I stood by a desk with three rotary-dial telephones, expecting someone to greet me. After five minutes, a person entered the room and pointed for me to sit with the other men. He returned with a welcome cup of tea. Ten minutes later, a middle-aged man sat at the desk and began to make phone calls. I approached and stood before him, but he took no notice of me and was fully engaged in a long conversation. He put down that phone, took up another phone, and dialed and began another long conversation. Eventually, he put the phone down, looked up, and said, "What do you want?"

I stuttered a few words and handed him the piece of paper.

He studied it and said, "What does this mean?"

I explained the situation, and he said, "I think you are in the wrong place." Then suddenly, he recalled, "Oh, the young man from the hotel in Rishikesh. Yes, I remember the phone call."

He called out names and gave instructions. Two of the young men jumped up and left. He then went on to make another phone call. The young men came back, and he indicated that I should follow them. They took me to a small room where they had made a bed ready and showed me where to find the toilet and the sink. The room looked like a grungy prison cell, but I was glad for it, fell into bed, and lost consciousness.

I had been invited to attend a 4:00 a.m. meditation the next morning, which was not going to happen. At 9:00 a.m., the guru was going to give a darshan, a blessing. So I arrived fifteen minutes early, and there was a circle of young men and one middle-aged woman seated on chairs outside with a throne-like high-back chair left empty. The person next to me spoke very fine English, and I immediately felt relieved. Out of the house stepped a figure who walked up to the throne. I looked into his face, and I saw it was the middle-aged man who had been on the phone at the desk the night before. This was not what I was expecting. He performed the whole darshan in Sanskrit, with commentary in the local language. His only English comment was to introduce me as "Mr. Ramaniji. Maybe...Sri Ramaniji. No...Ramaniji is good." Then he just got up and left.

I turned to the young man next to me and asked if he could explain what was said. The guru, he said, was reading from the scriptures and giving his interpretation. This young man turned out to be a student working on his dissertation for a university. He shared that he was so grateful to be in this environment of peace and quiet and to be able to dedicate himself to his work without distraction. We immediately became friends.

Within a day, I began to form a positive opinion of the guru. This was a very small ashram, and the guru did most of the administration himself. He relied on a few devotees to man the kitchen, take care of the general house duties and gardens, and to help him to perform the religious rites. I found out he was organizing free hospitals, clinics, pharmacies, and schools for the local people in the villages nearby who were mostly poor but, I would add, rich in spirit. A dedicated and formidable force, this guru commanded the respect of the most influential and powerful members of the community, from which he extracted the majority of donations to the cause.

In the ten days I was there, I had very few words with the guru. He was always busy. So the student took me under his wing and one day invited me to his cabin. He embodied a sense of strength and softness, and it encouraged the same in me. I enquired about his studies. In the conversation, I found out that he lacked several books. As I was interested in the subject myself, I asked him if he would take me to his bookstore. He said there was just one in Uttarkashi specializing in academic books. So we took a rickshaw into town to that store. You could pay to read books there as well as buy them. The owner spoke English. He pointed us in the direction of our interest and found two books for us, which were key to the subject. I asked my companion if he had these books, and he said, hesitantly, "No." While he was looking at the books, I spoke with the owner and enquired about the price. I realized this was way above what my friend could afford, but easily within my means. So I purchased them. After a few protests, he received them with gratitude. We returned to the ashram, and the next day, he presented me with a hand-carved wooden pen. He said these two books were the ones he needed to complete his thesis, and they would be passed on in the same spirit to other students when he was finished with them.

One day, while I was at the ashram, the guru and all eighteen of the sannyasins, disciples, were sitting around in the back room in a circle, making an Ayurvedic recipe for rejuvenation. At dawn, they had been out in the foothills to collect these herbs and roots. In front of them were bowls where they were grinding and mixing. Half would chant the mantra, and the other half would repeat it, call and response. I sat down with them. Then I noticed the guru looking at his wristwatch. One of his disciples jumped up and turned the television on. Appearing on the small tube screen was a cricket match. Immediately, mantras were replaced with the cheers of enthusiastic fans.

I spent the rest of my time at the ashram in nature and in contemplation and meditation. I had read about the ancient healing system of Ayurveda. I wanted to experience the twenty-one-day full detox and healing for myself. In the United States, it would cost four, five, even six thousand dollars. The Indian economy would be gentler on my pocket. I asked the guru if he would recommend someone. He made a telephone call. Jotting down a name, he told me he was going into town the next day, and I could ride with him.

In the morning, before leaving, I walked down to the icy, cold, gently flowing river, Bhagirathi, which fed the Ganges below. I stepped from slippery stone to slippery stone to the middle. Sitting down with the sound of the waters surrounding me, I was drawn into meditation. A light mist rose off the water as the sun came up, the sacred river embracing me in one of its many forms. I got ready to leave, said my good-byes to the guru's devotees, and made a special last visit to the cook, who was twenty-two and as handsome and noble as any god. I jumped into the car with the guru and company, and we were off.

The Doctor of Uttarkashi

I was deposited, with all my belongings, on the outskirts of the marketplace, which was in full swing, with hundreds of vendors, and even more people going about their business, in what could only be described by my small mind as total chaos. But it wasn't chaos—it was a miracle of humanity's ability to weave their lives around each other with surprisingly few collisions.

On the scrap of paper, I had the name of the doctor. The guru had not given me an address or directions. All the shops blurred into one mass of banners, signs, shapes, merchandise, and services. After approaching a few people with the question, "Doctor?," I was pointed in the right direction and soon found myself outside his practice.

The windows were boarded up, and the door had a pull-down metal protection panel over it. There were places to sit, so I rested my one suitcase on its wheels with my backpack on top, and people watched for half an hour. In that wait time, people started to arrive. Mothers with their babies and children and two young men in their mid-twenties waited with me.

A man speeded up on his motorbike and took off his helmet, revealing his fiftyish face. He sputtered out a few sentences in the local language, which brought one of the two men to attention. He proceeded to take over the motorbike and wheeled it up the street, while the motorist unlocked the metal sliding cover to the door, opened up, and, without missing a beat, marched to the back, disappearing into a room. He sent out a command to the other young man, who immediately went into action.

I could see he would soon be busy with his patients, and I needed to act quickly. So I approached him and introduced myself as the person the guru had called him about. In his excellent English, he calmly said I could leave my baggage in the back of his office and asked me to please come back in two hours. So I went to the market with the idea of hunting down some fruit for breakfast. I was fascinated by the hill people selling their handmade wares in their traditional garb. This was the first time I had seen them. It was now time to return to the doctor's office.

He had instructed one of his assistants to sit me down and send for a cup of tea from a street vendor. I love the way that tea is made in India. The vendor always has a large pot with tea and another with sugar and milk, both on the boil. He pours a portion of each into a hand-made ceramic cup. Then, lifting it up over his head, he proceeds to pour it into another cup held three feet below in the other hand, without spilling a drop. He then alternates sides, lifting the lower cup to the top and the top to the bottom and pouring between the two once again. This he does several times, so the tea, still near boiling, has been aerated, and it is light and refreshing.

The doctor signaled for me to come in and sit down in his office. A mother was there with her five-year-old son. He addressed the mother, and she relaxed. The doctor proceeded to examine the boy. He lightly squeezed the boy's head, shoulders, and back and looked intently into his eyes. Without shifting his gaze, he told me that the boy was complaining of pain on the right side of his head near his ear and upper jaw. He sat back, thinking for a moment, and then took hold of the boy's left arm and gently squeezed just above the elbow. The boy winced, and the doctor smiled. He said something in their language and then rapidly shouted to one of the assistants out front where all the medications and formulas were. The mother seemed to be very pleased and gave him something wrapped in paper. With boy in hand, she picked up the recommended prescription from the assistant. The doctor told me the pain the boy was getting was from a tension on the right side of his neck and shoulder that was referring to the left side. So he prescribed that the boy stop heading the soccer ball for a week and gave him a natural relaxant and rubbing ointment. He also gave his mother a tonic because he said she looked overtired, adding, "Most of the women here work too hard for too long."

It was now the end of his morning surgery hours. After a few minutes of shuffling around papers and bags, he drew his eyes from the clutter of the room and, first, looked at me, really looked at me, and me at him. He had a broad face, his complexion light brown, with soft, kind, dark-brown eyes. They had dark circles around them, revealing a person who lived on the edge of his stamina. His hair was thick and full, with the vitality of a young man, except that it was graying. He looked strong and solid. At the same time, there was a lightness of being. There are people who, for whatever reason, I take to straightaway. That was true here. I am not sure if he even made a judgment of what he thought of me. I suspected he was the type of personality who left that part to his intuition until shown otherwise.

A black car from the late eighties came and picked us up. We arrived, and he ushered me into his home, filled with his boy of fourteen, his girl of twelve, two visiting nephews, their mothers, a sister-in-law and a happy small black dog. More often than not, when I enter an Indian home, there is no question about my presence. I'm immediately included in whatever is going on. It feels as though I am in scene 14 of a play where I have been in all thirteen scenes before. Such was the case here. My bags were whisked away behind a sofa. His son was showing one of his cousins a game, and I was invited to join in. The doctor had gone somewhere to change. Meanwhile, I noticed the women making a few quick peripheral glances to check me out. At my mature age, I figured it wasn't to see if I were a possible match for one of their single female family members or friends. Because I am a mixed breed of Tamil father and Gujarati mother, but my body language is Western, I am obviously different. The women were probably curious and wanted to know, "Who is this man, and where is he from?"

The doctor came out looking refreshed and told me that his wife was also a doctor, who specialized in OB/GYN and worked primarily with women. She was out doing her rounds and would be back shortly. When she returned, we all sat down to a simple dinner. It was now getting late, and the doctor said he would drive me to the retreat center. In the morning, he would describe the details of the cleansing program he had planned for me.

The retreat center was about ten miles south of Uttarkashi on a winding road that passed between hills on both sides with the river to the left. It was uniquely designed, with the attributes of both a Western castle and an Eastern palace. Brand new, painted white, it shone brilliantly in the light of a three-quarter moon. We turned off the road, and we were met by a middle-aged man who opened the gate so we could pass from the gravel turnoff into the courtyard.

A younger man greeted us, took my belongings, and escorted us past an arch at the front door, through a foyer with a sixteen-foot-high ceiling and into the reception area. Tile and marble covered the floor and walls to waist height as far as the eye could see. The doctor noticed I was tired and asked someone to show me to my room, which was fit for a king. I collapsed on the bed and, closing my eyes, listened to the call of a night bird. A knock on the door brought me out of my reverie to a great cup of chai, sweet tea with milk and spices.

I fell asleep and woke up during the night. The moon had gone down, so it was close to pitch black. I stepped out onto a walkway that circumnavigated the whole of the second floor. The night sky revealed the full glory of its planets and stars and the awesome presence of the Milky Way.

It was in the moments of this wonder I knew I had arrived. Until then, no matter where I was throughout my life, and no matter how long I stayed, there was always something I was looking for. Maybe I would never find it in my lifetime, but now here I was, after several very scary illnesses, a history of debilitating chronic diseases from childhood, in my Mother India, for twenty-one days in this sanctuary. Hopefully, this ancient science based on nature and knowledge would go deep into the core of my being and heal me. In the process, maybe I would even find myself.

A Doctor's Dedication and Uncle

The doctor returned the next morning and took me for an extensive tour of the building and grounds. He led me up to the roof, where I was met with a stunning view. The sun had not yet touched the mountainside, leaving it purple in the rising mist. Sparkles reflected off the river flowing through the valley, which was now bathed in every hue of green and sprinkled with patches of color from wildflowers. The doctor declared, "This is where I was born and raised. It's a part of me. After I graduated, I returned to serve my community. I had the dream of creating a healing center. When I saw this place, I knew the center had to be right here. My wife and I had it built from the ground up."

We found a shaded area, and he described his twenty-one-day *Panchakarma* detox program. We discussed the price, and I was satisfied. We went downstairs, and he gave me a thorough two-hour Ayurvedic examination and diagnosis, including astrology in his consideration. From this, he proposed a customized treatment plan for me. His warmth and sincerity made me feel cared for and safe. He mentioned that the main season for visitors was over, and I would have the whole center to myself.

So I was the only guest in this huge palace with seven to eight people attending me. I received a massage every other day over the next eight days, with less frequency over the course of the program. Two men escorted me to a room with a wooden table covered in plastic. They saturated my body with a pitcher of medicinal oil with spicy, earthy tones, including calamus root, cedar, nutmeg, and clove in a base of sesame oil. One man stood on each side of me and placed his hands on my shoulder. Following each other with precision, they used rhythmic, repetitive strokes with medium pressure to cover the whole of my body, counting out a different number of strokes for each part. This lasted for two hours, and I was in heaven.

On the in-between days, I received other treatments, like a head massage, facial, *Shirodhara*, where oil is poured on the forehead, and one where I was pounded with bags full of heated herbs. I was also given a deep enema to detox the digestive system, which, I was informed, was beneficial for the mental and emotional state. In the first few days, I was on a strict diet of rice, lentils, and ghee. Then gradually, vegetables and fruit were added in. Herbal formulations were specially concocted for me, some to drink and some to eat. During this time, I was instructed on the principles of Ayurveda, as well as the importance of yoga, *Pranayama* (breathing techniques), meditation, exercise, and rest. They asked me to include these practices in my program. Those that I already knew I did for myself, and they guided me with those I did not.

The cleanse drew out emotional and mental skeletons from my closet. Many questions emerged about my past decisions, my purpose, and the beauty and futility of my life. My mood swung back and forth, strings pulled like a marionette doll. Sometimes I wished I wasn't alone, so there would be someone to process with. Though I could feel their kindness, none of the staff spoke more than a few words of English. The doctor came every third day. The Internet didn't work, and I had to wait to go into town to speak to Jenny. So there were times when my sense of isolation was overwhelming. This lessened over time and evaporated toward the end.

The staff member delegated to oversee the program was referred to as Uncle. He was in his mid-fifties. From the first time our eyes met, we formed a nonverbal connection. His English comprised of a few words, mostly gestures, doing diagrams with his hands. One day he communicated that he was going up into the foothills to pick herbs, and that he'd like me to join him.

We set off in the early afternoon, ascending the hill on a narrow beaten track that had been created by the passage of people and creatures over time. Within half an hour, it became steeper, and we were nearly climbing. It leveled out after about an hour. We were high enough that I was at eye level with circling winged predators, possibly eagles or falcons. The path widened. He left the trail and, inspecting a grouping of plants, he carefully selected and plucked some leaves, which he put in a bag that was slung over his shoulder. As we continued, Uncle pointed out and harvested flowers, berries, roots, and fresh twigs, speaking in his native tongue. In the beginning, I thought he was talking to me, but I soon realized he was talking directly to the plants. He took each individual, held it close to his face, turning it in his hand while whispering softly. I became aware that I was being taught something important about listening with intuitive openness.

We came to a clearing on a gentle slope, and he invited me to sit on a rock and just relax. Behind us was a stone structure. It looked as though it had been there for a long time. By now, it must've been about four o'clock in the evening, and as this was winter, the sun was just at the horizon of the opposing hills. He started to walk around, inspect the parameters of the open space, and scrutinize the ground. He came back to me and pointed to the stone building and, with a few words and gestures, indicated that this was a place where animals were brought to graze. At nighttime, the animals were sheltered in the stone building, and the door was blockaded to keep out mountain tigers. This he conveyed, by making claws with his hands and growling loudly. Then he showed me some bones that he had collected as he was walking around and signed to me that these were the results of the tiger hunting. He made an imitation of the tiger biting his arm. Then jumping forward, he mimed the tiger biting me and laughed very loudly.

He pointed to his wristwatch. Then he pointed at the sun and motioned the sun going down, covering his eyes and holding his hands out as if he couldn't see. He mimed the international walking movement of two fingers one after the other, making it quite clear that we needed to go now before the tigers came out. I was in the domain of one of the greatest predators in the world, soon to be looking for supper, yet being with Uncle, I was without fear. We descended quickly down the trail, and I was relieved to return to the safety of the center.

During my stay at the retreat, when the doctor came to visit, he would invite me into the office, and we would speak very personally about many subjects that were close to our hearts. A few times, he took me to his home to eat with them. His fourteen-year-old boy became my tour leader around town. In India, there are always festivals. Not one week goes by without at least one or two happening somewhere. Such was the case in Uttarkashi. With the doctor's son as my companion and guide, I enjoyed music, parades, lots of lights, dancing, and singing. Everywhere, I was in a sea of smiling faces—mothers with their babies, dogs running around, and the sense of gaiety and happiness. Indians are obsessed with cricket. One can always find a cricket match with enthusiastic schoolboys setting up their wickets, gathering in herds to play the game. My escort was no less a fan. He also guided me through the open market so I could stock up on things.

I told the doctor that when I was finished with my retreat, I was going to stay for a week to ten days more. He said, in that case, he would like to invite me into the Himalayan foothills to experience what it was like to be a doctor for the regional tribal peoples of the area.

The Doctor and the Hill People

True to his word, the doctor asked me if I would accompany him to see the medical center he had established for the tribal people. I was excited and agreed. He picked me up at dawn the next morning. Everything except the river was asleep. We drove to his house, first passing vistas of shadowed hills and fields, edging down to the bubbling waters that divided the valley. It wasn't long before the sounds of the morning hustle and bustle on the fringes of town met our ears. The doctor explained that we were going to take an hour's ride on a bus and then walk the rest of the way. He had a large backpack and a case. I was told to take something to eat and drink, and we were off.

The bus took us farther north, so I could see the snowy tops of the mountains as the air began to warm from the chill of the morning. It was my first glimpse of the Himalayas. I saw peak after peak, ranging to the horizon. We took a turn onto a minor road, and after another fifteen minutes, the bus reached its terminal.

As I got off the bus and looked around, I was greeted by a multitude of hills, covered with thick undergrowth and clutches of evergreen trees. The morning mist was still lingering, waiting to be burnt off by the direct sun. The doctor started to walk, and I followed. He led us up a narrow road, which turned into a sloping cobbled path that hugged the side of the hill. We ascended from left to right, spiraling as we climbed. After a few minutes, I was winded and had to ask him to slow down. The air was thin, and at sixty-five years old, this body was not used to the exertion. As we carried on, I got into the rhythm and could pace myself and focus on breathing slower and deeper.

We had been climbing for about half an hour when I saw a girl descending from higher up, leading a donkey. On its back was a large rolled carpet. The doctor stopped and exchanged a few words with the girl, and we continued as they passed us by on their way down. The doctor told me that there was a very sick person rolled in the carpet. This was the safest way to transport people in serious condition from the mountain to the hospital in Rishikesh.

An hour passed, and we came to the first village, consisting of five houses on the side of the path and a few more scattered around. A woman came out and greeted the doctor, and he took a box from his backpack and gave it to her. The woman and I exchanged a nod, and we were off again, walking up and up, about fifty paces, and turning left around a bend, then fifty paces, and then turning right. Up and up. It was getting hot, not only because of the sunshine, but also from the sheer strain of the climb. In a way, I welcomed it. It was testing me. Did I still have some semblance of the younger man I was who could run at full speed to catch a bus or goat-hop down the side of a hill, landing for a second on each descending rock till I reached the bottom? We had been walking uphill for two hours, and I was still in the game.

We stopped every so often at a village, and he passed out more boxes. I suspect they were medicines. After another good hour, we reached an open area and a well-weathered small wooden house. About twenty locals were gathered, sitting on the ground. The doctor unlocked the door and showed me into the house. It had two rows of shelves with a walkway in between. The shelves on one side were mostly empty, except for a scattering of boxes and trays. On the shelves on the other side were dark bottles with tinctures and other things I couldn't identify. Bunches of wild herbs hung curing from the ceiling above. He asked me to help him carry some chairs and a small table and set them up outside. He sat by the table, leaving two chairs for his patients and a chair for me.

One by one, they came. Alone, as a couple, or mothers with their children. He had asked a patient to get an x-ray, which she produced. I marveled to see an x-ray on the side of a mountain, bridging a traditional tribal life reaching back into prehistory with the modern world. The doctor looked at it, showed it to me, and explained that he had told them I was visiting and was interested in what he did. That seemed to be enough.

I noticed that on completing a consultation, the patient would give him a small wrapped object or a few paise, one-hundredth of a rupee. He explained to me that this was a gesture of acknowledging his service and creating a balance of respect for him and themselves. Or they would give him wild-crafted herbs, healing flowers, and roots, which were light in weight and easy for him to carry down. I could see that being invited to sit as an equal with a doctor who cared about them and treated them with dignity was very special for them. I watched each sacred exchange in reverence and felt this was the highest service a human being can give to another human.

All the patients left. We packed, and he locked up. It was now midday. The pairs of eagles had stopped circling below us in the valley, and we started our three hour's walk down, leaving this clinic in the sky.

One day, the doctor said he wanted to show me something, and I needed to be ready at 5:00 a.m. the next morning. He picked me up, and we drove to his house, where he exchanged his car for his motorbike. I got on behind him, and we wound in and out, until we stopped at a temple with a stone maze in front of it. He took my hand (which is not unusual in India among male friends) and led me through the maze, until we came to the entrance of the temple and went inside. Here he left me and prayed. He then took my hand again and led me back out of the maze, and we hopped onto the motorbike. Then at lightning speed, he drove through narrow alleys, weaving and turning until we came to another temple. He told me this temple had one of the five Shiva Lingams in India that had descended from the sky. We entered. There were multiple statues of deities. Again, leading me by the hand, he took me into the inner sanctum, where a puja was in progress. It was hot from the heat of the sacred fire. We sat with the priest. The doctor gave his offering to him, and he started to chant a mantra and then put the offering into the fire. The mantra was the same as the priest had chanted on my first visit to India, one of the three mantras I knew out of the millions. I learned that the doctor would visit the hill tribe clinic twice a week. Every day he would get up early and go to both temples before opening his practice.

The night before my departure, the doctor and the family threw a farewell party for me. I was sad, yet I felt satisfied. He ceremoniously presented me with a silk Kashmir shawl. When the opportunity presented, he took me aside and made a request. Would I visit his guru's ashram in Varanasi? He said he would make a call to introduce me.

Varanasi, the Path to Sarnath

Varanasi, also known as Benares, was 960 kilometers away. It took just under nineteen hours by several trains. I arrived late in the afternoon. As had become the norm, I had only the address of the ashram scribbled on a scrap of paper.

It was getting dark by the time I hailed an open rickshaw taxi. After several mistaken locations, I was deposited outside what looked like a palace that had gotten lost on a side street in a slum. Glowing lights came from behind immaculately painted walls on either side of an ornamental gate fit for royalty. Through this gate, I could see a grandiose temple of gold and white marble. I waited there with sacred cows on one side and garbage on the other. Finally, someone approached and eyed me up and down. After mentioning where I had come from, I was ushered in. I was told the guru was away on business, and I was shown to my plain yet adequate room on the second floor.

The cook took me under his wing. He seemed to be the person who ran the whole place. After two days, the guru turned up. I waited to be introduced to him, but it never happened. The cook, realizing this, asked one of the staff, who could speak a little English, to show me around.

It is not possible to describe Varanasi in one book, or even a volume of books. There were temples so old that nature had worn them down to a mere hint of their original structure. Thousands of visiting pilgrims bathed in the sacred river Ganga day and night, with the hope of liberation from the karmic wheel of reincarnation. My escort encouraged me to bathe, but I was not brave enough to test the waters.

Over the week I was there, the few times I saw the guru at a distance, he looked more like an actor playing a role, troubled and not so holy. There were about 10 devotees and as many people managing the temple and ashram. We gathered together at morning meditation, breakfast, light lunch, and evening prayers. The cook said he would take time off the next day to show me a very special place. I should be ready for a 6:00 a.m. taxi ride.

I was up and very excited as 6:00 a.m. came and went. The whole ashram seemed to be in a commotion about something important, with several staff running here and there. Mumbles and shouts echoed in the great hall. The cook finally appeared, and as he whizzed by me, I asked about our special trip. He stopped and took a breath and said that he couldn't. He thought for a second and said he would send me with one of his assistants, and then he ran on.

Within ten minutes, a young man in his late teens approached me and beckoned me to follow him out of the compound of the ashram. There, taxis were parked, and he signaled me to get in. It was then that I realized he didn't speak English, but his broad smile and friendly gestures were reassuring. He instructed the driver of our destination, and we were off.

It was going on 7:00 a.m., and traffic was a multidirectional stampede. I still didn't know where we were going, but as the shops thinned out, replaced by houses and then open fields, I decided to sit back and trust. We had been on the road for less than an hour, when we stopped in a town. I negotiated the fare and received an even bigger smile from the cook's assistant as he left in the taxi.

RAMANI RANGAN

By now it was very hot. Finding the closest restaurant, I asked, "Where am I?"

Three men invited me to sit, and with their broken English, my few Hindi words, and international signing, they helped me order breakfast.

I knew I had to leave the un-happenings of the ashram. I thought this would be a good place to land. I returned to the ashram to collect my belongings. I offered a donation through the cook, as it was obvious the guru hadn't wanted to see me. The cook set up an audience without the guru's knowledge, so I walked in on him muttering to himself. I thanked him for my stay. On hearing that I was making a donation, he half turned, gave me a side glance and pointed to a table. I set it down and left. The cook said something enthusiastic about Sarnath, the name of the town where I was going to stay. "Very sacred, very sacred," he repeated as I left.

I stayed overnight in a government hostel and heard about a small ten-room hotel, which I went to see the next day. I entered into a large round garden, divided by four walkways to a circular center, where there were two benches to sit on. A profusion of wonderful flowers were interspersed with herb and vegetable companions. The owners were an older couple and welcomed me with calming smiles, inviting me in out of the heat of the morning. They led me to my room and asked me if I'd like to come down and share a refreshment when I was ready. As I sat and sipped limeade, they revealed to me where I was. It was nothing I had expected. Sarnath, this little dusty town, was the place where, over 2,500 years ago, a wandering homeless man arrived with his five students. He told them he had a realization and shared this knowledge, which became the foundation of a world religion of over 500 million people. It was a wonderful shock that I was here and I was going to walk on the same ground, drink from the same spring as the Enlightened One, the Buddha.

I wanted to go out straightaway, but the heat pushed me back into the shade. The couple suggested I wait till the cool of the evening. I returned to my room, showered, sat in a reclining chair under a group of trees, closed my eyes, and daydreamed. Evening could not come quick enough. As soon as I saw other people walking by the hotel, I stepped out. I followed the others, turning the corner. There in front of me was a street of temples, each one very different from the other. Behind them, I could see even more temples peeking out. Over the next several evenings, I visited temple after temple of breathtaking beauty, many with giant statues of the Buddha, some sumptuously adorned and covered with gold leaf. There were temples representing China, Japan, Thailand, Vietnam, Myanmar, Sri Lanka, South Korea, Taiwan, Cambodia, and India. Each reflected the unique architecture of its culture, like an ambassador displaying the highest respect for this most sacred of sacred grounds.

I noticed that Hindus came by the busload to acknowledge this ancient son of Nepal. There was a clear sense of inclusiveness, Hinduism embracing Buddhism and honoring its founder. One night, I saw a Hindu grandfather teach his grandson to meditate in the courtyard of the Thai temple. Another night, I saw a man in a business suit take off his jacket and practice yoga on the marble floor of another temple. On the main street during the day, I could watch five young apprentices painting highly intricate *Thangkas*, Tibetan Buddhist religious scrolls, each adding the part corresponding to their skill level. The master performed the finishing touches, while the youngest helped where he was needed. All the goods sold on the street were specifically focused on the history of Sarnath. Some were trinkets, but many were for meditation and healing. This was not the usual Indian bazaar.

Leaving the temples one day, I came across a walkway over a small lake. People were standing looking down into the water. More and more people came. I thought they would be looking at ducks, but when I looked down, I saw nothing. Then suddenly, I realized they were looking at the lotus flowers that were floating on the surface. I then remembered the lesson the Buddha gave us. Not to stay focused on the flower and the beauty and the things on the surface that distract us but to follow the roots of the lotus where they go deep into the mud. This is where we will find our true nourishment. Here I was, perhaps standing on the same spot where the Buddha made this connection. I looked up and saw a herd of deer. This was the Deer Park, where Buddha first taught the Middle Way, moderation between the extremes of self-indulgence and self-mortification through practice of the Noble Eightfold Path: right view, right resolve, right speech, right conduct, right livelihood, right effort, right mindfulness, and right samadhi (union with the divine).

After a week had passed, I woke up and saw the streets were filled with hundreds of red-robed monks milling about. Monks continued to arrive by the busload, and truck after truck delivered large, thick bamboo poles. I went and sat at my favorite outdoor tea and biscuit shop, strategically placed on the corner so I could see all the goings-on. One of my new friends told me that the Dalai Lama was coming and the town was going to grow by thirty thousand in ten days. I rushed back to the hotel and asked if I could extend my stay. He laughed and told me that the hotel had been booked for two years ahead. They had a flat roof. I mentioned this and asked if I could sleep there, and he laughed some more.

On the morning of my reluctant departure, I sat silently with the deer herd and watched the mirroring of the sky at the lotus lake. Returning to my hotel, I asked for a taxi and was told it would take a few hours. My bags were in the office, and I decided to walk through the paradise garden to the gates. The bamboo deposited by the trucks had been erected into temporary lodging for the multitude of monks. The heightened energy was tangible.

I was watching passersby when my eyes refocused to see that the enormous doors of the building across from the hotel had opened. Inside sat hundreds of Tibetan monks with as many lit butter lamps, awaiting the arrival of their beloved leader. I crossed the road and stood, with a magnetic pull to go in. At that very moment, one of the monks slowly turned and gave the slightest indication for me to enter. I stooped down to create the least distraction and stepped in. I found a place to sit at the back and was captured immediately by the deep-throat chanting of what must have been three hundred or more monks. It encompassed my body and mind, and I was submerged into a timeless world. I could have been there for an hour—or more, or less, I don't know. At some point, a monk turned in my direction, our eyes met, and I was free to leave.

Just as I stepped out of the temple, the taxi arrived. I thanked my hotel couple, and as we weaved our way past all the organized chaos, I thanked Sarnath. I gave a special thanks to Siddhārtha Gautama, Shakyamuni Buddha. The Buddha.

There Are Rhythms

There are rhythms that are unknown to us. They are constant. Our closest companions through this brief encounter with the earth vehicle we call a body. Some of these rhythms originate far out in the universe, and maybe even beyond. As we wake and sleep, the moon is dancing with the vast oceans of this world. We too, as bodies of water, are constantly being massaged by not only lunar influences, but also by the sun, planets, stars, and galaxies. Then there are the more intimate dynamics of this earthly planet. The whole of life pulsates together, exchanging frequencies, each a unique instrument in an infinite symphonic cosmic orchestra.

I stretch my imagination right now and look at my hand. I see stories of the journey of this lifetime ingrained in the major and minor lines on the surface of this palm. My mind says, *This is my hand.* Then another voice whispers very softly, *These eyes are looking at form, but what is being seen are qualities, beyond color and sound, rhythms playing back so life can experience life itself.* There is no need to seek the Mystery. All is in all. We sleepwalk in the concept of love being something we have to achieve. Yet our true nature is and has always been...*We are that which we seek.*

The prayer flags blow on the mountain,
The prayers call out,
The wind blows,
Nevertheless, Know,
The wind is enough.

Epilogue

Timeless Traveler, Ramani Rangan

The Timeless Traveler

Does life pass through us or we through it?
Clocks tick a measure for us to fit.
Time tangos with space in an eternal dance,
Our spirit invites us to awake from our trance.

We are all Timeless Travelers, no manual in hand,
No instructions given when we land.
Scraps of distorted memories parents lay on,
From the mirage of a broken mirror view all gone.
They gleaned the right and wrong imprisoned mind,
Passed down from ancestors of the humankind.

We are already members to the cosmos club,
No need to pay a fee . . . This is your home...that is the rub.
Our thoughts are strokes of mind brush surface met,
On canvas of unlimited creativity set.
So we ride on the surface of "why, where from, and where to?"
The artist with infinite rainbows within and beyond is You.

Look away, Timeless Traveler, look in to your Core of Peace,
Take the reins and then trust and release.
There! There you are, all limitless and whole,
Love is your true nature, You are the goal.

We Are Here, Ramani Rangan

Dedicated to All Those Who Are Seeking and Dancing the Way

I dedicate this work to all those mentioned in this book and to all those who over the years brought light into my world, so that, by chance, I have gained some stillness in the storm and thunder in the stillness. I would like to give special thanks for all the lessons I have learned from being wrong, being opinionated, and tested by the heat of anger, jealousy, and, mostly, fear. I thank all who have seen me or made me visible in their lives. Who have seen their beauty in me and thus revealed the unlimited beauty in all of us. I thank my mother and my father for showing me perfect examples of how to be and not be in the world. Their lives gave me the initiative to investigate greater potentials. I honor their incredible struggle and few moments of success.

My beloved sister, Charmaine—she is in my sacred private temple, yet must be mentioned. A short journey, a young and early loss.

My son, David, who saw in my essays a book worthy of publishing. I thank you for your inspiration and support and for your love.

My wife, Jenny, who rewrote, revised and edited this book with me over a period of three years. I thank you for all your input and technical involvement. Your talent, knowledge, encouragement, enthusiasm, super human patience, and perseverance made this book possible.

A special thanks to Chris Williams, for taking my paintings and creating a photographic masterpiece of each one. An extraordinarily talented Renaissance man, fixer of all things, fellow Brit, and beloved friend.

My family in Denmark, England, and South Africa, all my children and grandchildren, my wife's family, who have been my family. Your presence in my life has been a blessing. Thank you for your patience with me as I figure out who I am. Wherever you are in your endeavors, you are always in my heart.

The Rose Baker Senior Center Memoirs Group in Gloucester, Massachusetts. These twice-monthly sharings were the engine to capture moments of inspiration. The time and space to sit down, go inside, and encourage a story to surface gave the influence and foundation necessary to create this book. You know who you are, and I thank you.

Feel the love. At last, my breath, I give thanks for. Without the spontaneous movement of these two lungs, none of this is possible.

When I began my life, we were at war. Now in 2019, seventy-seven years later, I feel we are again at war. Our environment is being poisoned, and the brakes are not being put on fast enough to avoid catastrophe. I am deeply concerned for the state of our home, this planet we call Earth. I pray with all my heart that, together, we may cherish, honor, and protect the wondrous gift and miracle that is life.

My Dad Sonnee at the Piano

Sonnee and the Leopard

Portrait of Sonnee Rangan

My Mother Dorothy and Her Sister Irene

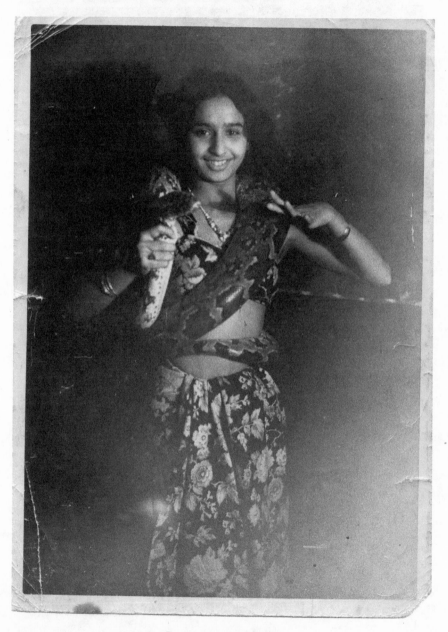

Dorothy and the Python

DOORLAY'S NON-STOP-REVUE „TROPICAL-EXPRESS

Dorothy's Finale Costume